Frege

D1343153

Frege

A Critical Introduction

Harold W. Noonan

Polity

Copyright © Harold W. Noonan 2001

The right of Harold W. Noonan to be identified as author of this work has been asserted in accordance with the Copyright, Designs and Patents Act 1988.

First published in 2001 by Polity Press in association with Blackwell Publishers Ltd

Editorial office:
Polity Press
65 Bridge Street
Cambridge CB2 1UR, UK

Marketing and production:
Blackwell Publishers Ltd
108 Cowley Road
Oxford OX4 1JF, UK

Published in the USA by
Blackwell Publishers Inc.
Commerce Place
350 Main Street
Malden, MA 02148, USA

All rights reserved. Except for the quotation of short passages for the purposes of criticism and review, no part of this publication may be reproduced, stored in a retrieval system, or transmitted, in any form or by any means, electronic, mechanical, photocopying, recording or otherwise, without the prior permission of the publisher.

Except in the United States of America, this book is sold subject to the condition that it shall not, by way of trade or otherwise, be lent, re-sold, hired out, or otherwise circulated without the publisher's prior consent in any form of binding or cover other than that in which it is published and without a similar condition including this condition being imposed on the subsequent purchaser.

ISBN 0-7456-1672-0
ISBN 0-7456-1673-9 (pbk)

A catalogue record for this book is available from the British Library and has been applied for from the Library of Congress.

Typeset in $10\frac{1}{2}$ on 12 pt Palatino
by Best-set Typesetter Ltd., Hong Kong
Printed in Great Britain by MPG Books Ltd, Bodmin, Cornwall

This book is printed on acid-free paper.

Undergraduate Lending Library

Key Contemporary Thinkers

Published

Forthcoming

Maria Baghramian, *Hilary Putnam*
Sara Beardsworth, *Kristeva*
Mark Cain, *Fodor: Language, Mind and Philosophy*
James Carey, *Innis and McLuhan*
Rosemary Cowan, *Cornell West: The Politics of Redemption*
George Crowder, *Isaiah Berlin: Liberty, Pluralism and Liberalism*
Thomas D'Andrea, *Alasdair MacIntyre*
Eric Dunning, *Norbert Elias*
Jocelyn Dunphy, *Paul Ricoeur*
Matthew Elton, *Daniel Dennett*
Nigel Gibson, *Frantz Fanon*
Graeme Gilloch, *Walter Benjamin*
Karen Green, *Dummett: Philosophy of Language*
Espen Hammer, *Stanley Cavell*
Keith Hart, *C. L. R. James*
Sarah Kay, *Žižek: A Critical Introduction*
Paul Kelly, *Ronald Dworkin*
Carl Levy, *Antonio Gramsci*
Moya Lloyd, *Judith Butler*
Dermot Moran, *Edmund Husserl*
Steve Redhead, *Paul Virilio: Theorist for an Accelerated Culture*
Chris Rojek, *Stuart Hall and Cultural Studies*
Wes Sharrock and Rupert Read, *Kuhn*
Nick Smith, *Charles Taylor*
Nicholas Walker, *Heidegger*

Contents

Contents

Preface

In this book I present a study of the most important themes in the work of the great German philosopher and logician Gottlob Frege. The exposition follows the order in which these themes appear in Frege's work. Thus, after an introductory chapter outlining the background to Frege's thought and setting him in the context of his time, the second chapter explains his fundamental advances in logic, as found in his first book, *Conceptual Notation*. The third chapter is devoted to his discussion of number in his masterpiece, *The Foundations of Arithmetic*, and its successor *The Basic Laws of Arithmetic*, including an account of the inconsistency discovered in his system by Bertrand Russell, 'Russell's Paradox'. The remaining two chapters are concerned with the most significant and influential of his writings on philosophical logic and meaning: 'Function and Concept', 'On Concept and Object', 'On Sense and Reference' and 'Thoughts'.

I am grateful to my colleagues at the University of Birmingham, particularly Joss Walker, for the patience with which they have read and commented on successive redraftings of this material.

H. W. N.

Acknowledgements

The author and publishers are grateful to the following for permission to quote from copyrighted material:

Blackwell Publishers for *Translations from the Philosophical Writings of Gottlob Frege*, ed. P. Geach and M. Black, Oxford, 1969; *Posthumous Writings*, trans. P. Long and H. White, Oxford, 1979; and *Collected Papers on Mathematics, Logic and Philosophy*, ed. B. McGuinness, trans. M. Black et al., Oxford, 1984.

Blackwell Publishers and Northwestern University Press for Gottlob Frege, *The Foundations of Arithmetic*, trans. J. L. Austin, Oxford and Evanston, Ill., 1968.

Oxford University Press for Gottlob Frege, *Conceptual Notation and Related Articles*, ed. and trans. T. W. Bynum, Oxford, 1972.

Every effort has been made to contact copyright holders, but if any have been inadvertently overlooked, the publishers will be pleased to make the necessary arrangements at the first opportunity.

1

Introduction: Frege's Life and Work

Biography

Friedrich Ludwig Gottlob Frege was the founder of modern mathematical logic, which he created in his first book, *Conceptual Notation, a Formula Language of Pure Thought Modelled upon the Formula Language of Arithmetic* (*Begriffsschrift, eine der arithmetischen nachgebildete Formalsprache des reinen Denkens* (1879), translated in Frege 1972). This describes a system of symbolic logic which goes far beyond the two thousand year old Aristotelian logic on which, hitherto, there had been little decisive advance. Frege was also one of the main formative influences, together with Bertrand Russell, Ludwig Wittgenstein and G. E. Moore, on the analytical school of philosophy which now dominates the English-speaking philosophical world. Apart from his definitive contribution to logic, his writings on the philosophy of mathematics, philosophical logic and the theory of meaning are such that no philosopher working in any of these areas today could hope to make a contribution without a thorough familiarity with Frege's philosophy. Yet in his lifetime the significance of Frege's work was little acknowledged. Even his work on logic met with general incomprehension and his work in philosophy was mostly unread and unappreciated. He was, however, studied by Edmund Husserl, Bertrand Russell, Ludwig Wittgenstein and Rudolf Carnap and via these great figures he has eventually achieved general recognition.

Frege's life was not a personally fulfilled one (for more detailed accounts of the following see Bynum's introduction to Frege 1972 and Beaney's introduction to Frege 1997). His wife died twenty years before his own death in 1925 (he was survived by an adopted son, Alfred) and, ironically, his life's work in the philosophy of mathematics, to which he regarded all the rest of his efforts as subordinate, that is, his attempted demonstration that arithmetic was a branch of logic (the 'logicist thesis' as it is now called), was dealt a fatal blow by Bertrand Russell, one of his greatest admirers, who showed that it entailed the inconsistency that now bears his name ('Russell's Paradox'). Nevertheless, Frege perhaps gained some comfort from the respect accorded to him by Russell and by Wittgenstein, who met Frege several times and revered him above all other philosophers. In retrospect, indeed, many would perhaps say that in philosophy generally, as distinct from the narrower branches of logic and the philosophy of mathematics, Frege's greatest contribution was the advance in the philosophy of logic and language which made Wittgenstein's work possible.

Little is known of Frege's personality and life outside philosophy. Apparently his politics and social views, as recorded in his diaries, reveal him to have been, in his later years, extremely right-wing, strongly opposed to democracy and to civil rights for Catholics and Jews. Frege's greatest commentator, Michael Dummett, expresses great shock and disappointment (1973: xii) that someone he had revered as an absolutely rational man could have been imbued with such prejudices. But a more generous view is the one expressed by another great Frege scholar, Peter Geach. Geach writes that while Frege was indeed imbued with typical German conservative prejudices, 'to borrow an epigram from Quine, it doesn't matter what you believe so long as you're not sincere. Nobody can really imagine Frege as an active politico devoted to some course like Hitler's' (1976c: 437).

We have, however, a presentation of the more attractive side of Frege in an account Wittgenstein gives of his encounters with him:

> I was shown into Frege's study. Frege was a small, neat man with a pointed beard who bounced around the room as he talked. He absolutely wiped the floor with me, and I felt very depressed; but at the end he said 'You must come again,' so I cheered up. I had several discussions with him after that. Frege would never talk about anything but logic and mathematics, if I started on some other subject, he would say something polite and then plunge back into logic and mathematics. He once showed me an obituary on a colleague, who,

it was said, never used a word without knowing what it meant; he expressed astonishment that a man should be praised for this! The last time I saw Frege, as we were waiting at the station for my train, I said to him 'Don't you ever find any difficulty in your theory that numbers are objects?' He replied: 'Sometimes I *seem* to see a difficulty but then again I *don't* see it.' (Included in Anscombe and Geach 1961)

Rudolf Carnap, who attended Frege's lectures in 1914, also presents a vivid image:

> Frege looked old beyond his years. He was of small stature, rather shy, extremely introverted. He seldom looked at his audience. Ordinarily we saw only his back, while he drew the strange diagrams of his symbolism on the blackboard and explained them. Never did a student ask a question or make a remark, whether during the lecture or afterwards. The possibility of a discussion seemed to be out of the question. (Carnap 1963: 5)

Frege was born in 1848 in Wismar on the German Baltic coast. He attended the Gymnasium in Wismar for five years (1864–9), passed his Abitur in the spring of 1869 and then entered Jena University.

There Frege spent two years studying chemistry, mathematics and philosophy. He then transferred to the University of Göttingen (perhaps influenced by one of his mathematics professors, Ernst Abbe), where he studied philosophy, physics and mathematics.

In 1873 Frege presented his doctoral dissertation, *On a Geometrical Representation of Imaginary Figures in a Plane* (in Frege 1984: 1–55), which extended the work of Gauss on complex numbers, and was granted the degree of Doctor of Philosophy in Göttingen in December of that year.

Frege then applied for the position of Privatdozent (unsalaried lecturer), at the University of Jena. Among the documents he supplied in support of his application was his Habilitationsschrift (postdoctoral dissertation required for appointment to a university teaching post), 'Methods of Calculation Based upon an Amplification of the Concept of Magnitude' (in Frege 1984: 56–92). In this piece there first emerges Frege's interest in the concept of a *function* which, as we shall see, was to play an absolutely central role throughout his philosophy.

Frege's work was judged acceptable by the Jena mathematics faculty, and in a prescient report Ernst Abbe speculated that it contained the seeds of a viewpoint which would achieve a durable advance in mathematical analysis. Frege was therefore allowed to proceed to an oral examination, which he passed, though he was judged to be neither quick-witted nor fluent. After a public disputation and trial lecture in May 1874 he was appointed Privatdozent at Jena, where he remained for the rest of his career.

Initially Frege had a heavy teaching load and he only published four short articles (see Frege 1984: 93–100), three of them reviews and one an article on geometry, before 1879, when *Conceptual Notation* was published. Nevertheless, these were probably the happiest years of his life. He was young, ambitious, with a plan of his life's work (as we see from the Preface to *Conceptual Notation*) already formed. He was, moreover, well thought of by the faculty and by the best mathematics students at Jena. The description of his 'student friendly' lecturing style quoted from Carnap earlier fits with Abbe's evaluation of Frege for the university officials in 1879. Abbe reported that Frege's courses were little suited to please the mediocre student 'for whom a lecture is just an exercise for the ears'. But 'Dr Frege, by virtue of the great clarity and precision of his expression and by virtue of the thoughtfulness of his lectures is particularly fit to introduce aspiring listeners to the difficult material of mathematical studies – I myself have repeatedly had the opportunity to hear lectures by him which appeared to me to be absolutely perfect on every fundamental point' (quoted in Frege 1972: 8).

Absolute perfection on every *fundamental* point was indeed the aim – and the achievement – of Frege's *Conceptual Notation*, which he conceived as the necessary starting point of his logicist programme. It appeared in 1879 and partly as a result Frege was promoted to the salaried post of special (*ausserordentlicher*) Professor. The promotion was granted on the strength of a recommendation by Frege's mentor Ernst Abbe, who wrote with appreciation of *Conceptual Notation*. His remarks were again prescient. He thought that mathematics 'will be affected, perhaps very considerably, but immediately only very little, by the inclination of the author and the content of the book'. He continued by noting that some mathematicians 'will find little that is appealing in so subtle investigations into the formal interrelationships of knowledge', and 'scarcely anyone will be able, offhand, to take a position on the very original cluster of ideas in this book . . . it will probably be understood and appreciated by only a few' (quotations from Frege 1972: 16).

Abbe's pessimism about the immediate reception of Frege's work was wholly justified. It received at least six reviews, but none showed an appreciation of the book's significance, even though some of the reviewers were eminent logicians. The reviews by Schröder in Germany and Venn in England must have been particularly bitter disappointments. Frege's work was judged inferior to the Boolean logic of his leading contemporaries and his 'conceptual notation' dismissed as 'cumbrous and inconvenient' (by Venn) and 'a monstrous waste of space' which 'indulges in the Japanese custom of writing vertically' (by Schröder).

It was an unfortunate outcome but neither without precedent, nor, in retrospect, surprising. The extent of Frege's achievement was something that could not possibly have been expected by a reviewer asked to give an initial assessment of his work. One is reminded of the similar reception of David Hume's *Treatise of Human Nature* which, likewise, as Hume famously put it, 'fell dead-born from the press'. And, as also in the case of Hume, the poor reception of Frege's work was partly his own fault – arising from the 'manner rather than the matter' of presentation, to use Hume's words – and something that could have been anticipated. Frege did not explain clearly and thoroughly the purpose of *Conceptual Notation* and did not justify and illustrate the advantages of his bizarre-looking two-dimensional notation and its superiority to those available at the time. One can thus sympathize with the first reviewers. As a recent commentator has put it: 'The odds that Frege's work was the production of a genius rather than a crackpot may have seemed long indeed to his colleagues and contemporaries' (Boolos 1998: 144).

As a result of the poor reception of *Conceptual Notation*, Frege postponed his plan, announced in its preface, to proceed immediately to the analysis of the concept of number. Instead he attempted to answer his critics. He wrote two papers comparing his logical symbolism with that of Boole. The first, 'Boole's Logic Calculus and the Concept-Script' (now published in Frege 1979: 9–46) was rejected by three journals. The second, a much shorter version of the first, 'Boole's Logical Formula Language and my Conceptual Notation' (now in Frege 1979: 47–52) was also rejected. Finally Frege managed to get published a more general justification of his conceptual notation, 'On the Scientific Justification of a Conceptual Notation' (now in Frege 1972: 83–9), and was able to deliver a lecture, also subsequently published, at a meeting of the Jenaischüe Gesellschaft für Medicin und Naturwissenschaft, in which he compared his symbolism with Boole's ('On the Aim of the Conceptual Notation', now in Frege 1972: 90–100).

The disappointing reviews of *Conceptual Notation* thus side-tracked Frege into a frustrating episode of self-justification. But they also had the effect of making him more aware of how he must present his work if it was to be appreciated. Instead of proceeding straight from *Conceptual Notation* to a formal demonstration, in his symbolic notation, of the derivability of arithmetic from logic, as anticipated in the Preface to *Conceptual Notation*, Frege decided to produce an informal sketch of his derivation in ordinary German, set out against the background of a critique of traditional (including Kantian and empiricist) views of number. The result was his masterpiece, *The Foundations of Arithmetic: A Logico-Mathematical Enquiry into the Concept of Number* (*Die Grundlagen der Arithmetik: eine logische mathematische Untersuchung über den Begriff der Zahl*) published in 1884 (Frege 1968).

Once again, as in the case of *Conceptual Notation*, Frege viewed this only as a preliminary stage in his logicist project. He thought that he had made the 'analytic character of arithmetical propositions' (i.e. their derivability from logical laws by definition) 'probable', but to *prove* his thesis he needed to produce 'a chain of deductions with no link missing' using principles of inference all of which could be recognized as purely logical (Frege 1968: 102).

Frege could have hoped that after *Foundations* his achievement of this project would have been eagerly awaited by scholars. For *Foundations* is indeed, as Frege intended, a brilliantly written exposition of his views, both negative and positive. In fact, it received only three reviews, all of them hostile (one, by Cantor, criticizing Frege on the basis of the misunderstanding that he took numbers to be sets of physical objects), and remained largely unread and unnoted for nearly twenty years. A partial explanation of this situation is perhaps the poor reception of *Conceptual Notation*, which could not have added to Frege's reputation or predisposed mathematicians and philosophers to think his subsequent work worthy of the effort needed to understand it. But whatever the case, the result was that Frege had no choice but to persevere with his logicist project unacknowledged and unsupported by any encouragement from his peers.

The next stage in this project appeared as volume 1 of *The Basic Laws of Arithmetic* (*Grundgesetze der Arithmetik*) in 1893 (see Frege 1962, translated in part in Frege 1964). However, in the intervening nine years Frege's views on the underlying philosophy of language and logic of *Foundations* developed rapidly, necessitating a complete rewriting of a large preliminary manuscript for *Basic Laws*. It was in this period that he published, in the early 1890s, his three best known papers 'Function and Concept' (*Funktion und Begriff*), 'On Sense and Reference' ('Über Sinn und Bedeutung') and 'On Concept and Object' ('Über Begriff und Gegenstand') (all in Frege 1969). All three of these are now regarded as classic works in the philosophy of language, and the second, in particular, must be read by anyone who wishes to understand twentieth-century analytic philosophy at all, but their importance for Frege was that they set out the changes in his views from the time of *Foundations* and prepared their readers for *Basic Laws*.

In this period, also, notice began to be taken notice of Frege's works when the Italian logician Peano cited them in print and Husserl began to correspond with Frege.

With volume 1 of *Basic Laws* written, Frege should now have been able to look forward to its publication and the recognition his work had for so long gone without. However, so poorly had his previous work been received that no publisher would print the lengthy manuscript as a whole. Frege eventually got an agreement from Hermann Pohle of Jena, who had published 'Function and Concept', to publish it in two volumes, with the publication of the second volume being conditional on the success of the first. In this way volume 1 was eventually printed in 1893.

Frege evidently anticipated that his work was likely, once more, to fail to gain the recognition it deserved. He acknowledged that:

> An expression cropping up here or there, as one leafs through these pages, may easily appear strange and create prejudice . . . Even the first impression must frighten people off: unfamiliar signs, pages of nothing but alien looking formulas . . . I must relinquish as readers all those mathematicians who, if they bump into logical expressions such as 'concept', 'relation', 'judgement', think: *metaphysica sunt, non leguntur*, and likewise those philosophers who at the sight of a formula cry: *mathematica sunt, non leguntur*; and the number of such persons is surely not small. Perhaps the number of mathematicians who trouble themselves over the foundations of their science is not great, and even those frequently seem to be in a great hurry until they have got the fundamental principles behind them. And I scarcely dare hope that my reasons for painstaking rigour and its inevitable lengthiness will persuade many of them. (Frege 1964: xi–xii)

For this reason Frege made great efforts to make his work more accessible to his readers. He gave hints in the Preface as to how to read the book to achieve a speedy understanding and in the text he prefaced his proofs with rough outlines to bring out their significance. He also attempted to provoke other scholars to respond to his work by attacking rival theories.

It was all to no avail. Volume 1 of *Basic Laws* received just two reviews, both unfavourable, one of only three sentences, and was otherwise ignored. As a result the publisher refused to publish the remainder of Frege's work and volume 2 eventually had to be published a decade later by Frege at his own expense.

Nevertheless, publication of volume 1 at least led to an improvement in Frege's material circumstances, with his promotion in 1896 to the rank of Honorary Ordinary Professor. This was unsalaried but without administrative duties. Frege was able to accept this post because he was offered a stipend from the Carl Zeiss Stiftung, founded and sustained by his mentor Ernst Abbe. Consequently Frege now had more time for his research, and in the decade preceding the publication of volume 2 of *Basic Laws* engaged in correspondence with a variety of scholars, and published a number of articles and reviews of other authors as well as carrying forward his work on the *Basic Laws*.

One of the scholars Frege corresponded with in this period was Peano, who had written the longer of the two reviews of volume 1 of *Basic Laws* The review started an exchange of views and led Peano to make modifications in his logical symbolism (Frege's correspondence with Peano is published in Frege 1980: 108–29; his two pieces explaining the superiority of his logical notation to that of Peano are published in Frege 1980: 112–18). Another fateful result of Frege's coming to the notice of Peano was that Russell, who adopted Peano's notation, learned of his work. As Russell himself tells the story (Russell 1959: 65):

> I did not read [the *Begriffsschrift*] . . . until I had independently worked out a great deal of what it contained . . . I read it in 1901. . . . What first attracted me to Frege was a review of a later book of his by Peano [Peano's review of volume 1 of the *Grundgesetze*] accusing him of unnecessary subtlety. As Peano was the most subtle logician I had at that time come across, I felt that Frege must be remarkable.

Apart from Peano, another scholar on whom Frege had some influence during this period prior to the publication of the second volume of *Basic Laws* was Husserl, the founder of the continental phenomenological school. Husserl began as a disciple of Brentano and an advocate of psychologism (the attempt to base logic and arithmetic on psychology). In 1891 he published the first volume of his *Philosophy of Arithmetic*. This contained criticisms of Frege and Frege responded in 1894 with a scathing review. Husserl was converted from psychologism and became henceforth its strong opponent, developing the notion of the *noema* of an act of thought, which corresponds to, but is intended to generalize, Frege's notion of sense.

Thus, although his own work was still neglected, Frege could at least take comfort from the fact that he was now known and respected by some of the most eminent scholars of the day, and look forward to a better reception for volume 2 of *Basic Laws*. Despite the neglect of his work, he himself never doubted its achievement. In the final paragraph to the Preface of volume 1 of *Basic Laws* he raises the question of the possibility of someone deriving a contradiction in his system, but dismisses it with total confidence:

> It is *prima facie* improbable that such a structure could be erected on a base that was uncertain or defective. . . . As a refutation in this I can only recognize someone's actually demonstrating either that a better, more durable edifice can be erected upon other fundamental convictions, or else that my principles lead to manifestly false conclusions. But no one will be able to do that. (1964: xxvi)

Disaster struck in the form of a modestly expressed letter from Russell which arrived in June 1902, as the second volume of *Basic Laws* was in press. Russell's letter pointed out that the contradiction now known as 'Russell's Paradox' was derivable in Frege's logical system. After expressing his admiration for Frege's work and his substantial agreement, Russell writes:

> I have encountered a difficulty only on one point. You assert (p.17) that a function could also constitute the indefinite element. This is what I used to believe, but this view now seems to me dubious because of the following contradiction: let w be the predicate of being a predicate which cannot be predicated of itself. Can w be predicated of itself? From either answer follows its contradictory. We must therefore conclude that w is not a predicate. Likewise, there is no class (as a whole) of those classes which, as wholes, are not members of themselves. From this I conclude that under certain circumstances a definable set does not form a whole. (Frege 1969: 130–1)

Frege recognized at once the seriousness of the difficulty Russell had explained and identified Basic Law (V) as its origin. He wrote back to Russell:

> Your discovery of the contradiction has surprised me beyond words and, I should almost like to say, left me thunderstruck because it has rocked the ground on which I meant to build arithmetic. It seems accordingly that the transformation of the generality of an equality [*Gleichheit*] into an equality of value ranges is not always permissible, that my law (V) is false, and that my explanations do not suffice to secure a reference [*Bedeutung*] for my combination of signs in all cases. I must give some further thought to the matter. It is all the more serious as the collapse of my law (V) seems to undermine not only the foundations of my arithmetic but the only possible foundations of arithmetic as such. (Frege 1969: 132–3)

Frege attempted to develop a response to the paradox and published an amendment in an appendix to volume 2 of *Basic Laws*. However, the amended system can also be proved to be inconsistent (see Quine 1955; Geach 1956) and although it is unclear when Frege finally accepted that his work had been fatally undermined, the third volume of *Basic Laws* was never published and at the end of his life Frege admitted that his logicist programme had been a failure, and attempted in his last years to found arithmetic on geometry.

After the discovery of the paradox Frege was now to suffer personal tragedy. His wife died, leaving him to bring up his adopted son, Alfred, on his own. He published little following this, apart from several articles on the foundations of geometry which arose from his correspondence with Hilbert before the disclosure of Russell's Paradox, and three articles against 'formalist' arithmetic in response to an attack by his Jena colleague Johannes Thomae. However, Frege did engage in extensive correspondence during this period and continued his lectures at Jena. And this was the time that he met Wittgenstein, who wrote to him after reading an account of his views in Russell's *Principles of Mathematics*. The correspondence led to a meeting and as well as discussing his own views with Wittgenstein Frege also made the suggestion that Wittgenstein should go to Cambridge to study with Russell.

It was also during this period that Rudolf Carnap attended Frege's lectures. Like Wittgenstein, Carnap greatly admired Frege's work and developed and disseminated his ideas when he subsequently became influential.

Frege retired from lecturing in 1918 and moved from Jena to Bad Kleinen, near his home town of Wismar. He did not cease working and appears to have gained renewed vigour in this later period. At any rate he wrote a series of papers, of which the first, 'Thoughts' ('Der Gedanke'), has had more influence and attracted more discussion than any of Frege's papers apart from 'On Sense and Reference'. During this time, too, Frege came to believe that arithmetic must have a geometrical foundation. In a piece entitled 'Numbers and Arithmetic' written in the last year of his life he wrote:

> The more I have thought the matter over, the more convinced I have become that arithmetic and geometry have developed on the same basis – a geometrical one in fact – so that mathematics in its entirety is really geometry. Only on this view does mathematics present itself as completely homogeneous in nature. Counting, which arose psychologically out of the demands of practical life, has led the learned astray. (Frege 1979: 275–7)

Thus Frege at last abandoned the view he had held ever since his first publication, that arithmetic, unlike geometry, was a source of *a priori* knowledge requiring no foundation in intuition.

However, Frege did not have the time left to pursue his new ideas and he died in 1925, aged seventy-seven, before he was able to know of the widespread influence his work was to have.

He bequeathed his unpublished writings to his son Alfred with the following note attached (now printed in Frege 1979: ix):

> Dear Alfred,
> Do not despise the pieces I have written. Even if all is not gold, there is gold in them. I believe there are things which will one day be priced much more highly than they are now. Take care that nothing gets lost.
> Your loving father.
> It is a large part of myself that I bequeath to you herewith.

Alfred handed over Frege's papers to Heinrich Scholz of the University of Münster in 1935. Unfortunately the originals were destroyed by Allied bombing during the war. However, copies had been made of most of the important pieces and eventually, after a long delay, due to Scholz's own illness and death, they were published in German in 1969 and in English in 1979. Meanwhile Frege's correspondence was edited and published in German in 1976 and in English (in an abridged edition) in 1980.

The Origin and Development of Frege's Philosophy

It is clear that from the start of his career Frege was interested in seeking a foundation for arithmetic. How important he took it to be for a mathematician to be clear about the fundamentals of his subject is made very obvious in a harsh review, his first publication after his appointment as Privatdozent at Jena, of a book on *The Elements of Arithmetic* by one H. Seager (in Frege 1984). Frege writes:

> After some particularly unfortunate explanations of the calculating operations and their symbols, some propositions are presented in the second and third chapters under the title of 'the fundamental theorems and most essential transformation formulas'. These propositions, which actually form the foundation of the whole of arithmetic, are lumped together without proof; while, later, theorems of a much more limited importance are distinguished with particular names and proved in detail. . . . The amplification of concepts which is so highly important for arithmetic, and is often the source of great confusion for the student, leaves much to be desired. . . . The result of all these deficiencies will be that the student will merely memorize the laws of arithmetic and become accustomed to being satisfied with words he does not understand.

Whether it was reading Seager's book that stimulated in Frege the ambition to set arithmetic on pure logical foundations we do not know. But we will understand this project better if we place it in the philosophical and mathematical context of his time. In particular, it will be illuminating to look briefly at the links between Frege's project and the Kantian doctrine of the synthetic *a priori* and the associated notion of pure intuition; the development of non-Euclidean geometry; and the arithmetization of analysis.

For Kant mathematics was an epistemological puzzle, combining two apparently irreconcilable features: necessity and substantiality. Mathematical propositions seem to state truths that could not be otherwise. But at the same time they appear to represent genuine extensions of our knowledge. In this respect, Kant thought, they were like the maxim of universal causation, that every event has a cause, whose problematic status Kant's predecessor Hume, the great British empiricist, had brought to his attention. Hume had operated with a dichotomy, between relations of ideas and matters of fact, which did not allow any place for a proposition of this character. Thus he claimed that the causal maxim was, in fact, a merely

contingently true statement of a matter of fact and that our ascribing to it the character of a necessary truth was a mistake whose psychological origin he took it to be one of his principal achievements
to have explained. Kant would not accept this, however, but neither
was he willing to accept that the causal maxim merely expressed a
Humean relation of ideas, and so, like the proposition that every
effect has a cause, was trivially true in virtue of its meaning. Both in
this case and the case of mathematics, Kant thought, what we had
to acknowledge was the existence of propositions which fell on
neither side of Hume's dichotomy.

Kant discusses this problem in *The Critique of Pure Reason* (1781)
within the framework of a pair of distinctions: (i) between *a priori*
and *a posteriori* knowledge and (ii) between *analytic* and *synthetic*
judgements. He explains the first term of the first distinction as
follows:

> We shall understand by *a priori* knowledge, not knowledge indepen-
> dent of this or that experience, but knowledge absolutely indepen-
> dent of all experience. (Kant 1929 A2/B3: 43)

A posteriori knowledge, then, is knowledge that does require
experience.

Kant's second distinction he explains as follows:

> Either the predicate B belongs to the subject A, as something which
> is (covertly) contained in this concept A, or B lies outside the concept
> A, although it does indeed stand in connection with it. In the one
> case I entitle the judgement analytic, in the other synthetic. (Kant
> 1929 A6/B10: 48)

In an analytic judgement, Kant says, in thinking the subject term
one thinks the predicate term, so no new knowledge can be
expressed in an analytic judgement. He illustrates this distinction
with the following example:

> Analytic judgement: All Bodies are Extended
> Synthetic judgement: All Bodies are Heavy

Thus for Kant, there are four possible categories of judgement.
The synthetic *a posteriori*, the synthetic *a priori*, the analytic *a posteriori* and the analytic *a priori*. The first category, illustrated by the
judgement 'All Bodies are Heavy' is unproblematic, as is the fourth,

illustrated by the judgement 'All Bodies are Extended', the third category is unproblematically empty. For Kant it is the second category, the synthetic *a priori*, which is of interest. It is in this category that he places the causal maxim and mathematical propositions, as extending our knowledge – since the concept of the predicate is not thought in thinking the concept of the subject – and at the same time as necessary and universally true and, therefore, knowable independently of the contingencies of particular features of our experience.

Kant's argument for the synthetic *a priori* character of mathematics is clearly expressed in his *Prolegomena* (1783) (Kant 1959). First he argues:

> properly mathematical propositions are always judgements *a priori*, and not empirical, because they carry with them necessity, which cannot be taken from experience. (1959: 18–19)

Next he argues, illustrating his point with his favourite mathematical proposition, that $7 + 5 = 12$ is synthetic because twelve can never be found in the analysis of the sum of seven and five:

> The concept of twelve is in no way already thought merely by thinking this unification of seven and five, and though I analyse my concept of such a possible sum as long as I please, I shall never find the twelve in it. We have to go outside these concepts and with the help of the intuition which corresponds to one of them, our five fingers for instance, (or as Segner does in his Arithmetic) five points, add to the concept of seven, unit by unit, the five given in intuition. Thus we really amplify our concept by this proposition $7 + 5 = 12$, and add to the first concept a new one which was not thought in it. That is to say, arithmetical propositions are always synthetic, of which we shall be the more clearly aware if we take rather larger numbers. For it is then obvious that however we might turn and twist our concept, we could never find the sum by means of mere analysis of our concepts without seeking the aid of intuition. (1959: 19–20)

Kant thinks that the same is true of geometrical truths, e.g. that a straight line is the shortest distance between two points:

> That the straight line between two points is the shortest, is a synthetic proposition. For my concept of *straight* contains nothing of quantity,

but only of quality. The concept of the shortest is wholly an addition, and cannot be derived, through any process of analogy, from the concept of the straight line. (1929 B16: 53)

And, as already indicated in the penultimate passage quoted, he thinks that the key notion to be appealed to in explaining how such synthetic *a priori* knowledge is possible is that of *intuition*.

An intuition for Kant is a singular representation of an object, a concept is a general representation. Concepts are the products of the understanding, to which individual representations are never given. So:

> Our nature is so constituted that our *intuition* can never be other than sensible; that is, it contains only the mode in which we are affected by objects. . . . Without sensibility no object would be given to us. (Kant 1929 A51/B75: 93)

However, Kant thinks, as well as empirical intuitions of the kind an empiricist such as Hume would recognize, we must also recognize pure intuitions which underlie our *a priori* knowledge of arithmetic and geometry. These pure intuitions constitute the *forms* supplied by the human mind, in which the *matter* of any empirical intuition must be given to us. And of these forms he says:

> there are two forms of sensible intuition, serving as principles of *a priori* knowledge, namely, space and time. (1929 A22/B63: 67)

Thus, Kant thinks, any sense experience we have of the world must conform to these forms of intuition. Any experience of outer sense (of objects other than ourselves) must conform to the form of space, and any experience at all, whether it presents itself as experience of something other than its subject or not, must conform to the form of time. Russell's famous analogy is of a man who because he wears blue spectacles sees everything blue (Russell 1946: 734). Using a similar analogy Bennett (1966: 15–16) compares the pure intuition of space, the form of outer sense, to the invariant form imposed on a piece of music by its being played on a piano. Whatever the world is like in itself, when it 'plays' on our sensibility, because of the nature of that 'instrument' the product must invariably have a spatio-temporal form. To rephrase the point in terms of Russell's analogy, we all wear spatio-temporal spectacles and so are constrained to perceive the world, however it is in itself, as spatio-temporal.

Kant finds in this doctrine an explanation of the synthetic *a priori* character of arithmetic and geometry (which he takes to be Euclidean geometry). As he explains in the *Prolegomenon*:

> But we find that all mathematical knowledge has this peculiarity, that it must first exhibit its concept *in intuition*, and do so *a priori*, in an intuition that is not empirical but pure: without this means mathematics cannot make a single step. Its judgements are therefore always intuitional. (1959: 36)

Kant illustrates the involvement of intuition in our mathematical judgements with the example of the proof that the angles of a triangle sum to two right angles. He maintains that no analysis of the concept of a triangle could ever yield this knowledge. Rather to arrive at it we must *construct* a triangle in intuition (draw one on paper or visualize one in the mind's eye) and then deduce the conclusion from the universal conditions governing the construction of triangles. In this fashion the mathematician arrives at his conclusions through a chain of inferences guided throughout by intuition (1929: 742–5).

It is the same with our arithmetical knowledge, Kant thinks. Both spatial intuition, as we saw earlier in the example of $7 + 5 = 12$, in the form of intuitions of fingers or points, and temporal intuition, in the form of counting, are involved in our acquisition of arithmetical knowledge (though Kant thinks that arithmetic is particularly related to the pure intuition of time as geometry is to the pure intuition of space). Thus we see that everything we can experience must conform to the forms of time and space, and as the features of these are spelled out in arithmetic and geometry, everything we experience must conform to the rules of arithmetic and (Euclidean) geometry. A world conforming to a different geometry or a different arithmetic is not *inconceivable* – it would involve no contradiction – but it is *unimaginable*, and we can therefore know in advance that no such world could be given to us in sensibility.

Crucial to this Kantian theory, then, is the assumption that our knowledge of both arithmetic and geometry depend upon our knowledge of space and time, and that in this respect geometry and arithmetic are epistemologically on a par.

The discovery of non-Euclidean geometries and the proof of their consistency relative to Euclidean geometry thus created a serious problem for this unified Kantian theory of mathematics in the absence of consistent alternative arithmetics (see also Detlefsen 1995, to which the following is indebted).

In the work of Gauss, Lobatchevsky, Bolyai and Riemann, non-Euclidean geometry was developed by replacing the Euclidean fifth axiom, the axiom of parallels (that through any point outside a straight line there is one and only one straight line coplanar with it, which does not intersect the given straight line in either direction) with an alternative axiom. When it was established that such alternative geometries were consistent if Euclidean geometry was consistent it became tempting to conclude that we do not, after all, have *a priori* knowledge of the truth of Euclidean geometry as we have of arithmetic, but can only know it *a posteriori* on the basis of empirical intuition. Thus Gauss wrote in 1821:

> My innermost conviction is that geometry has a completely different position in our *a priori* knowledge than arithmetic . . . we must humbly admit that, although number is purely a product of our intellect, space also possesses a reality outside the mind to which we cannot ascribe its laws *a priori*. (Gauss 1863–1903: vol. 8, 200)

And later in a letter to Bolyai's father he wrote:

> It is precisely in the impossibility of deciding *a priori* between [Euclidean geometry] and [the younger Bolyai's non-Euclidean geometry] that we have the clearest proof that Kant was wrong to claim that space is only the form of our intuition. (Gauss 1863–1903: vol. 8, 220–1)

As Detlefsen explained, there thus developed a belief among nineteenth-century thinkers that arithmetic was *not* epistemologically on a par with geometry, as Kant had thought, and that a philosophy of mathematics was required which recognized this fact.

The third feature of the nineteenth-century mathematical context which was importantly present in the background of Frege's thought was the reductive programme known as 'the arithmetization of analysis', that is the programme of definition of the real numbers in terms of rational numbers (and set theory) and thus, since rational numbers can easily be defined in terms of natural numbers, in terms of natural numbers. The arithmetization of analysis was actually the culmination of a movement to introduce greater rigour in the development of mathematical analysis and particularly to define the crucial notion of a 'limit' without appeal to the paradoxical notion of infinitesimals. This movement eventually led to a focus on real numbers, which were shown to be definable (by Weierstrass, Cantor and Dedekind) purely in terms of rational numbers without any appeal to geometrical notions (which had been the earlier basis of the account of real numbers).

Dedekind stresses the need to provide a non-geometrical foundation for analysis in his 'Continuity and Irrational Numbers' (1872):

> In discussing the notion of the approach of a variable magnitude to a fixed limiting value, and especially in proving the theorem that every magnitude which grows continually, but not beyond all limits, must certainly approach a limiting value, I had recourse to geometric evidences. Even now such recourse to geometric intuition in a first presentation of the differential calculus, I regard as extremely useful, from the didactic standpoint, and indeed indispensable, if one does not wish to lose too much time. But that this form of introduction into the differential calculus can make no claim to being scientific, no one will deny. For myself this feeling of dissatisfaction was so overpowering that I made the fixed resolve to keep meditating on the question till I should find a purely arithmetical and perfectly rigorous foundation for the principles of infinitesimal analysis. (1909a: 1–2)

Given his achievement it seemed to him that he had reduced the whole of analysis to a study of natural numbers. As he puts it himself in 'The Nature and Meaning of Number' (1888):

> every theorem of algebra and higher analysis, no matter how remote, can be expressed as a theorem about natural numbers, – a declaration I have heard repeatedly from the lips of Dirichlet. (Dedekind 1909b: 135)

Given that this was so, as it seemed obvious that it was in the 1870s, the natural next question to ask was about the natural numbers themselves. And Dedekind himself made this transition, putting forward independently of Frege a version of logicism which he states thus:

> In speaking of arithmetic (algebra, analysis) as a part of logic I mean to imply that I consider the number-concept entirely independent of

the notions or intuitions of space and time. That I consider it an immediate result from the laws of thought. . . . It is only through the purely logical process of building up the science of numbers and by thus acquiring the continuous number domain that we are prepared accurately to investigate our notions of space and time by bringing them into relation with this number-domain created in our minds. (1909b: 31–2)

With this philosophical and mathematical context in mind, let us now return to the development of Frege's own thought.

From the start Frege's work had an epistemological motive and was set against a Kantian background. He begins his doctoral dissertation by insisting that geometry rests on intuition.

By contrast, he insists in his Habilitationsschrift:

It is quite clear that there can be no intuition of so pervasive and abstract a concept as that of magnitude. There is therefore a remarkable difference between geometry and arithmetic concerning the way in which their basic laws are grounded. The elements of all geometrical constructions are intuitions, and geometry refers to intuition as the source of its axioms. Because the object of arithmetic is not intuitable, it follows that its basic laws cannot be based on intuition. (Frege 1984: 57)

The same point, that the object of arithmetic is not intuitable, is made in section 105 of the *Foundations*:

In arithmetic we are not concerned with objects which we come to know as something alien from without through the medium of the senses, but with objects given directly to our reason and, as its nearest kin, utterly transparent to it. (Frege 1968)

Frege attempted to establish a philosophy of mathematics which respected what he took to be the fundamental difference, demonstrated by the existence of non-Euclidean geometries, between geometry and arithmetic: that arithmetic, in contrast to geometry, is not merely applicable to everything that is intuitable, but to everything that is numerable, that is, to everything that is *conceivable*.

This generality of arithmetic is something he stresses in section 14 of *Foundations* where his recognition of the consistency of non-Euclidean geometries is also indicated:

Empirical propositions hold good of what is physically or psychologically actual, the truths of geometry govern all that is spatially intuitable, whether natural or product of our fancy. The wildest visions of delirium, the boldest inventions of legend and poetry, where animals speak and stars stand still, where men are turned to stone and trees turn into men, whence the drowning haul themselves up by their own topknots – all these remain, so long as they remain intuitable, still subject to the axioms of geometry. Conceptual thought alone can after a fashion shake off this yoke, when it assumes, say, a space of four dimensions or positive curvature. To study such conceptions is not useless, by any means, but it is to leave the ground of intuition entirely behind. If we do make use of intuition even here, as an aid, it is still the same old intuition of Euclidean space, the only space of which we have any picture. Only then the intuition is not taken at its face value, but as symbolic of something else; for example, we call straight or plane what we actually intuit as curved. For purposes of conceptual thought we can always assume the contrary of some one or other of the geometrical axioms, without involving ourselves in any self-contradiction when we proceed to our deductions, despite the conflict between our assumptions and our intuitions. The fact that this is possible shows that the axioms of geometry are independent of one another and of the primitive laws of logic and consequently are synthetic. Can the same be said of the fundamental propositions of the science of number? Here, we have only to try denying one of them, and complete confusion ensues. Even to think at all seems no longer possible. The basis of arithmetic lies deeper, it seems, than that of any of the empirical sciences, and even that of geometry. The truths of arithmetic govern all that is numerable. This is the widest domain of all; for to it belongs not only the actual, not only the intuitable, but everything thinkable. Should not the laws of number then, be connected very intimately with the laws of thought? (Frege 1968: 20–1)

To explain the universal validity of arithmetic was the fundamental motive behind Frege's philosophy. To do so he believed he needed to establish the independence of arithmetic from intuition, and hence geometry, and to do that, in turn, he needed to establish that at no point did intuition need to be appealed to in arithmetical proof (see also Demopoulos 1994, to which the following is greatly indebted). It was for this purpose, he explains in *Foundations*, that he invented his conceptual notation (*Begriffsschrift*), to give 'gapless' mathematical proofs:

In proofs as we know them, progress is by jumps, which is why the variety of types of inference in mathematics appears to be so excessively rich . . . the correctness of such a transition is immediately self-evident to us ... whereupon, since it does not obviously conform to any of the recognized types of logical inference, we are prepared to accept its self-evidence forthwith as intuitive, and the conclusion itself as a synthetic truth – and this even when obviously it holds good of much more than merely what can be intuited.

On these lines what is synthetic and based on intuition cannot be sharply separated from what is analytic ...

To minimize these drawbacks, I invented my conceptual notation. It is designed to produce expressions which are shorter and easier to take in, ... so that no step is permitted which does not conform to the rules which are laid down once and for all. It is impossible, therefore, for any premiss to creep into a proof without being noticed. In this way I have, without borrowing any axiom from intuition, given a proof of a proposition which might at first sight be taken for synthetic which I shall here formulate as follows:

> If the relation of every member of a series to its successor is one- or many-one, and if m and y follows in that series after x, then either y comes in that series before m, or it coincides with m, or it follows after m. (1968: 102–3)

This proposition is number 133 in *Conceptual Notation*, to the proof of which Frege devotes the whole of its part III. In his introductory comments in this part of *Conceptual Notation* he once again stresses the way in which intuition can be shown by the use of his conceptual notation to be inessential to arithmetical proof:

> Throughout the present example [the proof of 133] we see how pure thought, irrespective of any content given by the senses or even by an intuition *a priori*, can, solely from the content that results from its own constitution, bring forth judgements that at first sight appear to be possible only on the basis of some intuition. (1972: 167)

Alerted by this, the significance of Frege's apparently casual reference to 'something intuitive' in the Preface to *Conceptual Notation*, in which he explains how the idea of his conceptual notation arose, will not be missed:

> we divide all truths which require a proof into two kinds: the proof of the first kind can proceed purely logically, while that of the second kind must be supported by empirical facts ... not the psychological mode of origin, but the most perfect method of proof underlies the classification.
>
> Now while considering the question to which of these two kinds do judgements of arithmetic belong, I had first to test how far one

would get in arithmetic by means of logical deductions alone, supported only by the laws of thought, which transcend all particulars. The procedure in this effort was this: I sought first to reduce the concept of ordering-in-a-sequence to the notion of *logical* ordering, in order to advance from here to the concept of number. So that something intuitive could not squeeze in unnoticed here, it was important to keep the chain of reasoning free of gaps. As I endeavoured to fulfil this requirement most rigorously, I found an obstacle in the inadequacy of the language; despite all the unwieldiness of the expressions, the more complex the relations became, the less precision – which my purpose required – could be obtained. From this deficiency arose the idea of the 'conceptual notation' presented here. Thus, its chief purpose should be to test in the most reliable manner the validity of a chain of reasoning and expose each presupposition which tends to creep in unnoticed, so that its source can be investigated. (1972: 103–4)

So far I have been stressing the anti-Kantian motivation of Frege's work: his desire to demonstrate that arithmetic, in contrast to Euclidean geometry, is applicable to everything conceivable and does not require any ground in intuition. The link between Frege's thought and the arithmetization of analysis is related and can be better understood with this fundamental motivation in mind. As we saw in the passages quoted from Dedekind, the separation of analysis from geometry and the definition of the notion of a real number without appeal to geometrical concepts was one of the chief aims of this programme. And in extending this programme to the natural numbers, and thus putting forward his own version of logicism, Dedekind again stresses that he considers 'the number concept entirely independent of the notion or intuitions of space and time'. In fact, this is part of what 'logicism' means for Dedekind: 'In speaking of arithmetic (algebra, analysis) as part of logic I *mean to imply* that I consider the number-concept entirely independent of the notions or intuition of space and time' (1909b: 31, my italics). Logicism is thus not defined positively, in terms of what logic includes, but rather negatively, in terms of what it uncontroversially excludes – Kantian intuition.

Thus Frege's logicism was not a novel addition to nineteenth-century mathematics or philosophy, but rather belonged to an accepted tradition and had a comprehensible motivation in the context of its time. Later, particularly in the writings of the logical empiricists of the Vienna Circle, logicism came to be thought of as a way of demonstrating that the Kantian synthetic *a priori* need not be acknowledged at all, even in the domain of mathematics, in which it seemed most plausible to apply it. But such a *global* anti-Kantianism was never Frege's position: as we have seen, he remained wedded throughout his life to the synthetic *a priori* character of Euclidean geometry.

So far we have been considering the original motive of Frege's work. This remained constant until the time, after he became convinced that Russell's Paradox presented an insuperable roadblock (probably in 1906), that he abandoned his fundamental interests (only resuming them in the last years of his life, when he finally came to accept the Kantian view he had for so long opposed). However, Frege's thought nonetheless underwent important changes and developments during this time.

Initially, in *Conceptual Notation* Frege's aim appears to have been the relatively modest one of showing that *some* mathematical propositions, such as his number 133, which had previously been thought to be establishable only by an appeal to Kantian intuition, could be given gap-free proofs in his logical system and thus demonstrated without appeal to intuition. In this way the aim of *Conceptual Notation* was to establish that Kant's view of mathematics was mistaken, since that view implied that intuition was indispensable in (at least some) cases where it could be proved that this was not so. But either during the writing of *Conceptual Notation*, or soon after, Frege became convinced that intuition could be seen to be unnecessary *throughout* arithmetic and that the latter could be given a wholly logical foundation. Thus he announces at the end of its Preface:

> arithmetic was the point of departure for the train of thought that led me to my ideography. And that is why I intend to apply it first of all to that science, attempting to provide a more detailed analysis of the concepts of arithmetic and a deeper foundation for its theorems. For the present I have reported in the third chapter some of the developments in this direction. To proceed further along the path indicated, to elucidate the concepts of number, magnitude and so forth – all this will be the object of further investigations, which I shall publish immediately after this booklet. (1972: 107)

The 'further investigations' here referred to, of course, appeared, after a lengthy delay, in *Foundations*. The logic, philosophical logic and theory of meaning of the *Foundations* are those of *Conceptual Notation* applied to the development of Frege's logicist thesis.

After its publication, however, important developments took place in Frege's system. *Conceptual Notation* and *Foundations* operated with a notion of the conceptual content of a sentence or subsentential expression. In his article 'On Sense and Reference' Frege distinguished within this notion the two notions of *Sinn* (sense) and *Bedeutung* (reference) (in Frege 1969). This distinction became central to Frege's thought thereafter and is perhaps his most important contribution to philosophy.

Secondly, in his article 'Function and Concept' (also in Frege 1969) Frege develops and makes explicit the identification of concepts with functions mapping arguments on to truth-values which then becomes incorporated into his formal treatment of arithmetic in *Basic Laws*. In *Conceptual Notation* Frege operates with the notion of a function, but his explicit definition of what a function is restricts it to linguistic expressions, and in *Foundations*, though the notion of a concept is central to Frege's argument – one of his fundamental contentions being that a statement of number is an assertion *about* a concept – he does not give the notion any analysis or identify concepts with functions.

Associated with Frege's distinction between sense and reference and his identification of concepts with functions is another doctrine Frege introduced after *Foundations* – the doctrine that sentences are proper names of truth-values. Since Frege had now distinguished the earlier notion of conceptual content into the two components of sense and reference, and since he applied this distinction across the board, he was led to distinguish between the sense of a complete sentence (which he called a 'thought') and its reference. Regarding concepts (the reference of predicates) as functions he was then led to the conclusion that sentences, as a particular kind of completed complex functional expression, must have as their references truth-values.

Also associated with the other doctrines introduced by Frege after *Foundations* was his definite adherence to the identification of numbers with the extensions of concepts (classes). In *Foundations* Frege's concern had been to explain how numbers, as objects, could be given to us otherwise than in intuition. He was led to identify them with extensions of concepts, taken to be logical objects already understood, by a line of thought we will examine later. But he is quite explicit that this identification is tentative and not central. After *Foundations*, given the explicit identification of concepts with functions, he is able to explain extensions of concepts as a special case of value ranges of functions – objects defined by his Basic Law (V) – and commits himself to the identification.

Apart from these changes Frege's system remains the same after *Foundations* and in the prolegomenon to *Basic Laws* he gives a precise statement of the philosophical logic developed after *Foundations* in terms of which he then proceeds to the development of the gapless system of proofs required to demonstrate his logicism.

After the discovery of the vulnerability of his system to Russell's Paradox the one departure he makes is the rejection of value ranges as fictions of our language: the distinction between sense and reference, the characterization of concepts as functions and all the associated elements of the system are retained.

Frege's Contributions to Philosophy

Frege's contributions to philosophy fall into four areas – logic, philosophy of mathematics, philosophical logic and the theory of meaning – and it will be convenient now to summarize them.

Frege's definitive contributions in logic, as we have noted, were already present in *Conceptual Notation*. Logic before Frege had been dominated by the Aristotelian theory of the syllogism, which was concerned with the validity of inferences involving general sentences, that is those containing such expressions as 'every', 'some', 'no' and their synonyms. An example of a syllogism is:

> Every swan is an animal
> Every animal is a living thing
> *Ergo*: Every swan is a living thing

In each of these sentences there is a subject term (in the first sentence this is 'swan') and a predicate term ('animal' in the first sentence). The term which occurs in both premisses ('animal') is called the 'middle term'.

Thus Aristotelian logic is a logic of *terms*. It is concerned with the various patterns of argument which can be exhibited by combining the expressions 'every', 'some', 'no' and their synonyms with terms. For example, the pattern exhibited by the above argument is 'A belongs to all B and B belongs to all C therefore A belongs to all C' in which 'A', 'B' and 'C' stand in for any terms whatever.

A competing logical theory, developed by the Stoics, was a logic of sentences, or propositions. The Stoics were interested in the validity of arguments like the following:

> If it is day then it is light
> It is day
> *Ergo*:   It is light.

The pattern this exhibits, in virtue of which the argument is valid, is expressed as follows by the Stoics: 'If the first then the second, the first, therefore, the second.' Thus Stoic logic was concerned with the validity of those patterns of argument which can be exhibited by replacing sentences occurring in more complex sentences by symbols ('the first', 'the second') which stand in for any sentence whatever. The patterns the Stoics studied were those whose validity depended on the occurrence in them of the sentential operators: negation ('It is not the case that'), conjunction ('Both . . . and . . . '), disjunction ('Either . . . or . . . ') and the conditional ('If . . . then . . . '), which are used to construct more complex sentences from simpler ones.

These two theories of logic were merged in the work of George Boole (1815–1864), who developed an algebraic system whose formulae, differently interpreted, could be taken either as expressing the general propositions which were the subject matter of the Aristotelian logic of terms or the complex propositions which were the subject matter of Stoic logic. Boole called propositions of the former type 'primary propositions' and propositions of the latter type 'secondary propositions'. This indicated his view of their relative priority. He thought that secondary propositions could be understood as generalizations about classes of occasions or times and so could be reduced to primary propositions.

The greatest weakness of logic as developed before Frege was its inability to deal with sentences containing expressions for *multiple generality*, sentences like 'Every boy loves some girl', or 'some girl is admired by every boy', in which two or more general expressions ('every boy', 'some girl') are joined by an expression for a relation. Such sentences, which are, of course, commonplace in mathematics (e.g. 'Every even number is the sum of two primes'), are frequently ambiguous. Medieval logicians elaborated theories of 'supposition', in part to deal with multiple generality and explain the ambiguities, but could not provide a convincing account.

In addition, even in Boole's system, in which both the traditional Aristotelian logic of terms and the Stoic logic of propositions can be represented, the validity of inferences from the one type of proposition to the other cannot be represented – precisely because for

Boole term logic and propositional logic are *two* interpretations of the *same* algebraic system.

The logical system Frege introduced in *Conceptual Notation* resolved these difficulties once and for all. Its key was the replacement of the *grammatical* notions of subject and predicate, central to Aristotelian syllogistic, by the *mathematical* notions of argument and function.

Thus Frege viewed the sentence:

Carbon dioxide is heavier than hydrogen

not as asserting of the subject 'carbon dioxide' the predicate 'is heavier than hydrogen' but as the value of the function 'is heavier than hydrogen' for the argument 'carbon dioxide', or again as the value of the function 'carbon dioxide is heavier than' for the argument 'hydrogen', or again as the value of the third function 'is heavier than' for the pair of arguments 'carbon dioxide' and 'hydrogen'. Analogously, 2 + 3 (that is, the number 5) can be regarded as the value of the function designated by '( ) + 3' for the argument 2, or as the value of the different function designated by '2 + ( )' for the argument 3, or as the value of the third function designated by '( ) + ( )' for the pair of arguments 2 and 3.

On the basis of this innovation Frege was then able to introduce his most important logical discovery – the quantifier. We can express the fact that carbon dioxide is heavier than hydrogen, using Frege's function/argument language, in some such way as follows:

The function 'is heavier than hydrogen' is a fact for the argument 'carbon dioxide'

And, since hydrogen is the lightest gas (and we are only considering gases):

The function 'is heavier than hydrogen' is a fact whatever we take as its argument

This, of course, states the general claim that *everything* is heavier than hydrogen. Using now familiar logical symbolism, which is not different in essentials from Frege's, we can express this as follows: $(\forall x)(x$ is heavier than hydrogen). Here the *universal quantifier* '$(\forall x)$', captures the generality of Frege's phrase 'whatever we take as its argument'.

As we shall see in more detail later, the introduction of the quantifier (and its associated variable) enables Frege to express unambiguously, in a perspicuous notation, not only singly general propositions like the one in the example, but also multiply general propositions like 'Every gas is heavier than some gas'. When combined with Frege's innovations in propositional logic (the branch of logic studied by the Stoics), it also enables him to express unambiguously in his symbolism *every* proposition expressible in Aristotelian syllogistic and *every* multiply general proposition no matter how complex. The essential insight which made this possible for Frege was his reversal in the order of explanatory priority of Boole's 'primary' and 'secondary' propositions. (It is this reversal Frege expresses by his repeated statement that, unlike other logicians, he proceeds from judgements rather than concepts.)

Frege's other great contribution to logic in *Conceptual Notation* was his construction of the first formal system. A formal system has three parts: a precisely specified language in which the propositions of the system can be expressed, a set of axioms, and a specification of rules by which theorems can be deduced from the axioms in accordance with purely formal or syntactic constraints (i.e. on the basis of their shapes). The formulae of the formal system will express particular propositions under the intended interpretation, but it will be unnecessary to know what propositions are expressed by the formulae in a derivation in order to check whether that derivation is in accordance with the rules. That can be done mechanically simply by attending to the shapes of the formulae. Frege's system as presented in *Conceptual Notation* is not quite flawless, since it employs a rule of inference (a rule of substitution) which is not explicitly stated, but this defect is remedied in *Basic Laws*. Given a formal system it makes sense to ask whether it is complete, whether all the logical truths it is intended to capture can indeed be derived from its axioms via its rules. Frege's formulation in *Conceptual Notation* (with the implicit rule of substitution made explicit) is a complete axiomatization of first-order logic and contains a complete axiomatization of propositional logic as a subsystem.

In the philosophy of mathematics, as we have already seen, Frege's primary aim was to establish the independence of arithmetic from intuition and thus to refute Kant's contention that it is synthetic *a priori*. In *Foundations* he consequently expresses the thesis he wishes to defend in the Kantian terminology as the thesis that arithmetic is analytic. But he is equally concerned to refute the empiricism of John Stuart Mill, whose position, in Kantian terms, is that arithmetic is synthetic *a posteriori*. Thus he devotes the first part of *Foundations* to a critique of these two philosophies and elaborations of them. His criticisms, which we shall examine later, are devastating, and enable him to proceed to his positive contentions from the firmly established basis of several conclusions about what numbers are *not*: they are not subjective ideas, nor physical objects, nor collections or properties of such. Frege's first and most famous positive contention he expresses in his claim: 'The content of a statement of number is an assertion about a concept.'

If I say, for example, 'Venus has 0 moons', I am not making a statement about the moons of Venus (which do not exist if I am right). Rather I am assigning a property to the concept *moon of Venus*. I am saying how many things there are falling under that concept. Another way of putting this fundamental point is to say that a statement of number is a statement about a *kind of thing* – a statement about how many things there are of that kind.

It is an important implication of this point that the fundamental method of referring to numbers is via descriptions of the form 'the number belonging to the concept F' or, more briefly, 'the number of F's': for example, 'the number of moons of Venus'. This apparently trivial linguistic claim is crucial for Frege, because it enables him to provide an answer other than the Kantian one to Kant's question: 'How are numbers given to us?'

For Kant the only possible answer to this question is: they are given to us in intuition. For numbers, he thinks, are objects and objects can only be given in intuition. Frege accepts the Kantian distinction between objects and concepts, and indeed states as a fundamental principle in *Foundations* 'never to lose sight of the distinction between concept and object', but he also insists that numbers are objects. Thus he is faced with the need to explain how numbers are given to us 'if we cannot have any ideas or intuitions of them' (1968: 73). His answer appeals to the second fundamental principle he states at the outset of the *Foundations*, his famous 'context principle': 'never to ask for the meaning of a word in isolation but only in the context of a sentence.' The precise meaning and status of this principle in Frege's philosophy has become the most controversial question in Fregean scholarship. But its significance for Frege at the point in his discussion we are concerned with is that it enables him to make what Michael Dummett has called 'the linguistic turn' (Dummett 1991a: 111–12): to convert what is plainly for Kant an epistemological question into a question about language. 'Since', Frege writes, 'it is only in the context of a sentence that words have any meaning, our problem becomes this: to define the sense of a sentence in which a number word occurs.'

Since numbers are objects, Frege now goes on to say, the most important form of sentence whose sense must be explained is one asserting identity: 'if we are to use the symbol *a* to signify an object, we must have a criterion for deciding in all cases whether *b* is the same as *a*' (1968: 73). But given that the fundamental way to refer to a number is as the number associated with a certain concept, it follows that what needs explaining is the sense of sentences of the form:

> the number which belongs to the concept F is the same as that which belongs to the concept G

To explain this is to give the *criterion of identity* for numbers.

The criterion Frege proposes is *one–one correlation*. A one–one correlation holds between the F's and the G's if and only if every F can be paired with exactly one G and every G with exactly one F so that no F or G is left over. Frege is able, appealing to the treatment of relations in *Conceptual Notation*, to give a purely logical definition of one–one correlation, and so is able to put forward what has now come to be called Hume's Principle (because Frege introduces it with a quotation from Hume):

> The number of F's is identical with the number of G's if and only if there is a one–one correlation between the F's and G's

as a definition of numerical identity in purely logical terms.

It is at this point that things start to get murky. For Frege now rejects Hume's Principle as an adequate account of numerical identity on the ground that it does not allow us to determine whether Julius Caesar is a number! This objection has come to be known as 'the Julius Caesar objection'. Nevertheless Frege does not dismiss Hume's Principle completely but treats its derivability as a criterion of adequacy of the explicit definition of number he goes on to give in terms of extensions of concepts (classes). However, recent work on Frege's philosophy of arithmetic has made it clear that the role of Hume's Principle is arguably more significant than this suggests. For first, it can be proved that if Hume's Principle is added as the sole additional axiom to second-order logic, that is, the logic of *Conceptual Notation*, then axioms sufficient for arithmetic (Peano's axioms or Frege's own set, which are equivalent) can be derived (see Parsons 1965; Wright 1983; Boolos 1998). This thesis has come to be known, following a proposal made by George Boolos, as 'Frege's Theorem'. Secondly, it can be seen by attention to the actual structure of Frege's informal proof sketches in *Foundations* and his formal proofs in *Basic Laws* that Frege only ever makes essential appeal to his explicit definition of number in terms of extensions of concepts to derive Hume's Principle. Everything else is derived from Hume's Principle. Thus Frege himself proved Frege's Theorem (Boolos 1998; Heck 1993).

The importance of these mathematical and historical facts is disputed. Some modern commentators (notably Crispin Wright (1983 and 1998) and Bob Hale (1994)) take them as implying that, despite Russell's Paradox, Frege's essential insights can be defended: Hume's Principle can be taken as explanatory of our concept of number and since its addition to second-order logic is all that is required for arithmetic, arithmetic can be seen, not indeed merely as logic, but at least as a body of analytic truths. Other commentators, notably Michael Dummett (1991a) and George Boolos, deny this, and take it that Frege's logical project must be seen as a, doubtless magnificent, failure. One major issue in this debate is whether the Julius Caesar problem, which caused Frege to move to his explicit identification of numbers with the extensions of concepts, can be solved without taking this step, or legitimately ignored.

Two more of Frege's achievements in the philosophy of mathematics may be mentioned at this point: his definition (introduced in *Conceptual Notation*) of the notion of the ancestral of a relation (that relation which stands to the given relation as *being an ancestor of* stands to *being a parent of*) and his definition of the natural, or finite, numbers in *Foundations* as those which stand to zero in the ancestral of the relation of *immediate successor of*.

The general definition of the ancestral of a relation was very important to Frege's anti-Kantian project because it enabled him to explain the general notion of *following in a series* in purely logical terms, without any appeal to spatial or temporal intuition, and his definition of the *natural numbers* as the objects which stand to zero in the ancestral of the relation *immediate successor of*, given his definition of the ancestral in general (in terms, as we shall see, of the notion of a 'hereditary' property), enables him to establish immediately the *logical* validity of proof by induction in mathematics (since, in effect, his definition of the natural numbers is: the objects for which mathematical induction works).

Turning now to Frege's contribution to philosophical logic, first and foremost must be mentioned his functional theory of predication. We have already looked briefly at this in connection with Frege's logical contribution in *Conceptual Notation*. However, after *Conceptual Notation* Frege extends the theory and makes it much more precise. In *Conceptual Notation* the proposal is that a sentence like 'Hydrogen is lighter than carbon dioxide' may *itself* be seen as the value of a function for an argument, in fact, as we have seen, as the value of the different functions for different arguments, just as the number 2 + 3 (i.e. 5) may be seen as the value of different functions for different arguments. Thus Frege's focus at this stage is on *linguistic* items: sentences, the names they contain and the functions which we can regard as mapping names as arguments on to sentences as values. There is no explicit development of the thought that not only linguistic items but also the extra-linguistic items corresponding to them should be regarded similarly as functionally related. After *Foundations* this development takes place. Frege now suggests that in a sentence such as 'Socrates is wise' (to keep to a simple example) we can discern a proper name 'Socrates' and a 'concept word' or predicate ('is wise'). Corresponding to the name is the object for which it stands and corresponding to the 'concept word' is the concept for which it stands, and this concept is *itself* a function mapping objects onto values. In particular, just as the function designated by '( ) + 3' maps the number 2 onto the number 5, that is, the number which is designated by '2 + 3', so the concept for which '( ) is wise' stands maps the man Socrates onto that which is designated by the sentence 'Socrates is wise'. But what is designated by this sentence? Frege's answer is: the truth-value True (since the sentence *is* true). Thus he arrives at the conclusion that concepts are functions mapping arguments onto truth-values. Similarly, relations, which are analogous to the addition function, map *pairs* of arguments onto truth-values.

This functional theory of predication is fundamental to Frege's philosophy of logic; whether it can be sustained, or whether in the end it can only be seen as an illuminating analogy depends on whether Frege's view of truth-values as objects can be defended. But whichever is the case, it enables Frege to achieve a second fundamental insight which allows him to sweep aside as irrelevant thousands of years of debate about the distinction between universals and particulars. According to traditional doctrine the sentence 'Socrates is wise' introduces, via the predicate 'is wise', the universal *wisdom* into our discourse, as something said of Socrates. And *the very same item* may be introduced into our discourse, via the name 'wisdom', as something about which something else is said, for example, in the sentence 'Wisdom is a characteristic of the old'. Particulars, like Socrates, are then those items about which other things may be said but may not *themselves* be said of other things – they are the ultimate subjects of predication. Frege rejected this traditional view entirely. For he maintained that concepts are essentially predicative. What the predicate (or as he prefers to say, concept-word) '( ) is wise' stands for is a concept, and as such cannot be the reference of a proper name like 'Wisdom'. 'Wisdom' is a perfectly good proper name, and there is no need to deny it a reference, but its reference cannot be the same as that of any predicate, even the predicate '( ) is wise'.

The reason for this is that predicates, unlike proper names, are essentially incomplete. A predicate must be written with an indication of the gap(s) to be filled, not as a matter of convention, but because a predicate is not itself a quotable bit of a sentence, as a proper name is, but a pattern exhibited by the sentences which contain it. Thus proper names and predicates are of a fundamentally different character and simply could not play the same linguistic role. And correspondingly, Frege maintains, concepts and objects are ontologically of a fundamentally different character. No concept could be an object, because no concept could be the reference of a proper name.

Given Frege's functional theory of predication, the incompleteness of concepts emerges straightforwardly as a special case of the, perhaps at first sight more intuitively appealing, incompleteness of functions. That a function, as a mapping from objects or functions to objects, is itself awaiting completion, or saturation, by arguments has an initial appeal that the idea of the essential incompleteness of concepts (thought of as the references of concept-words or predicates) does not possess. Thus Frege's espousal of the functional theory of predication made it easy for him to accept the incompleteness, and therefore essentially predicative nature, of concepts. However, Frege's arguments for the incompleteness of concepts do not depend upon the functional theory of predication. What is essential is rather Frege's insight, expressed in his rejection of the traditional doctrine of subject and predicate, that the very same sentence can be analysed equally legitimately as saying different things of (the same or different) things, and that certain sentences, on certain analyses, need not contain any quotable part corresponding to what is said. Thus, to use Frege's own example, what 'Cato killed

Cato' says of Cato when broken up into 'Cato' and '( ) killed ( )' does not correspond to any quotable part of the sentence, but rather to its exhibiting the pattern of containing the verb 'killed' preceded and followed by two occurrences of the *same proper name*: thus we say the very same thing of Socrates with the sentence 'Socrates killed Socrates'.

Frege's insistence on the essentially predicative nature of a concept leads him into paradox, however. For he is led to deny that the concept *horse* is a concept – since 'the concept *horse*' is not an incomplete expression. This 'awkwardness of language', as Frege calls it, has been much debated. But it seems clear that Frege's conclusion (at least in 'Concept and Object') is that what we must recognize here is that there are fundamental ontological divisions in the world corresponding to fundamental linguistic divisions, and that these divisions cannot be put into words – cannot be stated, but are recognized implicitly by any competent language-user.

Finally, in this brief look at Frege's fundamental contributions, we must now turn to his theory of meaning; and first of all, of course, to his argument for his distinction between sense and reference.

In *Conceptual Notation* and *Foundations* Frege operated with an undifferentiated notion of the 'content' of a linguistic expression. But in 'On Sense and Reference' he distinguishes within this notion the two notions of sense and reference. His argument for this distinction starts from the puzzle of identity: the fact that identity statements can be both true and informative. Thus 'The Morning Star is the Evening Star' can convey new information to someone who has not heard it before. 'The Morning Star is the Morning Star' cannot.

Yet both 'the Morning Star' and 'the Evening Star' stand for the same thing, the planet Venus. If we consider only what the expressions in the two identity statements stand for, therefore, we cannot account for the difference in potential informativeness – or 'cognitive value' – of the two. Frege's solution is to say that associated with each of the two names 'the Morning Star' and 'the Evening Star' there is, as well as a reference, a sense – which is what someone understands when they grasp the expression – and the difference in cognitive value is accounted for by the different senses of the two names.

Once Frege has introduced the distinction between sense and reference in this way he applies it generally, not only to singular terms, but also to predicates and to sentences. In the case of predicates he insists on distinguishing the concept which is the reference of the predicate both from its extension – the class of objects it applies to – and from its sense. The former distinction is made on the grounds that concepts are incomplete whereas extensions are complete, and the latter on the grounds that concepts, unlike senses, have extensional identity conditions – two predicates, for example '( ) is a creature with a heart' and '( ) is a creature with kidneys', which differ in sense, because what it is to grasp one differs from what it is to grasp the other, might apply (as in this case) to exactly the same items and thus will stand for the same concept. In the case of sentences, Frege again makes the distinction between sense and reference – introducing the name 'thought' for the sense of a sentence and arguing that the reference of a sentence must be regarded as its truth-value. A key premiss in his argument for this conclusion is his compositionality principle for reference: that the reference of a complex expression is determined by the references of its components. Frege is able to argue powerfully that nothing else can be the reference of a sentence since nothing else remains unchanged when component expressions are replaced by others with the same reference.

The distinction between sense and reference is initially appealing but it has, in fact, become a focus of intense debate and its tenability and precise nature are a matter of considerable controversy. We shall be exploring the reasons for this in the last chapter of the book. But now we must return to look with more care at Frege's logic, which is the foundation on which all of his work rests.

2

Logic

The Purpose of *Conceptual Notation*

As we have seen, the purpose for which Frege invented his logical system was to enable him to give gap-free proofs in arithmetic to ensure that no appeal to Kantian intuition might squeeze in unnoticed. Initially, as he explains, he had attempted such proofs in ordinary language, but found it inadequate. Thus he was led to the construction of his 'conceptual notation', whose 'purpose should be to test in the most reliable manner the validity of a claim of reasoning and expose each presupposition which tends to creep in unnoticed so that the source can be investigated' (1972: 104).

The purpose of *Conceptual Notation* is thus quite special; Frege suggests that its relation to ordinary language might be usefully compared to that of the microscope to the eye:

> The latter, because of the range of its applicability and because of the ease with which it can adapt itself to the most varied circumstances, has a great superiority over the microscope. Of course, viewed as an optical instrument it reveals many imperfections, which usually remain unnoticed only because of its intimate connection with mental life. But as soon as scientific purposes place strong requirements upon sharpness of resolution, the eye proves to be inadequate. On the other hand, the microscope is perfectly suited for just such purposes; but for this very reason it is useless for others. Similarly, this 'conceptual notation' is devised for particular scientific purposes, and therefore one may not condemn it because it is useless for other purposes. (1972: 105)

As the microscope allows the smallest detail in a physical structure to be examined, so Frege's conceptual notation enables the smallest detail in proofs to be examined and any presuppositions exposed. Thus, though it would be absurd to think of it as a substitute for ordinary language, it is, Frege claims, the perfect instrument for its assigned task.

Frege also suggests that his conceptual notation may be seen as a partial realization of Leibniz's ideal of a universal characteristic, a *calculus philosophicus* or *ratiocinator*, 'a method of notation which fits things themselves'. Frege says that the symbolisms of arithmetic, geometry and chemistry may be seen as realizations of the Leibnizian ideal in particular areas. His own conceptual notation adds, he suggests, a new domain to these, 'indeed, the one situated in the middle between all the others' (1972: 105). Hence, Frege goes on, we can begin to fill in the gaps in the existing formula languages, connecting their hitherto separate domains to the province of a single formula language and extending it to fields which up to now have lacked such a language.

Frege's thought is that by supplementing as necessary his conceptual notation with the symbolism of particular domains – arithmetic, geometry, chemistry, mechanics, mathematics and physics – all that is known in each of these areas of science will be capable of being adequately expressed in such a way that all deductive relations within each area will be capable of being exhibited in gap-free proofs and furthermore, the same will be true of all deductive relationships *between* the areas. The implicit claim is thus that the system of *Conceptual Notation* is a *complete* system of logic – whatever deductive relationships obtain within or between any area of knowledge can be exhibited in *Conceptual Notation* without any additions. Whether this is a correct claim depends on the extent of what may properly be called 'logic': if modal logic (the logic of necessity and possibility) and temporal logic (the logic of tense), for example, are properly so called, the claim is over-ambitious. But the possibility of such extensions was something Frege did not perceive, unsurprisingly, given his predominantly mathematical interests.

The logic of *Conceptual Notation* is the logic now standardly taught to students in introductory logic classes – predicate logic with identity. Because it is so familiar in its modern stream-lined form, it is difficult to appreciate what a huge leap Frege took in his first book, despite the awkwardness and unnecessary complexity of some of his explanations. Nevertheless, in order to understand the significance of Frege's work in logic, such appreciation is crucial.

We can begin by recalling that logic is the study of *argument*. Its aim is to give an account of the distinction between *valid* and *invalid* arguments. A valid argument is one in which, if the premisses are true, the conclusion must be true; an invalid argument is one in which it is not guaranteed that if the premisses are true the conclusion is true, i.e. in which in some possible circumstances all the premisses are true but the conclusion is false. Sentences may differ in various ways which do not affect their contributions to the validity of any arguments in which they occur, i.e. which are such that when one replaces the other in any valid argument the validity of the argument is preserved. Since in *Conceptual Notation* Frege is interested *only* in validity he introduces a special name, 'conceptual content', for what two such equipollent sentences have in common. He immediately goes on to draw from this narrow focus of interest a conclusion of the utmost importance:

A distinction between *subject* and *predicate* does *not occur* in my way of representing a judgement. To justify this I note that the contents of two judgements can differ in two ways: first, it may be the case that [all] the consequences which can be derived from the first judgement combined with certain others can also be derived from the second judgement combined with the same others; secondly this may not be the case. The two propositions, 'At Plataea the Greeks defeated the Persians' and 'At Plataea the Persians were defeated by the Greeks', differ in the first way. Even if one can perceive a slight difference in sense the agreement [of sense] still predominates. Now I call the part of the content which is the *same* in both *conceptual content*. Since *only this* is meaningful for [our] 'conceptual notation', we need not distinguish between propositions which have the same conceptual content. If one says 'The subject is the concept with which the judgement is concerned' this applies also to the object. Therefore, we can only say: 'The subject is the concept with which the judgement is chiefly concerned'. In [ordinary] language, the subject place has the significance in the word order of the *special* place where one puts what he wishes the listener to particularly hold. This can serve, for instance, to indicate a relation of this judgement to others, thus facilitating for the listener an understanding of the whole context. Now all aspects of [ordinary] language which result only from the interaction of speaker and listener – for example, when the speaker considers the listener's expectations and tries to put them on the right track even before speaking a [complete] sentence – have nothing corresponding to them in my formula language, because here the only thing relevant in a judgement is that which influences its *possible consequences*. Everything that is necessary for a correct inference is fully expressed, but what is not necessary usually is not indicated: nothing is left to guessing. (1972: 113)

What Frege puts in the place of the distinction between subject and predicate is the distinction between argument and function. And it is this which is the fundamental innovation in *Conceptual Notation* and allows Frege to introduce, for the first time in the history of logic, the device of quantification. In the Preface to *Conceptual Notation* he modestly indicates the importance he himself attaches to this innovation: 'I believe that the replacement of the concepts of *subject* and *predicate* by *argument* and *function* will prove itself in the long run' (1972: 107).

Logic before Frege

In the logical system which was dominant before Frege, Aristotelian syllogistic played a fundamental role. The four basic forms of sentence of which Aristotelian syllogistic treated were the A, E, I and O forms exemplified in the following:

All men are mortal (A)
No men are mortal (E)
Some men are mortal (I)
Some men are not mortal (O)

Aristotelian syllogistic specifies a set of rules by which arguments composed of sentences of these forms may be assessed for validity. Thus, for example,

Every swan is an animal
Every animal is a living thing
Ergo: Every swan is a living thing

is a valid syllogism by the Aristotelian rules.

As noted in the previous chapter, Aristotelian syllogistic is a logic of terms; more particularly it is a logic of *general* terms. Singular terms and sentences containing them (like 'Socrates is a man') had to be dealt with as an afterthought and were usually assimilated to universal sentences. As we shall see, it is of a piece with

Frege's supplanting the distinction between subject and predicate by the distinction between argument and function that this order of priority is reversed in *Conceptual Notation*.

As we also saw in the previous chapter, Aristotelian logic was recognized, long before Frege, as not covering the whole field of logic because it did not account for the validity of forms of argument such as 'If the first then the second, the first; therefore the second', which can be turned into valid arguments by replacing the place-holders 'the first' and 'the second' by *sentences*. The Stoics studied such arguments but did not think of themselves as offering a *supplement*, but rather a *competitor*, to Aristotelian syllogistic, whose champions in turn rejected Stoic logic.

However, in the work of George Boole these two theories of logic were merged. Boole developed a system of algebraic logic whose formulas could be interpreted either as expressing propositions which were the subject matter of Aristotelian logic or as expressing propositions which were the subject matter of Stoic logic. Boole called propositions of the former type 'primary' and propositions of the latter type 'secondary' because he thought that 'secondary' propositions could always be interpreted as a form of primary proposition. Thus 'If it is day then it is light' could be interpreted as 'Every time it is true to say that it is day is a time when it is true to say that it is light'.

This is how logic stood before Frege; and it involved multiple inadequacies.

The first inadequacy (see also Rumfitt 1994, to which the following is indebted, for useful elaboration) is a consequence of the assumption, implicit in Aristotelian syllogistic and retained by Boole, that every simple sentence has just *one* subject and *one* predicate. Consider the two-stage argument:

> (1) Everybody killed himself
Ergo: (2) Cato killed Cato
Ergo: (3) Somebody killed Cato

To account for the validity of the inference of (3) from (2) on the assumption that every simple sentence has a unique subject and a unique predicate we must regard the subject of (2) as 'Cato' and its predicate as 'killed Cato'. Since so understood (2) may be read as ascribing to Cato the property of *having killed Cato* we can infer that someone has that property, as (3) says. However, if we read (2) in this way we have no way of accounting for the validity of the inference of (2) from (1). For the subject in (1) is 'everybody' and the predicate is 'killed himself'. Thus the property ascribed to everybody in (1) is the property of *having killed oneself*, which is quite distinct from the property of *having killed Cato*. Why then should it be possible to infer from the fact that everybody has the former property, the conclusion that Cato, in particular, has the latter, quite different, property?

The second inadequacy in pre-Fregean logic was its inability to account for the validity of inferences from sentences of the form Stoic logic was designed to deal with, to sentences of the form Aristotelian term logic was designed to deal with. Obviously, neither of these two systems considered individually could deal with such inferences, but even in the Boolean synthesis they could not be accounted for, precisely because in Boolean logic secondary propositions and primary propositions constituted two different interpretations of the same algebraic formulae. This point is very clearly brought out by Dudman (1976), who is able to illustrate it with an example of Boole's own devising. Boole writes, in his chapter on hypotheticals in the *Mathematical Analysis of Logic* (1847) (Boole 1973: 58ff.):

> Note that there is a family of disjunctive and conditional Propositions which do not, of right, belong to the class considered in this chapter [the class of secondary propositions]. Such are those in which the force of the disjunctive or conditional participle is expended upon the predicate of the Proposition, as if, speaking of the inhabitants of a particular island, we should say, that they are all either Europeans or Asiatics, meaning, that it is true of each individual, that he is either a European or an Asiatic.... Very different from the above is the proposition, Either all the inhabitants are Europeans, or they are all Asiatics. Here the disjunctive particle separates Propositions.... The distinction is real and important. Every Proposition which language can express may be represented by elective symbols, and the laws of combination of these symbols are in all cases the same; but in one class of instances the symbols have reference to collections of objects, in the other to the truth of constituent Propositions.

The two sentences:

(1)   Every inhabitant is either European or Asiatic
(2)   Every inhabitant is European or every inhabitant is Asiatic

can be symbolized by Boole, but not in such a way that the same symbols bear the same interpretation. Thus Boole is unable to exhibit the argument from (2) to (1), which is *valid*, in a way that reveals its validity. Frege notes this, remarking that in Boole's system 'Any transition from one type of judgement to the other [from secondary to primary or vice versa] – and such transitions happen often enough in actual thought, after all – is cut off' (1972: 93).

Though (2) implies (1), (1) does not imply (2). Thus (1) and (2) are not equivalent. Boole, noticing this, draws an important conclusion:

> Some writers . . . regard it as the exclusive office of a conjunction [two-place sentential operator] to connect *Propositions*, not *words*. In this view I am not able to agree. The Proposition, Every animal is either rational *or* irrational cannot be resolved into *either* every animal is rational *or* every animal is irrational. (1973: 59n)

Boole's conclusion here, that it is *not* the exclusive office of a 'conjunction' to connect propositions, is one Frege rejects. He is able to do so because he puts at the foundation of his logical system *singular* sentences (propositions), like '*Socrates* is a man' or '*This animal* is either rational or irrational'. As Boole himself notes, when the predicate in such a singular proposition contains a sentential operator, it *can* always be rewritten as a 'conjunction' of propositions:

> This animal is *either* rational *or* irrational, is equivalent to, *Either* this animal is rational *or* it is irrational. This peculiarity of singular Propositions would almost justify our ranking them, though truly universals, in a separate class. (1973: 59n)

This is precisely what Frege does, rejecting the traditional and Boolean view of singular propositions as 'truly universals' (i.e. correctly assimilated to propositions of the Aristotelian A form), and by doing so is able, via the device of quantification, to bridge the gap between primary and secondary logic which for Boole is uncrossable.

The third, and most famous, inadequacy of pre-Fregean logic was its inability to cope with sentences containing multiple generality – sentences like 'Every boy loves some girl' – and arguments containing sentences of this form are abundant in mathematics. A famous example of a valid argument which traditional logic could not account for containing (implicitly) such multiple generality was the following:

(1) All horses are animals
Ergo: (2) All horses' heads are animals' heads

As we noted in the previous chapter, medieval logicians developed complicated theories to account for such multiple generality, but nothing approaching a solution was found. What was required was an explanation of the ambiguities present in such sentences and a notation in which the different meanings could be perspicuously exhibited.

Fregean Logic

With this sketch of the background to Frege's logic, and the needs it had to fulfil, we can now turn to Frege's own development of his system in *Conceptual Notation*.

Frege begins by distinguishing sharply between a *judgement* (or assertion) and its *content*. The expression of a judgement he indicates by writing the symbol

⊢

to the left of the symbol which gives the content of the judgement. The horizontal stroke without the vertical (which he calls the content stroke) indicates that what follows is expressed without being judged to be true.

Thus in

– A

the content that A is expressed without being judged (asserted). Whereas

⊢ A

expresses the judgement (assertion) that A.

The distinction Frege makes here is a fundamental one whose necessity can be indicated in various ways. Frege illustrates it himself by alluding to the possibility of a *reductio ad absurdum* argument in which we make a supposition 'in order to derive some conclusions from it and with these test the correctness of the thought' (1972: 112). To make sense of such a process of reasoning it is essential to appreciate that a thought can be entertained without being asserted: otherwise the procedure will appear self-destructive – 'like trying to build a house by removing the foundations to build the upper floors' (Anscombe and Geach 1961: 133). As Anscombe and Geach explain, the procedure certainly is self-destructive and absurd if: 'Suppose that A; it follows that not A. So not A' must be represented as '⊢ A; ergo ⊢ not A. So ⊢ not A'. But Frege is able to represent it rather as '⊢ (If A then not A); so ⊢ not A', in which A is never asserted.

The distinction between asserted and unasserted occurrences of sentences is also needed to account for the validity of arguments in which the same sentence occurs free-standing, as an asserted sentence, and unasserted as a component of a complex sentence. Once again Anscombe and Geach illustrate the point (which Geach has called 'the Frege point'):

> Does 'A' mean the same both times in 'B, if B then A, ergo A', or again in 'not B, B or A, ergo A'? If it does there is no inference, for the assertion 'A' is already part of the premisses; if it does not, the inference is vitiated by the ambiguity of 'A'. Frege would write such inferences as follows '⊢ B, ⊢ (if B then A), ergo ⊢ A'; '⊢ not B, ⊢ (B or A), ergo ⊢ A'. The content asserted in '⊢ A' occurs also in the premiss '⊢ (if B then A)', but is not asserted in this latter context. (Anscombe and Geach 1961: 133; 'p' and 'q' replaced by 'A' and 'B')

Having drawn the distinction between asserted and unasserted occurrences of sentences Frege now goes on to argue, in opposition to the traditional view, that the distinction between *universal* and *particular*, and again the distinction between *affirmative* and *negative*, belongs to contents as such, whether asserted or not. It is not the judgement which is particular or universal, rather 'these properties belong to the content even when it is put forth not as a judgement, but as an [unasserted] proposition' (1972: 114). The same, Frege argues, holds for negation: 'Negation attaches to the content, whether or not it occurs as a judgement' (1972: 114). He makes the point, once again, by reference to the possibility of supposition. If we say 'Suppose that the line segments AB and CD were not equal' we do not assert that the line segments AB and CD are not equal, but the content which is entertained nevertheless 'contains a negation' (1972: 114). Anscombe and Geach elaborate Frege's point. By recognizing that the same negative content can occur asserted and unasserted we are able to acknowledge that 'if not A, then B, not A; *ergo* B' and 'if A then B, A *ergo* B' are of the same form (*modus ponens*). If we maintained instead that negation belonged to the level of assertion, representing, perhaps, an act of rejection, as assertion represents an act of acceptance, we could not recognize the identity of form here; indeed we could not account for the occurrence of negation within the antecedent of a conditional ('if not A then B') at all.

Frege now goes on to introduce a notation for conditional propositions. If A and B are propositions, he notes, there are four possibilities:

(1) A is affirmed and B is affirmed
(2) A is affirmed and B is denied
(3) A is denied and B is affirmed
(4) A is denied and B is denied

He introduces a special symbol (see Appendix), for which the modern equivalent is 'B → A' and stipulates that (his equivalent of)

$\vdash (B \to A)$

expresses the judgement that 'the third of these possibilities does not occur, but one of the other three does' (1972: 133).

If the initial vertical strike is omitted the (unasserted) content is expressed.

What Frege has in effect done here is define the material conditional of modern logic by its truth-table.

In a modern symbolism a *truth-table* definition of the material conditional would be presented as follows:

A	B	B → A
T	T	T
T	F	T
F	T	F
F	F	T

Truth-tables were first explicitly employed in Wittgenstein's *Tractatus Logico-Philosophicus* (1961), but that Frege here anticipates Wittgenstein can be seen if it is noted that (a) later in *Conceptual Notation* Frege writes not of contents which *are* affirmed or denied but of contents which *are to be* affirmed or denied, and that (b) it is a consequence of Frege's own views on assertion that the antecedent and consequent of a conditional sentence *always* express contents which are unasserted (unaffirmed) even if the conditional sentence itself expresses a content which is asserted (affirmed). Thus 'is affirmed' and 'is denied' here have to be read as 'is true' and 'is false' to make sense of what Frege says.

Frege's equivalent of the modern symbol

$$B \rightarrow A$$

represents the *material conditional* of modern logic, i.e. the sentence that is true if B is false or A is true. In some circumstances, as Frege notes, it is appropriate to read this as 'if B then A'. For example, if it is asserted in ignorance of whether A and B are true or false, but on the basis of the consideration that some causal connection excludes the possibility that B is true and A false:

We can make the judgement

$$\vdash (B \rightarrow A)$$

without knowing whether A and B are to be affirmed or denied. For example, let B stand for the circumstance that the moon is in quadrature [with the sun] and A the circumstance that it appears as a semicircle. In this case we can translate

$$\vdash (B \rightarrow A)$$

with the aid of the conjunction 'if': 'If the moon is in quadrature [with the sun], it appears as a semi-circle'. (1972: 115–16; I have replaced Frege's symbol with its present-day equivalent)

However, in other circumstances one may assert the material conditional in the absence of any knowledge of any causal connection between antecedent and consequent. Thus, knowing only that $3 \times 7 = 21$ one may assert:

$$\vdash (\text{The sun is shining} \rightarrow 3 \times 7 = 21)$$

or knowing only that perpetual motion is impossible one may assert:

$$\vdash (\text{Perpetual motion is possible} \rightarrow \text{the universe is infinite})$$

In such cases Frege would deny that

$$- (B \rightarrow A)$$

is appropriately read as 'if B then A' because he holds that there is a causal connection implicit in the word 'if' which is not expressed in the symbol. Whether Frege is right about this is a matter about which there has been some doubt. For Frege's purposes, however, the matter is unimportant. 'If B then A' and the material conditional constructed from B and A have at least this in common: from either together with B one may infer A. This minimum of content is all that needs to be retained in a logical symbolism capable of expressing in a gap-free way deductive proofs in logic and mathematics.

Frege next goes on to introduce a symbol for negation:

> If a small vertical stroke is attached to the underside of the content stroke, this is to express the circumstance that *the content A* does not occur. (1972: 120)

The equivalent in modern symbolism is '$\neg$'. Thus

$$\vdash \neg A$$

is the denial of A, that is the assertion that it is not the case that A.

Like the material conditional, negation can be defined by a truth-table: using modern notation this can be set out as follows:

A	$\neg A$
T	F
F	T

Negation is thus, like the material conditional, a *truth-function*, to use the standard terminology first introduced by Russell, that is, its expression represents a way of forming complex sentences from simpler sentences in such a way that the truth-value (the circumstance of being true or false) of the compound proposition is wholly determined by, that is, is a function of, the truth-values of the simpler sentences. Frege does not note this in *Conceptual Notation* because he does not, in fact, there introduce the notion of a function at all until after he has given his accounts of negation and the conditional, and once he has introduced it, he does not go back to revise his accounts of negation and the conditional in the light of it. Nevertheless, Frege does go on to explain how the other truth-functions standardly symbolized in modern systems of logic can be defined in terms of negation and the conditional. Thus 'A or B' in the inclusive sense ('A or B or both') can be represented by

$\vdash (\neg B \to A)$

('If not B then A'). And 'A or B' in its exclusive sense ('A or B but not both') can be represented by the conjunction of

$\vdash (\neg B \to A)$ and $\vdash (B \to A)$

'A and B' can be symbolized

$\vdash \neg(B \to \neg A)$

('It is not the case that if B then not A').

Frege points out, however, that he could equally well have started with a symbol for conjunction and defined the conditional in terms of it and negation (as 'It is not the case that B and not A').

What Frege has thus done is to introduce a symbolism, with the symbols for negation and the conditional as primitives, adequate for truth-functional logic. Later he introduces a set of nine kernel propositions (axioms) of which the first six (numbers 1, 2, 8, 28, 31 and 41 in his system) concern only negation and the conditional. In modern notation they can be represented thus:

(1) $A \to (B \to A)$
(2) $[C \to (B \to A)] \to [(C \to B) \to (C \to A)]$
(8) $[D \to (B \to A)] \to [B \to (D \to A)]$
(28) $[(B \to A) \to (\neg A \to \neg B)]$
(31) $\neg\neg A \to A$
(41) $A \to \neg\neg A$

Together with the rule of *modus ponens* (introduced in section 6 of *Conceptual Notation*) and an implicit rule of substitution (allowing us to derive any formula from one already derived by uniform substitution of any correctly formed formula for one of the variable letters in the original formula) these six axioms form a complete set of axioms for truth-functional logic, allowing for the derivation of all valid formulae of truth-functional logic (i.e. all tautologies).

The next piece of symbolism Frege introduces is a sign for what he calls 'identity of content' '≡'. He defines this as follows:

let ⊢ (A ≡ B) mean: the symbol A and the symbol B have the same conceptual content, so that we can always replace A by B and vice versa

Here A and B can be replaced by singular terms or sentences. The notion of conceptual content was introduced earlier, as what is common to two sentences which are such that all the consequences that can be derived from one combined with certain others can always be derived from the second combined with the same others (1972: 112). Frege here extends this notion to singular terms. In doing so, he introduces the problem of informative but true identity statements (for example, 'the Evening Star is the Morning Star') to which later, referring back to this section of *Conceptual Notation*, he appeals in introducing his distinction between sense and reference.

In *Conceptual Notation*, however, Frege attempts to use an undifferentiated notion of content in explaining the informativeness of true identity statements. The key to understanding how such statements function, he suggests, is to recognize that in identity statements the symbol for identity of content (which in mathematics is expressed by '=' and in ordinary English by 'is') joins expressions which appear, not as representatives of their content, but '*in propria persona* . . . for this signifies that the two names have the same content' (1972: 124). Thus, Frege suggests, in an identity statement such as (to use his own later example)

The Morning Star is the Evening Star

or

$2 + 5 = 7$

the names ('The Morning Star', 'The Evening Star', '2 + 5' and '7') stand for themselves, not for their contents. An identity statement is thus a statement *about* names: it signifies that the two names flanking the sign of identity have the same content, and so are replaceable one by the other. It might be thought, Frege goes on to say, that this implies that we have no need for a symbol for identity of content at all, since we have no need for multiple expressions of the same content. This is mistaken, however, he argues, precisely because there are such things as true but informative identity statements. He illustrates the point with an unnecessarily complicated geometrical example, but it can be made with the example of 'The Morning Star' and 'The Evening Star'. These two names have the same content, the planet Venus, but this content is determined in two different ways: as the heavenly body visible in the morning and as the heavenly body visible in the evening. The name 'The Morning Star' corresponds to the first of these two modes of determination, the name 'The Evening Star' to the second:

> Thus the need of a symbol for identity of content rests upon the following fact: the same content can be fully determined in different ways, but that the *same content*, in a particular case, is actually given by *two different modes of determination* is the content of a judgement. Before this [judgement] can be made, we must supply two different names, corresponding to two [different] modes of determination, for the thing thus determined. But the judgement requires for its expression a symbol for identity of content to combine the two names. It follows from this that different names for the same content are not always an indifferent matter of form; but rather, if they are associated with different modes of determination, they concern the very heart of the matter. (1972: 126)

We will be looking later at the inadequacies of this account when we came to Frege's introduction of the sense/reference distinction. But it will be worthwhile to indicate briefly here the instability of Frege's position at this point in *Conceptual Notation*. On the one hand it is clear from Frege's examples that the 'content' of a name is the object for which it stands, so that the common content of the names 'The Morning Star' and 'The Evening Star' is the planet Venus. On the other hand, however, it is also clear from Frege's original introduction of the notion of conceptual content as applied to sentences, as what two 'equipollent' sentences have in common, that he would not, at this stage, have held that all sentences with the same truth-value have the same conceptual content. Yet this is the conclusion to which we are driven if we take it, as Frege clearly intends, that when two names with the same content replace one another in a sentence, the conceptual content of the whole sentence will remain undisturbed. This tension is only resolved when Frege introduces the sense/reference distinction (in 'Function and Concept' and 'On Concept and Object'); the notion of 'content' then falls apart, conceptual content as first introduced being identified with sense, and conceptual content, as illustrated in the example of informative but true identity statements in *Conceptual Notation*, being identified with reference. It is useless to try to find a resolution of the tension within the theory of *Conceptual Notation* itself; there is none. Frege's thought at this time was still in motion and every attempted snapshot of its momentary state will reveal only a blur.

The same is true of the next idea introduced in *Conceptual Notation*, the function/argument analysis of sentences. We have noted the importance Frege assigns to the replacement of the *grammatical* notions of subject and predicate by the *arithmetical* notions of argument and function. It is now time to give it a more careful examination.

Frege's starting point is the mathematical notion of a function, but we can approach his position most easily by considering his view of how arithmetical *expressions* are structured. In '2 + 3' we can recognize two types of expression: numerals ('2' and '3') and a symbol for a mathematical operation ('+'). The complex symbol '2 + 3' results from combining expressions of these two types in the appropriate way. Using other numerals and the same operator symbol we can construct other complex symbols, such as '3 + 7', and using the same numerals and other operator symbols ('×', '÷', '−') we can produce yet others ('2 × 3', '2 ÷ 3' and so on). Frege takes it that corresponding to these linguistic entities there are certain non-linguistic entities which they symbolize. The numerals symbolize *numbers* – objects which must be acknowledged, he thinks, as the subject matter of arithmetical truths – as do the complex arithmetical expressions formed from the numerals and the operator symbol. What the operator symbols, or rather, their occurrence in complex arithmetical expressions (the justification for this correction will appear later), symbolize are *functions*. Such a function is a mapping from numbers onto numbers; it is something which applied to a number or set of numbers as *arguments* yields another number as *value*.

So just as we can think of '2 + 3' as something formed by combining the numerals '2' and '3' with the operator symbol '+', so we can think of what '2 + 3' symbolizes, namely 5, as the value which results when the function '+' symbolizes is applied to the numbers symbolized by '2' and '3' as values.

However, we need not think of what '2 + 3' symbolizes in this way. If we compare '2 + 3' with

'3 + 4'   '7 + 4'   '33 + 61'   '98 + 2'

we will notice the pattern

'( ) + [ ]'

exhibited by an expression consisting of a numeral, followed by '+', followed by another numeral. Noting this pattern allows us to view '2 + 3' as symbolizing the value of the function symbolized by '+' for the pair of arguments symbolized by '2' and '3'.

If we compare '2 + 3' with

'2 + 5'   '2 + 92'   '2 + 13'   '2 + 16'

however, we notice another pattern

'2 + ( )'

exhibited by an expression consisting of the numeral '2' followed by '+' followed by another numeral. Noting this pattern allows us to view '2 + 3' as symbolizing the value of the function symbolized by '2 + ( )' – that is, the pattern thus exhibited – for the number 3 as argument.

Again, if we compare '2 + 3' with

'3 + 3'   '16 + 3'   '29 + 3'   '14 + 3'

we can notice a third pattern, that exhibited by an expression consisting of a numeral, followed by '+', followed by the numeral '3'. Noting this pattern allows us to view '2 + 3' as symbolizing the value of the function symbolized by '( ) + 3', for the number 2 as argument.

Consider another case. '3 + 3' may be compared with

'16 + 3'   '7 + 3'   '31 + 3'   '42 + 3'

and viewed as symbolizing the value of the function symbolized by '( ) + 3' for the number 3 as argument, or it may be compared with

'3 + 16'   '3 + 7'   '3 + 31'   '3 + 42'

and viewed as symbolizing the value of the function symbolized by '3 + ( )' for the number 3 as argument. Or it may be compared with

'7 + 6'   '14 + 2'   '6 + 8'   '15 + 7'

and viewed as symbolizing the value of the function symbolized by
'( ) + [ ]' for the pair of (as it happens identical) arguments 3 and 3.
But it may also be compared with

'5 + 5'   '7 + 7'   '14 + 14'   '56 + 56'

and viewed as symbolizing the value of the function symbolized by
'( ) + ( )' – that is, the pattern exhibited by a complex arithmetical
expression when it consists of a numeral, followed by '+', followed
by another occurrence of the *same* numeral – for the number 3 as
argument.

The particular importance of this last case is that it makes it clear,
as the previous examples do not, that it is no quotable part of the
complex arithmetical expression which symbolizes the function, but
the pattern it exhibits. For the part of the expression '3 + 3' left when
we remove both occurrences of the numeral '3' is '+' and this occurs
equally in, say, '2 + 7' which does *not* exhibit what it symbolizes as
a value of the function in question. And, in fact, Frege takes this to
be the case in general. The symbol for a function is never a quotable
part of the complex expressions which symbolize its values, but
always a pattern they exhibit. '+', '÷', '×' and '−' are thus not themselves symbols for functions, but rather auxiliary means for constructing expressions which exhibit the patterns which do
symbolize the functions in question.

With this account of Frege's understanding of the notion of a
function we can now go on to see how he extends it beyond its
mathematical application. And the first point to notice is that just
as we can regard what '2 + 3' symbolizes as the value of a function
for a particular argument, so we can regard the expression '2 + 3'
itself as the value of a function for certain arguments.

Comparing '2 + 3' with

'3 + 4'   '7 + 4'   '33 + 61'   '98 + 2'

we can recognize it as the value of a function which takes a pair of
numerals as arguments and yields complex arithmetical symbols as
values thus:

Arguments	Value
'2', '3'	'2 + 3'
'3', '4'	'3 + 4'
'33', '61'	'33 + 61'
'98', '2'	'98 + 2'

And just as in '2 + 3' '2' symbolizes 2 and '3' symbolizes '3', it seems right to say that it is this *linguistic* function that symbolizes in language the arithmetical function addition: we mention the arithmetical function by writing down some value or other of the linguistic function (compare Anscombe and Geach 1961: 143ff.). Earlier we spoke of the symbol for the arithmetical function being a linguistic *pattern*; the notion of a linguistic function seems an illuminating explication of this notion.

Now just as with arithmetical functions, so with linguistic functions, the very same item which can be regarded as the value of one function for one argument can equally well be regarded as the value of other functions for other arguments. So '2 + 3' can be viewed equally as the value for the argument '2' of the linguistic function which maps a numeral onto the result of writing that numeral followed by '+' followed by '3'; or as the value for the argument '3' of the linguistic function which maps a numeral onto the result of writing '2' followed by '+' followed by that numeral. And '3 + 3' can be regarded equally as (a) the value for the argument '3' of the linguistic function which maps a numeral onto the result of writing that numeral, followed by '+' followed by '3', or (b) as the value for the argument '3' of the linguistic function which maps a numeral onto the result of writing '3' followed by '+' followed by that numeral, or (c) as the value for the pair of arguments ⟨'3', '3'⟩ of the linguistic function which maps a pair of numerals onto the result of writing the first numeral followed by '+' followed by the second numeral, or (d) as the value for the argument '3' of the linguistic function which maps a numeral onto the result of writing that numeral followed by '+' followed by another occurrence of that same numeral.

The importance of the notion of a linguistic function is that it is linguistic functions Frege has predominantly in mind in the section of *Conceptual Notation* in which he introduces the notion of a function.

His principal example is the sentence:

Hydrogen is lighter than carbon dioxide

If we replace the symbol for hydrogen with a symbol for oxygen or nitrogen we obtain two new sentences:

Oxygen is lighter than carbon dioxide
Nitrogen is lighter than carbon dioxide

Comparing these three sentences we can regard them as values for the arguments 'Hydrogen', 'Oxygen' and 'Nitrogen', respectively, of the linguistic function which maps a singular term onto the result of writing that singular term followed by 'is lighter than carbon dioxide', just as we can regard '2 + 3' as a value for the argument '2' of the function which maps a numeral onto the result of writing that numeral followed by '+' followed by '3'.

Equally, if we compare

Hydrogen is lighter than carbon dioxide

with

Hydrogen is lighter than hydrogen chloride gas

and

Hydrogen is lighter than ammonia

we can see the sentence as the value for the argument 'carbon dioxide' of the linguistic function which maps a singular term onto the sentence that results from writing 'Hydrogen is lighter than' followed by that singular term. So viewed, the sentence can be understood as saying of carbon dioxide that it is heavier than hydrogen. We thus bring to prominence a particular analysis into argument and function by making the argument the grammatical subject of the sentence and, in fact, this is the principal role of the grammatical subject position in a sentence.

Hence Frege stresses:

Hydrogen is lighter than carbon dioxide

and

Carbon dioxide is heavier than hydrogen

have the *same* conceptual content. The different ways in which a sentence with a particular conceptual content can be considered as a function of this or that argument have nothing to do with the conceptual content itself, but only with our way of viewing it. That is, the recognition that

Hydrogen is lighter than carbon dioxide

can be regarded as the value, for the singular term 'Hydrogen' as argument, of the linguistic function which for a singular term as argument yields as value the result of writing that singular term followed by 'is lighter than carbon dioxide', is *not* essential to understanding the sentence. In so far as understanding the sentence is concerned, recognizing it as analysable in that particular way is of no importance. Where such recognition *is* of importance we shall see in due course.

Frege now introduces a second example, the sentence 'Cato killed Cato'. He points out that this sentence can be analysed as argument 'Cato', function 'killed Cato'; or argument 'Cato', function 'Cato killed'; or, if we think of 'Cato' as replaceable at both occurrences, as argument 'Cato', function 'killing oneself'. The example is analogous, of course, to the arithmetical example '3 + 3' introduced previously. We noted with respect to that example that its particular importance was that its analysis into argument: '3', function '( ) + ( )' (where the blanks are to be thought of as replaceable by the *same* numeral) made it clear that the symbol for an arithmetical function could not *always* be identified with a quotable bit of language, but must rather be regarded as a pattern, or a linguistic function. That Frege introduces the 'Cato' example here makes it unmistakably clear, in a way that his other examples do not, and despite his frequent references in the section to the function as the 'component' or 'part' of the expression which remains invariant, that he himself recognizes that the 'functions' he is concerned with, though linguistic items, cannot be identified with quotable parts of sentences, but must be regarded as patterns occurring in them.

Frege now gives a general statement of what his examples establish so far:

> If, in an expression (whose content need not be assertable), a simple or a complex symbol occurs in one or more places and we imagine it as replaceable by another [symbol] (but the same one each time) at all or some of these places, then we call the part of the expression that shows itself invariant [under such replacement] a function and the replaceable part its argument. (1972: 126)

Despite the fact that his examples have all concerned expressions for 'assertable' contents (e.g. 'hydrogen is lighter than carbon dioxide') Frege here indicates that his analysis applies more generally, to expressions for non-judgeable contents like '2 + 3' or 'the King of France'.

So far Frege has only considered replacements of one expression (perhaps at several occurrences) in a longer expression, but he now proceeds to generalize. If we view

Hydrogen is lighter than carbon dioxide

along with

Oxygen is lighter than nitrogen
Helium is lighter than hydrogen chloride gas
Nitrogen is lighter than oxygen

we can see this as a value of a linguistic function for a *pair* of arguments. Namely, we can see it as the value, for the arguments 'Hydrogen' and 'carbon dioxide', of the linguistic function '( ) is lighter than [ ]' which maps a pair of singular terms onto the sentence which results when we write the first, then 'is lighter than', then the second.

An indeterminate function of a single argument Frege suggests can be written:

$\Phi(A)$

An indeterminate function of two arguments can be written:

$\Psi(A, B)$

And

$\vdash \Psi(A, B)$

can be read: 'A stands in the Ψ-relation to B' or 'B is the result of an application of the procedure Ψ to the object A'.

Now we come to a crucial point, which Frege expresses as follows:

Let me warn here against an illusion to which the use of [ordinary] language easily gives rise. If we compare the two propositions: 'The number 20 can be represented as the sum of four squares' and 'Every positive integer can be represented as the sum of four squares' it appears possible to consider 'being representable as the sum of four squares' as a function whose argument is 'the number 20' one time and 'every positive integer' the other time. We can discern the error of this view from the observation that 'the number 20' and 'every positive integer' are not concepts of the same rank. What is asserted of the number 20 cannot be asserted in the same sense of [the concept] 'every positive integer', though, of course, in some circumstances it may be asserted of every positive integer. The expression 'every positive integer' by itself, unlike [the expression] 'the number 20', yields no independent idea; it acquires a sense only in the context of a sentence. (1972: 127–8)

What Frege is drawing attention to here is the difference between singular sentences, containing singular terms only, apart from predicates and sentential operators, and general sentences, and, in particular, between singular sentences and universal sentences. We earlier saw that George Boole contemplated the possibility of rejecting the traditional view that singular propositions were to be categorized as truly universal propositions of the Aristotelian A form, but did not do so. This is precisely what Frege does here. The singular sentence:

The number 20 can be regarded as the sum of four squares

he says, can be analysed as argument: 'the number 20', function: 'can be represented as the sum of four squares'. The universal affirmative sentence

Every positive integer can be represented as the sum of four squares

cannot be similarly analysed.

It is the purpose of the next section of *Conceptual Notation*, on generality, to explain how such sentences are to be understood, via the device of quantification. And in doing so Frege builds on his function/argument analysis of *singular* sentences and his exposition of truth-functional logic (the logic of the Stoics), thus completely reversing the traditional order.

The heart of traditional logic, syllogistic theory, is concerned with reasoning about *types* of thing – swans, animals, living things, etc. The interest is in inferences about all *swans*, some *animals*, no *living things*, etc. Frege, by contrast, takes as the fundamental form of a general sentence a sentence about *everything* – unrestricted as to type. General sentences about types of entity are then explained subsequently, with the aid of the truth-functional operators, thus reversing the order of priority Boole assigns to his primary and secondary propositions.

The fundamental form of general sentence is 'Everything is so-and-so'. Frege builds his explanation of this on his function/argument analysis of singular sentences.

The singular sentence

Hydrogen is lighter than carbon dioxide

may be analysed into argument: 'Hydrogen', function: 'is lighter than carbon dioxide', and we can express the fact that this sentence is true by saying that the function 'is lighter than carbon dioxide' *is a fact* (that is, expresses a truth) for the argument 'hydrogen'. Similarly this function is a fact for the argument 'helium', and it is a fact for the argument 'oxygen'.

Consider now the sentence stating that this function is a fact for *every* argument. This sentence is equivalent to one stating that *everything* is lighter than carbon dioxide. So, Frege proposes, in general, a sentence of the form

Everything is F

can be understood as saying that the function 'is F' is a fact for every argument.

We can express this in modern notation, deriving from Peano and Russell, as '$(\forall x)Fx$' ('for any x, x is F'), using the universal quantifier '$(\forall x)$'. Frege himself used old German letters embedded in a concavity to express universal quantification, and upper case Greek letters for function letters (see Appendix), but the notational difference is insignificant.

We can appreciate the power of this device by looking at an example involving multiple generality, in which two occurrences of quantifying expressions are linked by a relational expression. We have already encountered examples of this type of sentence, such as 'Every boy loves some girl', but at this stage this is too complicated, since it generalizes over restricted types of thing (boys and girls) and employs particular (or existential) quantification ('some girl'), as well as universal quantification ('every boy'). Let us consider instead the fundamental form of multiply general sentence:

Everything is related to everything

which in modern notation can be expressed:

$(\forall x)(\forall y)Rxy$

According to Frege's explanation this is the case if the function

    is related to everything

is a fact whatever we take as its argument. We are thus directed to consider the *singly* quantified sentences

    Adam is related to everything
    Eve is related to everything
    Cain is related to everything
    Abel is related to everything

and so on, for every object in the universe.

Our original sentence is true if and only if each of these is true, that is, if and only if their, possibly infinite, conjunction is true.

Now consider

    Adam is related to everything

which is also general, but contains only one quantifying expression. This is true, according to Frege's explanation if the function

    Adam is related to

is a fact whatever we take as its argument. Thus we are directed to consider the *singular* sentences

    Adam is related to Adam
    Adam is related to Eve
    Adam is related to Cain
    Adam is related to Abel

and so on, for every object in the universe.

Our singly quantified proposition 'Adam is related to everything' is true if and only if each of these singular sentences is true.

The same reasoning can be applied to each of the remaining singly quantified sentences

Eve is related to everything
Cain is related to everything
Abel is related to everything

and so on that Frege's explanation of universal quantification directed us to when we began with our original multiply general sentence. The outcome is that

Everything is related to everything

is true if and only if each of the singular sentences

Adam is related to Adam
Adam is related to Eve
Adam is related to Cain
Adam is related to Abel
etc.

Eve is related to Adam
Eve is related to Eve
Eve is related to Cain
Eve is related to Abel
etc.

Abel is related to Adam
Abel is related to Eve
Abel is related to Cain
Abel is related to Abel
etc.

Cain is related to Adam
Cain is related to Eve
Cain is related to Cain
Cain is related to Abel
etc.

and so on (for every pair of objects in the universe) is true.

Thus, Frege's explanation of universal quantification yields the correct account of the circumstances in which 'Everything is related to everything' is true, and it does so by allowing us at each stage of the explanation to consider a single occurrence of the symbol for generality, no matter how many occur in the original sentence.

The stages in the explanation correspond, in fact, to (the inverse of) an assumed constructional history of the sentence in which the symbols for generality are inserted, not simultaneously but successively, into the gaps left when singular terms are omitted from an original singular sentence (see also Dummett 1973: 8ff.). Thus if we begin with

Adam is related to Eve

we may analyse this as argument: 'Eve', function: 'Adam is related to'. Omitting the argument and replacing it with 'everything' we arrive at

Adam is related to everything

If we now analyse this into argument:'Adam', function: 'is related to everything', omit the argument and replace it by 'everything' we arrive at

Everything is related to everything

This is the constructional history that was assumed in the above account, in Fregean terms, of the truth-conditions of this sentence. But we could have assumed a different constructional history in which starting from

Adam is related to Eve

the name 'Adam' was first omitted so that the leftmost occurrence of 'everything' was the first introduced into the sentence. If we gave the Fregean account of the truth-conditions corresponding to this constructional history there would have been no difference in the end result.

But this is not so in general. If we consider the sentence

Everything is related to something

(or as a special case 'Everything is caused by something') it is possible to read it in two ways: as saying of everything that there is something or other to which it is related (everything is caused by something or other), or as saying of something in particular that everything is related to it (something in particular is such that everything is caused by it). The ambiguity brought out by these paraphrases in ordinary English corresponds to two different constructional histories for the sentence.

If we begin with

Adam is related to Eve

and omit 'Adam' to yield the function

is related to Eve

we can then insert 'everything' into the gap, resulting in

Everything is related to Eve

Omitting 'Eve' from this sentence and inserting 'something', we arrive at our original sentence:

Everything is related to something

If we introduce a symbol for existential quantification – '(∃x)' in modern notation – related to 'something' as the symbol for universal quantification is related to 'everything', so that

'(∃x)Fx' or 'something is F'

is read as saying that the function 'is F' is a fact for *some* argument, i.e. there is something which is F, then we can give a Fregean account of the truth-conditions of this sentence corresponding to this constructional history by dealing with the expressions of generality in the inverse order of their occurrence in the sentence.

So

Everything is related to something

will be true if and only if the function

Everything is related to

is a fact for some argument. We are thus directed to consider the singly quantified sentences

Everything is related to Adam
Everything is related to Eve
Everything is related to Cain
Everything is related to Abel

and so on, for every object in the universe.

Our original sentence is true if and only if *one* of these is true.

Now consider:

Everything is related to Adam

This is true, according to Frege's explanation if and only if the function

is related to Adam

is a fact whatever we take as its argument. So we are directed to consider the *singular* sentences

Adam is related to Adam
Eve is related to Adam
Cain is related to Adam
Abel is related to Adam

and so on, for every object in the universe.

Everything is related to Adam

is true if and only if *each* of these singular sentences is true.

The same reasoning can be applied to each of the remaining singly quantified sentences

Everything is related to Eve
Everything is related to Cain
Everything is related to Abel

and so on that we were directed to by the Fregean account of existential quantification given when we began with our original multiply general sentence. The outcome is that

Everything is related to something

is true if and only if *one of the sets* of singular sentences

Adam is related to Adam
Eve is related to Adam
Cain is related to Adam
Abel is related to Adam
etc.

Adam is related to Eve
Eve is related to Eve
Cain is related to Eve
Cain is related to Eve
etc.

Adam is related to Cain
Eve is related to Cain
Cain is related to Cain
Abel is related to Cain
etc.

and so on contains only true sentences.

The truth-condition of 'Everything is related to something' on its other reading can similarly be accounted for in a Fregean manner by first attending to the universal quantifier and then dealing with the existential quantifier (thinking, that is, of the sentence as being built up by first inserting the existential quantifier and then the universal quantifier). The notion of the 'scope' of a quantifier which Frege introduces in *Conceptual Notation* may now be explained. The two readings of 'Everything is related to something' (or again, 'Everything is caused by something') involve different scope assignments to the quantifiers: on the reading corresponding to the constructional history in which the existential quantifier is inserted last ('Something is such that everything is caused by it') the scope of the existential quantifier includes that of the universal quantifier; on the reading corresponding to the constructional history in which the universal quantifier is inserted last ('Everything is caused by something or other') the scope of the universal quantifier includes that of the existential. In general the scope of a quantifier inserted later in the constructional history of a sentence includes that of a quantifier inserted earlier; the same is true of the relative scopes of quantifiers and sentential operators, or pairs of sentential operators.

In fact, Frege does not proceed in exactly the way just explained since he introduces no existential quantifier. Instead he appeals to the equivalence: 'something is F if and only if it is not the case that everything is not F', to paraphrase existential sentences by negations of universal ones. But this does not alter matters significantly since the same opportunities for scope ambiguity arise when we consider sentences just containing universal quantification and truth-functional operators. Thus 'Everyone is not mortal' might be read as equivalent to 'Everyone is immortal' or as equivalent to 'It is not the case that everyone is mortal'. The two readings correspond to two possible constructional histories of the sentence. In the first we start with the singular sentence:

Adam is mortal

We then construct its negation:

It is not the case that Adam is mortal

We then omit the name 'Adam' to leave the linguistic function:

It is not the case that ( ) is mortal

Finally we insert the quantifier 'everything'.

So understood the sentence will be true on the Fregean account if and only if *each* of the sentences

It is not the case that Adam is mortal
It is not the case that Eve is mortal
It is not the case that Cain is mortal
It is not the case that Abel is mortal

and so on is true. And, given Frege's account of negation, the truth-value of each of these sentences is determined by the truth-value of the sentence to which 'It is not the case that' is prefixed.

On this account of its constructional history and truth-conditions, 'Everyone is not mortal' is a sentence in which the scope of the universal quantifier includes that of the negation symbol.

Alternatively, 'Everyone is not mortal' may be understood as being constructed by starting with

Adam is mortal

omitting the singular term 'Adam' to get the function

( ) is mortal

inserting 'everything' to get

Everything is mortal

and then forming its negation:

It is not the case that everything is mortal

If we follow through the Fregean account of the truth-conditions of the sentence so understood, in which the relative scopes of the universal quantifier and negation are reversed, a different truth-condition will emerge.

The important points to appreciate from the above are: (a) that Frege's account of generality explains how the truth-conditions of general sentences are determined by those of appropriately related singular sentences viewed as divided into argument and function, (b) that this account works by being applied to one expression of generality at a time, to yield at each stage a sentence with one less expression of generality, (c) that to apply this account to ordinary language sentences we must conceive of the sentence as built up in a sequence of stages, and (d) that in the Fregean account no *additional* explanation of the truth-functional operators is needed to explain their role when *not* connecting whole sentences (as in 'Everyone is not mortal' read as equivalent to 'Everyone is immortal'). It is in this way that Frege rejects Boole's contention noted above that it is *not* the exclusive office of a 'conjunction' (sentential operator) to connect propositions (Boole 1973: 59n).

We have been looking at Frege's account as applied to ordinary language sentences and noting how it can explain some ambiguities which are present in them. But in Frege's symbolism or its modern equivalents such ambiguities are impossible, and the relative scopes of quantifiers and sentential operators are utterly transparent. Thus, in a modern equivalent of Frege's symbolism the reading of 'everyone is not mortal' as 'everyone is immortal' is represented by

$(\forall x)\neg Fx$

(with the scope of the quantifier wider than that of negation) while the alternative reading is represented by

¬(∀x)Fx

(with the scope of negation wider than that of the quantifier). One simply cannot write down a well-formed scope-ambiguous formula.

Again, one reading of 'everything is related to something' will be represented in the modern equivalent of Frege's symbolism as

(∀x)(∃y)Rxy

in which the different variables ('x' and 'y') make clear the scopes of the two quantifiers. The other will be represented as

(∃x)(∀y)Ryx

So far we have looked only at how Frege's account works when applied to unrestrictedly general sentences possibly containing negation symbols. But we can now go on to see how it applies to sentences of restricted generality (the type of sentence dealt with in traditional Aristotelian logic) and to sentences containing expressions of unrestricted generality and other truth-functional connectives.

In fact, the two types of sentence reduce to one, for Frege is able to explain restricted generality in terms of unrestricted generality and truth-functions.

He illustrates this with the four types of proposition found in the Aristotelian square of opposition (1972: 133–5).

'Every F is G', he observes, is equivalent to 'If something has the property F, then it also has the property G', or 'Everything, if it is F is G'. And this may be expressed as follows in the modern equivalent of Frege's symbolism:

(∀x)(Fx → Gx)

Thus it will be true if nothing has the property F, i.e. if there are no F's.

'Some F is not G' is equivalent to 'Something is F and is not G', or, using universal quantification, to 'It is not the case that everything which is F is G'. This may be expressed as follows:

¬(∀x)(Fx → Gx)

This includes the case in which only one thing is F and G.

'No F is G' is equivalent to 'Everything which has F lacks G'

or:

$(\forall x)(Fx \rightarrow \neg Gx)$

Finally, 'Some F is G', which is equivalent to 'Not everything which has the property F lacks the property G' is symbolized as:

$\neg(\forall x)(Fx \rightarrow \neg Gx)$

Now we can note another feature of Frege's symbolism, which is introduced to allow a simpler expression of universally quantified propositions: a distinction between what modern logicians call 'free' and 'bound' variables. Frege makes this distinction by using italic letters for free variables and old German letters for bound variables.

As we have seen, the fact that his universal quantifier need not occur immediately after his judgement stroke, but can occur after a preceding universal quantifier, after the symbol for negation, or in the antecedent or consequent of a conditional, is what gives Frege's symbolism its richness, and allows him to symbolize existentially quantified sentences, and multiply general sentences. However, cases in which a universal quantifier does occur immediately after the judgement stroke, that is, in which it has maximal scope in the sentence, are especially important, since only in this case is substitution allowed. Thus from the sentence 'If everything is wet we cannot light a fire' (Kneale and Kneale 1962: 487), which, when translated into Frege's symbolism (i.e. as '$(\forall x)Fx \rightarrow P$'), would *not* involve a universal quantifier with maximal scope, we cannot infer, by substitution, 'If the wood is wet we cannot light a fire' (maybe we can, so long as the grass is dry). But from the sentence 'All men are mortal', which, when translated with Frege's symbolism does involve a universal quantifier with maximal occurrence, we can infer by substitution 'If Socrates is a man then Socrates is mortal'.

Frege consequently introduces 'free variables' (in his symbolism, italic letters), letters not linked to any explicit quantifier, to abbreviate sentences of the latter type by a stipulation that we may replace (his equivalent of)

⊢ (∀x)Fx

by (his equivalent of)

⊢ Fa

and move from the latter to the former, as long as the 'bound variable' (the 'x', in his symbolism an old German letter), i.e. the letter linked to an explicit quantifier, introduced in place of the free variable ('a') does not already occur in the latter judgement.

There is one final point to be made about Frege's logical symbolism to complete this exposition. So far, what has been explained is Frege's way of dealing with generalizations about individuals, that is, Frege's system of *first-order* predicate logic. But, in fact, Frege's *Conceptual Notation* includes a formulation of *second-order* logic, which also allows him to represent generalizations about *properties*. To see how Frege conceives of this we need to go back to his section 'The Function' and consider its final paragraph:

> Since the symbol Φ occurs at a place in the expression
>
> Φ(A)
>
> and since we can think of it as replaced by other symbols [such as] ψ, X – which then express other functions of the argument A – we can consider Φ(A) as a function of the argument Φ. This shows quite clearly that the concept of function in analysis, which I have in general followed, is far more restricted than the one developed here. (1972: 129)

Let us consider again the sentence:

> Hydrogen is lighter than carbon dioxide

As we have seen, if we conceive of 'Hydrogen' as replaceable, we can divide this as argument: 'Hydrogen', function: 'is lighter than carbon dioxide'. Or, if we conceive of 'carbon dioxide' as replaceable we can divide it as argument: 'carbon dioxide', function: 'hydrogen is lighter than'. Or again, we may conceive of both 'hydrogen' and 'carbon dioxide' as replaceable and then we can divide it as arguments: 'Hydrogen', 'carbon dioxide', function: 'is lighter than'. And, as we have noted, the functions here mentioned are not to be understood as quotable parts of the sentence, but as features, or linguistic functions.

There are, however, other ways of conceiving of the sentence 'Hydrogen is lighter than carbon dioxide' as divided into a replaceable and an invariant component. We may, for example, compare it with the sentences

Hydrogen is a gas
Hydrogen is inflammable
Hydrogen is an element

Here we are conceiving of the function

is lighter than carbon dioxide

which on the first analysis is the function of which the sentence is the value for the argument 'hydrogen', as *itself* the argument of a function which yields

Hydrogen is lighter than carbon dioxide

as the value in this case, and for the functions

is a gas
is inflammable
is an element

as arguments, yields the sentence listed above as values. This function expresses the property of being instantiated by hydrogen. It is the possibility of conceiving a singular sentence as the value of such a *second-level* linguistic function – a linguistic function mapping linguistic functions as arguments onto sentences as values – with which Frege is concerned in the last paragraph quoted.

Of course, if we try to write down such a second-level linguistic function we will fail. The only quotable part of all the sentences in which it occurs is the name 'Hydrogen'. But it is not identifiable with the name, any more than first-level linguistic functions are identifiable with the quotable parts of sentences which we exhibit when we write down *their* values.

Since

Hydrogen is lighter than carbon dioxide

conceived as split into argument: 'Hydrogen', function: 'is lighter than carbon dioxide' can be read as

Hydrogen has the property of being lighter than carbon dioxide

we can conceive of each of the sentences which are values of this second-level function as saying of hydrogen that it has a certain property. To say of hydrogen that it has every property is then to say that this function, 'is instantiated by hydrogen', is a fact whatever we take as its argument, which in a modern equivalent of Fregean symbolism can be written

$(\forall F)Fa$

using quantification over properties, and 'a' as a symbol for hydrogen. Frege draws attention to this possibility when he introduces his symbol for universal quantification: 'Since a letter which is used as a function symbol like Φ in $\Phi(A)$, can itself be considered as the argument of a function, it can be replaced by a German letter in the manner just specified' (1972: 130); but he does not think that he has to make any special provision for it in his axioms or rules of inference. As we shall see, for Frege's purposes the fact that his system includes a form of second-order logic is important, for it is via quantification over properties that he is able to define, in the third part of *Conceptual Notation*, the important notion of the ancestral of a relation.

Let us now return, however, to the inadequacies of traditional logic listed in the preceding section of this chapter and see how Frege's system overcomes them.

The first inadequacy we noted was the inability of traditional logic, given its commitment to the unique analysis of any single sentence into a single subject and predicate to account for the validity of *both* steps in the argument:

          (1) Everyone killed himself
Ergo: (2) Cato killed Cato
Ergo: (3) Someone killed Cato

On a Fregean account, which allows different, equally legitimate ways of viewing (2) as divisible into function and argument, the problem disappears. (1) translated into (a modern equivalent) of Frege's symbolism comes out as:

(∀x)Rxx

Its truth-condition is thus that the function

   ( ) killed ( )

– the function whose value for any name as argument is the result of writing that name followed by the verb 'killed' followed by another occurrence of the same name – is a fact whatever name is taken as its argument. Since this is so the truth of (2) is a necessary condition of the truth of (1) since (2) is a value of the function in question for the argument 'Cato'. (2), however, is also a value of the function

   ( ) killed Cato

for the argument 'Cato', and (3) is true iff that function is a fact for *some* name as argument. Therefore (2) entails (3).

The second inadequacy of traditional logic listed was its inability to account for inferences from such a truth-functionally complex sentence as

   Every inhabitant is European or every inhabitant is Asiatic

to such a general sentence as

   Every inhabitant is European or Asiatic

The key to the Fregean solution of this problem is its ability to account for the use of the disjunctive operator 'or' in both sentences on the basis solely of its explanation as a truth-functional *sentential* operator, i.e. its explicit role in the former sentence. Ignoring the irrelevant restriction of the generality to 'inhabitants' to get at the essence of the matter, the second sentence is true if and only if the function

   ( ) is a European or Asiatic

is a fact for every argument. But this is so if and only if the function

   ( ) is a European or ( ) is an Asiatic

– the function which maps a name onto the result of writing that name, followed by 'is a European or', followed by a second occurrence of the name, followed by 'is an Asiatic' – is a fact for every argument. But this is so just in case

> Adam is a European or Adam is an Asiatic
> Eve is a European or Eve is an Asiatic

and so on are all true.

Thus the truth-condition of the general sentence in which 'or' occurs connecting *non*-sentential components is fixed as determined by the truth of singular sentences in which 'or' occurs only connecting sentences. Given this, the validity of the inference of the second sentence from the first can now be justified straightforwardly by appeal to the truth-functional meaning of 'or' and the Fregean truth-condition of the first sentence.

The third inadequacy of traditional logic listed was the difficulty it had in dealing with sentences containing multiple generality. We have now seen in detail how easily Fregean logic enables sentences of this type, and the ambiguities they typically present in ordinary language, to be accounted for and provided with unambiguous perspicuous representations in logical symbolism.

Having explained his symbolism Frege goes on to set out a set of axioms and rules of inference. We have already looked at those which are exclusive to propositional logic. Frege introduces three others. Two (numbered (52) and (54) in *Conceptual Notation*) concern identity of content. Expressed in modern symbolism they are:

> (52) $(c = d) \rightarrow [Fc \rightarrow Fa]$
> (54) $c = c$

The first is a formulation of Leibniz's Law, the principle that identicals are indiscernible. The second axiom states that everything is identical with itself.

Frege's final axiom, numbered (58), deals with the universal quantifier. In modern symbolism it can be stated as:

> (58) $(\forall x)Fx \rightarrow Fa$.

Frege illustrates this with the example: 'If whatever is a bird can fly, then if this ostrich is a bird it can fly.'

Frege also introduces two rules governing the universal quantifier. One, already noted, is that we may move from a proposition containing a free variable (an italic letter) to one involving an initial universal quantifier so long as the bound variable (old German letter) introduced does not occur anywhere within the original sentence. The second rule Frege introduces is that from

'P → Fa' (in which 'a' is a free variable)

we may derive

P → ∀xFx

if 'P' is an expression in which 'a' does not occur and 'a' stands only in argument places of 'Fa' (*Conceptual Notation*, section 11).

These axioms and rules, together with the ones already introduced, constitute a complete set of axioms and rules for first-order predicate logic.

In this exposition of Frege's logical system, as it is presented in *Conceptual Notation*, I have been careful not to anticipate later developments in order to give the reader a sense of how *Conceptual Notation* would have appeared to Frege's first readers. But a sketch of these developments will now be appropriate.

The first change to note concerns the application of the notion of a function. Frege's later work involves what we might call the 'functionalization' of his logic. In *Conceptual Notation* the primary application of the notion of a function is to linguistic expressions, even if Frege occasionally deviates from this usage. After *Foundations* Frege explicitly distinguishes between the non-linguistic functions which are the references of expressions and the expressions themselves. But he did not forget the insights contained in *Conceptual Notation* and continued to think of expressions for functions as patterns exhibited by, rather than quotable parts of, the larger expressions in which they feature. However, he no longer refers to them as 'functions', reserving that term for their extra-linguistic correlates. Instead he refers to them as 'incomplete' or 'unsaturated' expressions. Thus in the later work Frege treats predicate expressions (which in *Conceptual Notation* are called 'functions') as names of a special type of function (called 'concepts', or 'relations' if they take more than one argument) – ones mapping arguments onto truth-values. He also treats the universal quantifier explicitly as a name of a function mapping first-level concepts onto truth-values, and so as itself a name of a second-level function. In *Conceptual Notation* Frege never describes the universal quantifier either as a function or as a name of a function. The same is true of the symbols for negation and the conditional introduced in *Conceptual Notation*. These are introduced prior to the section 'The Function' and never referred to as functions. Later, from 'Function and Concept' onwards, they are treated as names of functions mapping objects, including truth-values, onto truth-values (and so as concepts or relations). In fact, the only logical symbol which Frege introduces in *Conceptual Notation* which is *not* later regarded as a name of a function, and specifically as a name of a concept or relation, is the vertical judgement stroke and this is envisaged as not being a name at all.

In the logical system of *Basic Laws* two function names are introduced which are not names of concepts or relations. The most important is the symbol '$\acute{\epsilon}\phi(\epsilon)$', for the value range of the function $\phi(\zeta)$. Value ranges are objects paired with functions; since they are not, in general, truth-values, this function is not a concept. Its importance for Frege is immense, since when the function $\phi(\zeta)$ is a concept, it symbolizes the *extension* of that concept (the class of entities falling under it), and numbers are identified with the extensions of certain concepts. The second function-name Frege introduces in *Basic Laws* which does not stand for a concept is his substitute for the definite article, '$\backslash$', explained as a name for a function mapping objects onto objects. The function $\backslash$ is defined as follows: if the argument is the extension of a concept under which exactly one object falls, its value is that object, if the argument is any other type of object its value is the object itself. This guarantees a reference for Frege's symbolic equivalents of definite descriptions whether or not these would ordinarily be said to be satisfied. Thus Frege's substitute 'for the present King of France' is '$\backslash$(the extension of the concept *present King of France*)', and since there is no King of France this has as reference that very extension, whereas, in Frege's view, the ordinary language description has no reference.

The axioms of *Basic Laws* are those of *Conceptual Notation*, with some modifications and an explicit axiom concerning quantification over functions given separately. This says that whatever holds of *all* first-level functions of an argument holds of *any*, e.g. that if every property is possessed by Socrates, wisdom is possessed by Socrates. In addition there is an axiom introduced concerning value-ranges, the fatal Basic Law (V), which states that value-ranges are identical just in case the functions of which they are value-ranges always yield the same values for the same arguments, and an axiom governing Frege's substitute for the definite article

$$a = \backslash \acute{\epsilon} \, (a = \epsilon)$$

which asserts that the reference of the term '\(the extension of the concept *identical with a*)' is a itself.

Having set out his logical system in the first two parts of *Conceptual Notation* Frege turns in the third part to establish some mathematical results. His concern in this section is the concept of *following in a sequence*. This concept is essentially involved in our idea of a natural number: the natural numbers are just those objects which belong to the sequence which starts from 0 and is built up by successively adding one. But what is done successively is done in time. It thus appears that, if this manner of identification of a sequence is essential, the notion of a sequence and hence the notion of a natural number essentially depends upon that of time. Given that our knowledge of time rests on Kantian *a priori* intuition, then it follows that our knowledge of arithmetic cannot be free of intuition. It is this line of reasoning that the third part of *Conceptual Notation* is intended to block. Frege shows how to give a definition of *following in a sequence* (what is now known as the ancestral of a relation) in purely logical terms, without any appeal to intuition, spatial or temporal, and goes on to prove various general propositions about sequences also without any appeal to intuition.

In particular, Frege is able to establish (on the basis of the definition of the natural numbers as 0 itself plus the members of the sequence got from 0 by successive addition of 1) that mathematical induction is based on a logical truth and is not, as had been thought, a method of reasoning peculiar to mathematics. However, this last result is not established in *Conceptual Notation* but merely referred to in passing in a footnote (1972: 177); Frege spells it out in the *Foundations* where he states that: 'Only by means of this definition of following in a sequence [the definition of following-in-a-sequence given in *Conceptual Notation*] is it possible to reduce the inference from n to (n + 1), which on the face of it is peculiar to mathematics, to the general laws of logic' (1968: 93).

In order to define the notion of *following in a sequence* Frege first defines the notion of a hereditary property. A property F is said to be *hereditary in the R-sequence* if and only if: if x has F and x stands in the relation R to y then y has F. In modern symbolism we can express this as follows:

$(\forall x)(Fx \rightarrow ((\forall y)Rxy \rightarrow Fy))$

Frege illustrates this with the example of parenthood: if 'Rxy' means that x is a parent of y and 'Fx' means that x is human the displayed formula states that any child of a human being is a human being, which is true. Therefore, the property of *being human* is hereditary in the *parent–child* sequence. By contrast, the property, say, of *being wise* is not – wise parents can have foolish children.

Frege next defines what it is to *follow in the R-sequence*, that is, the relation which holds between y and x if y can be reached from x by a finite series of steps starting from x and moving at each step to something to which the object arrived at in the previous step stands in the relation R (in modern terminology this is called the 'proper ancestral' of the relation R). We can, of course, in a way, define this already. It is the relation which holds between y and x iff x bears the relation R to y, or to something which bears the relation R to y, or to something which bears the relation R to . . . something which bears the relation R to y. Thus my descendants are my children, or my children's children, or my children's children's . . . children, and so on. Frege's definition enables us to get rid of the dots and the 'and so on' and therewith any suspicion that a process essentially involving time is involved in the notion of *following in a sequence* (the proper ancestral of a relation).

His definition is:

y follows x in the R-sequence if and only if: every property hereditary in the R-sequence possessed by everything to which x is related by the relation R is also possessed by y

In modern symbolism (using 'Her(x)' to abbreviate 'F is hereditary in the R-sequence') this may be expressed:

$(\forall F)(Her(F) \wedge (\forall z)(Rxz \rightarrow Fz) \rightarrow Fy)$

Applied to the parent–child relation this tells us that y follows x in the parent–child sequence, i.e. y is a descendant of x, if and only if every hereditary property possessed by all x's children is also possessed by y. To see that this is intuitively correct, note first that all one's descendants will possess all hereditary properties possessed by all one's children (so the biconditional is correct left to right), and second, that *being a descendant of x* is itself a hereditary property, so that anyone possessing *all* one's children's hereditary properties will possess that property too, i.e. will be one's descendant (so the biconditional is correct right to left).

It is an easy consequence of these definitions that:

if x has a property F which is hereditary in the R-sequence, and if y follows x in the R-sequence, then y has the property F

This is Frege's own translation into ordinary language of his formula (81), to which he attaches the footnote: 'Bernouillian induction is based on this.'

Specializing to the natural number sequence, i.e. the sequence generated by the successor relation (addition of 1) starting from 0, we get:

if 0 has a property F which is hereditary in the successor-sequence, and if y follows 0 in the successor-sequence, then y has the property F

With the relation 'y belongs to the R-sequence beginning with x' (what is now called the 'ancestral proper' of the R-relation) defined as 'y = x or y follows x in the R-sequence' (Frege 1972: 186) and the natural numbers defined as those objects belonging to the successor-sequence beginning with 0 (Frege 1968: 96) this becomes:

if 0 has a property F which is hereditary in the successor-sequence and y is a natural number distinct from 0 then y has property F

Thus to establish that a property F is possessed by *all* natural numbers we have only to establish (a) that it is possessed by 0, and (b) that it is hereditary in the successor-sequence, i.e. is possessed by (n + 1) if possessed by n. But this is the reasoning characteristic of mathematical induction, which has therefore been shown to be, as Frege says, based 'on a general law of logic' (1968: 93).

3

Number

Aims of *The Foundations of Arithmetic*

The Foundations of Arithmetic, Frege's next substantial work after *Conceptual Notation*, is his masterpiece. It is not, however, for reasons explained in chapter 1, what a reader of *Conceptual Notation* would have expected. Instead of being written in Frege's logical symbolism it is entirely in German, and consists of both a negative part and a positive part, the former containing Frege's critique of the views of other philosophers and mathematicians, and the latter containing his own positive account of arithmetic, including informal sketches of some of the crucial proofs later given formally in *Basic Laws*. *Foundations* is, in fact, as Michael Dummett explains (1991a: 1) 'a philosophical justification of [Frege's] theory of natural numbers' – that is, of his mature theory of natural numbers formally expounded in part II of *Basic Laws* (contained partly in volume 1 and partly in volume 2). It relates to part II of *Basic Laws* as the first half of part III of that work relates to the second half. The first half of part III is a philosophical justification of Frege's theory of real numbers, consisting of a critique of alternative views, a summary of the requirements the critique has thrown up on a theory of real numbers, and an informal sketch of the formal derivations constituting the second half (see Dummett 1991a: 1–9 for a more detailed account). We must assume that as regards his account of the natural numbers Frege was satisfied, at the time he was writing the *Basic Laws*, with the philosophical justification provided by *Foundations*.

The aim of *Foundations*, as Frege expresses it in his conclusion, was to 'have made it probable that the laws of arithmetic are analytic judgements and consequently *a priori*' (1968: 99), or, as he states it in the introduction to *Basic Laws* 'in my *Grundlagen der Arithmetik* I sought to make it probable that arithmetic is a branch of logic and that no ground of proof needs to be drawn whether from experience or intuition' (1964: 29). Frege here signals his attitude to the two principal views opposed in *Foundations* – the Millian empiricist view according to which arithmetic is known through experience, and the Kantian, according to which it is known through (*a priori*) intuition.

The structure of *Foundations* is as follows. After an Introduction, there is a brief section in which Frege sets his project in the context of the mathematical work of the time and identifies in (redefined) Kantian terms the philosophical aim of his enquiry. He then examines, in part I, the views of certain writers, most importantly Kant and Mill (with whom he disagrees) and Leibniz (with whom he agrees) on the nature of arithmetical propositions. Part II is an examination of the concept of number, arguing against both the Millian view that number is a property of external things and the view that it is something subjective. Part III, which supplements part II, is concerned with the notions of unity and one, and culminates in Frege's presentation of his own position: that a statement of number is an assertion about a concept, which, he goes on to show, resolves all the difficulties in the theories about the nature of number previously examined. Part IV presents Frege's own positive account of the concept of number, and the book concludes with a restatement of the distinction between Kant's position and Frege's, and a recapitulation of what has been achieved so far and what has yet to be achieved (in the anticipated *Basic Laws*).

In his Introduction Frege begins by attempting to convince his reader of the need for his enquiry, for as he puts it: 'Many people will be sure to think this is not worth the trouble. Naturally, they will suppose, this concept [that of number] is adequately dealt with in the elementary text books where the subject is settled once and for all.... The first requisite for learning anything is thus utterly lacking – I mean the knowledge that we do not know' (1968: iii).

The Introduction opens with an imagined dialogue which is designed to impart this knowledge. It goes as follows:

Q.   What is the number one?
A.   Why, a thing!

Q. *Which* thing (since there are more than one)?
A. Anything you please – select it for yourself.

The respondent, he supposes, would attempt to justify this last answer by comparing the symbol '1' with the letter 'a', as it is used in arithmetic. But Frege insists on a distinction – 'a' so used does not mean some one definite number, but serves to express the generality of general propositions (i.e. it is a free variable): 'a+a–a=a' states that whatever number we put for a, so long as we put the same one each time, we will always get a true identity, '1+1=2', however, cannot be understood as stating that whatever we put for 1, so long as we put the same each time, we will always get a true identity. On the contrary, it looks as if we would have to put something *different* each time to ensure that this was so. In fact, though, to interpret the identity '1+1=2' as a generalization is mistaken, Frege suggests: '1' is not a free variable but a symbol for a definite particular object, with specifiable properties. Thus '1+1=2' asserts 'nothing of the Moon, nothing of the Sahara, nothing of the Peak of Teneriffe; for what would be the sense of any such assertion?' (1968: ii).

At the outset, then, Frege has already intimated two features of his developed view: numbers must be thought of as *objects*, and statements of arithmetic assert nothing of any *physical* objects.

He moves on to express a third fundamental element of his position. Against the suggestion that 'calculation is mechanical aggregative thought' he insists that thought is the same everywhere, whatever its subject matter – it is not that there are different kinds of thought to suit the objects thought about; and, referring to the achievement of the final part of *Conceptual Notation*, without yet mentioning that book by name, he denies the distinctiveness of mathematical induction: even an inference from n to n + 1 . . . is based on the general laws of logic' (1968: iv).

The rest of the Introduction is devoted to a polemic against psychologism in mathematics. Frege does not deny to psychology a place as a science in its own right, and he even acknowledges that it may 'serve some purpose to investigate the ideas and changes of ideas that accompany mathematical thinking' (1968: vi). But he insists that the description of psychological processes has nothing to do with mathematics: 'sensations are absolutely no concern of arithmetic. No more are mental pictures, formed from the amalgamated trace of earlier sense-impressions. . . . To the mathematician as such these mental pictures are . . . immaterial' (1968: v).

Frege's argument against psychologism has two main elements. First, he argues that whatever ideas, that is, whatever mental pictures, one has in one's mind when one hears or says, for example, 'one hundred' are irrelevant to what one means, since they may vary from speaker to speaker. One person may have in mind an image of the numeral '100', another an image of the letter 'C' (1968: vi). Others may have other images. One does not need to know, for what matters – that is, for what matters when one is doing mathematics and is not engaged in psychological investigation – is what is public and communicable. That one is expressing a thought concerning the number one hundred neither requires nor excludes the presence of any particular image accompanying one's utterance.

Apart from its importance for Frege's own position, this argument is important also for containing, when generalized, the germ of Wittgenstein's later definitive refutation of all ideational theories of meaning, and his profound rejection of any account of understanding as an 'inner process' – something occurring in one's mind at a particular time, which determines what one is then thinking. Wittgenstein expresses his rejection of this in the dictum 'If God had looked into our minds he would not have been able to see there whom we were speaking of' (Wittgenstein 1968: 217). Whatever occurs in one's mind at a time accompanying one's utterance or hearing of a word cannot determine *how* it is to be taken and therefore cannot determine how one *uses* the associated word. But *how I use it* is precisely what understanding it in a particular way consists of, so no account of understanding in terms of occurrent mental processes can be correct.

The second element of Frege's attack on psychologism in the Introduction is his argument that we must 'never . . . take a description of the origin of an idea for a definition' (1968: vi). There are two things to be distinguished: an account of a concept (say, the concept of number), and an account of the process of concept acquisition. The latter cannot be complete without the former and, more importantly, the latter cannot replace the former. An account of a concept is a definition and definitions in mathematics prove their worth in the construction of proofs (1968: ix). An account of the way in which a mathematical concept is arrived at can never be a necessary component of a mathematical proof. Such an account must then be sharply distinguished from an account, i.e. a definition, of a concept. Thus, while there is indeed what is known as 'the history of concepts' (1968: vii) it is wrongly so called. Concepts have no history:

there is only the history of our knowledge of concepts or of the meanings of words.

Once again, of course, Frege's argument generalizes beyond the mathematical domain, as Dummett explains (1991a: 14ff.). What one wants from an account of a concept, or a definition, is something that will enable one to determine the truth-value of a proposition. To be given a definition is to be told that 'X' means Y (in the simplest case of an explicit definition) and such a statement means nothing unless it tells one something about the contribution that 'X' makes to the truth-conditions of propositions containing it. But an account of the origin of a concept can never tell one anything of this sort. It is therefore no substitute for a definition.

Frege ends his Introduction by laying down three fundamental principles (1968: x):

> always to separate sharply the psychological from the logical, the subjective from the objective;
>
> never to ask for the meaning of a word in isolation, but only in the context of a proposition;
>
> never to lose sight of the distinction between concept and object.

The first is a summary of what has gone before. The second principle is the celebrated 'context principle', which has been a subject of huge debate and is appealed to by Frege, as we have briefly noted in chapter 1, at a crucial point in *Foundations* in defence of his claim that the key form of proposition to be defined in an account of number is that of an identity statement. Here Frege links it with his anti-psychologism, saying that rejection of it almost forces one to identify word meanings with mental pictures or individual acts of mind, and so to offend against the first principle as well. The thought here is appealing. If one appreciates that all one needs to know to understand a word is its contribution to the meaning of the propositions in which it occurs, one will be content with an account that provides that. But if not, one will want more, and, particularly in the case of terms like numerals, which are names of abstract objects, an account of the images in one's mind when one hears or utters the word, or the mental processes going on at the time, will seem to be all that is available that could possibly be relevant. (In the case of concrete objects, which one can encounter in perception, the temptation will not be so great, since one might be satisfied with an 'ostensive definition', pointing out the object, as providing an answer to one's request for the meaning of the word: but, of course, if the context principle is correct, such a 'definition' will either be irrelevant or will be construable as an account of the contribution of the meaning of the word to the meaning of propositions in which it occurs.)

The third principle, never to lose sight of the distinction between concept and object, is, at this stage in *Foundations*, hard to understand. Frege's sharp distinction between objects and functions (and, therefore, as a subclass, concepts) has not yet been made. But we see it at work later in *Foundations* where Frege insists on distinguishing a concept word from a proper name of an object even when the concept word (like 'satellite of the earth') applies to only one object. In general, his point is that a concept may have many instances, none, or exactly one instance. Whether a concept word is well defined is one question; whether any objects fall under it, and if so how many, is another. Thus 'the widely held formalist theory of functional, negative etc., numbers' (1968: x), which is discussed in the Conclusion of *Foundations*, is untenable: its error lying precisely in taking freedom from contradiction in a concept as a sufficient guarantee that something falls under it (1968: 119) – a mistake easily made if one fails to distinguish clearly between concepts and objects (1968: 108).

Rebuttal of Earlier Attempts

After the Introduction, Frege turns to his critique of rival views, but he begins by again setting out, in sections 1 and 2, a justification for his enquiry. First he addresses himself to the mathematician. He writes:

> The concepts of function, of continuity, of limit and infinity, have been shown to stand in need of sharper definition. Negative and irrational numbers, which had long since been admitted into a science, have had to submit to the closest scrutiny of their credentials ... Proceeding along these lines, we are bound eventually to come to the concept of Number and to the simplest propositions holding of positive whole numbers, which form the foundation of the whole of arithmetic. (1968: 1–2)

Here Frege presents his enquiry as the natural culmination of the 'revolution in rigour' which began with Cauchy in the nineteenth century, and attempted to introduce greater rigour into the foundations of mathematical analysis (differential and integral calculus), and dispel the suspicion hanging over it that its employment of such ideas as that of a Newton 'fluxion' or Leibnizian 'infinitesimal' was simply incoherent. The earlier stages of the movement, as Frege says, involved definitions of such key notions as functions, continuity and limit, and its later stage involved the arithmetization of analysis (the 'scrutiny of the credentials of negative and irrational numbers' which Frege refers to). Since, as we have seen, the latter involved a rejection of the traditional geometrical approach to real numbers, Frege's project, understood in the way outlined in chapter 1, as an attempt to account for the epistemological asymmetry between geometry and arithmetic revealed by the existence of consistent non-Euclidean geometries, is indeed a natural next step.

Frege goes on to explain how 'philosophical notions, too, have prompted one to enquiries of this kind' (1968: 3) (though, if the foregoing is correct, the 'too' suggests too sharp a distinction). Immediately he frames his enquiry in Kantian terms: are arithmetical truths *a priori* or *a posteriori*, synthetic or analytic?

For Kant the two distinctions belong to two different spheres, the former to epistemology, the latter to logic. Frege draws them both on the same basis, in terms of the kind of justification available:

> The problem becomes, in fact, that of finding the proof of the proposition, and of following it up right back to the primitive truths. If in carrying out this process, we come only on general logical laws and on definitions, then the truth is an analytic one, bearing in mind that we must take account also of all propositions upon which the admissibility of any of the definitions depends. If, however, it is impossible to give the proof without making use of truths which are not of a general logical nature, but belong to some special science then the truth is a synthetic one. For a truth to be *a posteriori*, it must be impossible to construct a proof of it without including an appeal to facts, i.e. to truths which cannot be proved and are not general, since they contain assertions about particular objects. But if, on the contrary, its proof can be derived exclusively from general laws, which themselves neither need nor admit of proof, then the truth is *a priori*. (1968: 4)

But he remarks in a footnote that he does not 'mean to assign a new sense to these terms, but only to state accurately what earlier writers, Kant, in particular, have meant by them' (1968: 3). At the end of *Foundations* he gives a justification for his departure from

Kant's definition of analyticity (in terms of 'containment' of the predicate concept in the subject concept) by pointing to the inadequacy of the Aristotelian logic in terms of which Kant framed it. Existential and singular propositions simply *have* no subject concept. But he also notes that Kant, too, hints at an epistemic basis for the analytic/synthetic distinction when he cites the principle of contradiction as the 'highest principle' of all analytic judgements and says that a synthetic proposition can only be seen to be true by the law of contradiction if *another* synthetic proposition is presupposed (1968: 100).

We can extract from the passage quoted the following Fregean definitions of the notions of an analytic (and hence *a priori*) truth, a synthetic *a priori* truth, and a synthetic *a posteriori* truth:

A truth is analytic if and only if it is provable from general logical laws which themselves neither need nor admit of proof.

A truth is synthetic *a priori* if and only if it is provable from general laws which themselves neither need nor admit of proof but belong to the sphere of some special science.

A truth is synthetic *a posteriori* if and only if it is not provable without an appeal to facts, i.e. truths which cannot be proved and are not general, since they contain assertions about particular objects.

The difference between an analytic truth and a synthetic *a priori* one for Frege, then, is simply that the latter is only provable from general laws with a restricted subject matter – 'logical' laws are just those which can be applied to any subject matter. This fits, of course, precisely with Frege's distinction between geometry and arithmetic as expressed in a passage already quoted in full in chapter 1: 'the truths of geometry govern all that is spatially intuitable . . . [But] the truths of arithmetic govern all that is numerable. This is the widest domain of all; for to it belongs not only the actual, not only the intuitable, but everything thinkable' (1968: 20–1).

Things of every kind can be counted: not just physical objects, not just temporal objects, but abstract objects including numbers themselves, and indeed concepts and functions. And to anything which can be counted arithmetic applies. Thus arithmetical terms and concepts have universal applicability, and are therefore logical ones. But it does not follow immediately that all arithmetical truths are analytic, for it remains possible that particular arithmetical truths, like 2+3=5, which deal with particular numbers, are facts, i.e. truths which cannot be proved and are not general, since they contain assertions about particular objects; in which case, according to Frege's classificatory scheme, they would be synthetic *a posteriori*. Another philosopher might resist this by denying that such arithmetical truths make assertions about particular objects, but Frege cannot do so since one of his principal contentions is that numbers *are* objects. Thus, to establish his thesis he needs to show that such arithmetical truths are provable from *general* laws, which do not contain assertions about particular objects. It is this which is the object of *Foundations*; not to establish arithmetic as a body of *logical* truths (for that that is so, given that it is a body of truths at all, is already established by the observation that it is universally applicable), but to establish, or more cautiously, to make it probable, that it is a body of *analytic* truths.

Frege thus first turns his attention to arithmetical propositions and begins his critique of other authors by focusing on the question: 'Are numerical formulae provable?'

Kant denies this, holding that numerical formulae are synthetic and known to be true only by the aid of intuition. To verify that $7+5=12$ we must 'call to our aid the intuition corresponding to one of them, say our five fingers' and then add unit by unit to 7 to get 12 (1929 B15: 152). Frege applies this proposal to large numbers to exhibit its inadequacy. It is not self-evident that $135664+37863=173527$. On Kant's theory it would be necessary to exhibit one of the concepts in intuition to verify the proposition as illustrated in the example of $7+5=12$. But first, this runs the risk of making the proposition appear to be empirical, for 'whatever an intuition of 37863 fingers may be it is at least not pure' (1968: 6). Secondly, it is doubtful that we have such an intuition at all – we cannot distinctly perceive or construct a mental picture of 37863 fingers in the way we can distinctly perceive or construct a mental picture of five fingers. But, thirdly, if we could have intuitions of such large numbers it ought to be self-evident what the value is of $33863+135664$, for an intuition 'is that through which an object is in *immediate* relation to us' (Kant 1929 A19/B33: 65). However, it is not.

Nor is it of any avail, Frege argues, to defend the Kantian theory for *small* numbers but to accept that numerical formulae concerning *large* numbers can only be known via proof. There is no sharp dividing line between small numbers and large numbers. This last argument is particularly important; it is one to which Frege returns, wielding it again against Kant and against Mill.

The upshot of the discussion is that to be known numerical formulae must be provable.

Leibniz had thought the same, and had argued that they could be proved solely from the *definitions* of each number in terms of its predecessors and an axiom which could also be viewed as a definition. Frege quotes his 'proof' that 2+2 = 4:

Definitions   (1) 2 is 1 and 1
              (2) 3 is 2 and 1
              (3) 4 is 3 and 1

Axiom: if equals be substituted for equals the equality remains:
Proof: 2+2+2+1+1 (by Def. 1)+3+1 (by Def. 2)=4 (by Def. 3)
Therefore 2+2=4 (by the Axiom)

He then points out that as it stands this proof is fallacious, because it requires for its validity mention of the associative law 'a+(b+c)=(a+b)+c' on which it depends. Thus not only definitions but *general laws* are required to prove numerical formulae, and their credentials need an investigation which Leibniz does not give.

Frege does, however, record his agreement that the individual numbers should be defined in Leibniz's way, from 1 and addition by 1 (or as he eventually explains, from 0 and addition by 1).

Frege next turns to John Stuart Mill. Mill believed that arithmetical truths were not *a priori*, but *a posteriori*. The proposition '2+2=4', for example, is based on such observations as that if I put two apples in a box and then another two, and count the total, I will get the answer four, or that if I take four apples from a box, put half in another box and the remainder in a third box and then count the contents of each of the other two boxes I will get the answer two in each case.

Mill himself states his position as follows:

Three pebbles in two separate parcels and three pebbles in one parcel, do not make the same impression on our senses, and the assertion that the very same pebbles may by an alteration of place and arrangement be made to produce either the one set of sensations or the other, though a very familiar proposition, is not an identical one. It is a truth known to us by early and constant experience – an inductive truth; and such truths are the foundation of the science of Numbers. The fundamental truths of that science all rest on the evidence of sense, they are proved by showing to our eyes and our fingers that any given numbers of objects, ten balls, for example, may by separation and rearrangement exhibit to our senses all the different sets of numbers the sum of which is equal to ten. All the approved methods of teaching arithmetic to children proceed on a knowledge of this fact. All who wish to carry the child's mind along with them in learning arithmetic, all who wish to teach numbers, and not mere ciphers – now teach it through the evidence of the senses in the manner we have described. (1936: 168–9)

Mill accepts Leibniz's definition of each number in terms of its predecessor, but claims that these definitions assert facts:

And thus we call 'Three is two and one' a definition of three, but the calculations which depend on that proposition do not follow from the definition itself, but from an arithmetical theorem presupposed in it, namely, that collections of objects exist, which while they impress the senses thus, o o o, may be separated into two parts, thus o o o. This proposition being granted, we term all such parcels Threes, after which the enunciation of the above-mentioned physical fact will serve also for a definition of the word Three. (1936: 169)

'What a mercy', Frege comments, 'that not everything in the world is nailed down; for if it were we should not be able to bring off this separation, and 2 and 1 would not be 3' (1968: 9).

Anyway, if this definition were correct, we could not count sensations or strokes of a clock or methods of solving an equation, for none of these are ever presented in parcels which impress the senses thus o o o. Thus, if we do Mill the credit of taking him at his word, his explanation cannot account for the universal applicability of number.

Moreover, even if we accept Mill's account for small numbers it is utterly implausible for large numbers:

What in the world can be the observed fact . . . which is asserted in the definition of the number 777864. . . . If the definition of each individual number did really assert a special physical fact, then we should never be able sufficiently to admire, for his knowledge of nature, a man who calculates with nine-figure numbers . . . who is actually prepared to assert that the fact which, according to Mill, is contained in the definition of an eighteen figure number has ever been observed, and who is prepared to deny that the symbol for such a number has nonetheless, a sense. (Frege 1968: 10–11)

The response might be that only the small numbers need to be defined in terms of physical facts, the large numbers being constructible out of these. But Frege now brings to bear the argument previously used against Kant. There is no sharp line between large and small numbers. Does the definition of eleven not presuppose a physical fact, while the definition of ten does so? Wherever the boundary between large and small numbers is proposed a question of the same unanswerable form can be asked.

Frege thus concludes from his discussion of Kant and Mill so far that there is no alternative to regarding numerical formulae as derivable from general laws and the definitions of the individual numbers in terms of 0 or 1 and the successor operation, and that they neither assert nor presuppose observed facts. The status of arithmetic thus turns on the status of its general laws. Are they *a posteriori*, synthetic *a priori*, or analytic?

Mill's view was that they were *a posteriori* inductive truths. Arithmetical laws are 'in reality physical truths obtained by observation' (1936: Book IV, ch. 24, sec. 5). We observe in very many instances, for example, that when an aggregate containing two units is put together with an aggregate containing five an aggregate containing seven units results. But this is not, Frege objects, the sense of the arithmetical proposition. The meaning of the '+' symbol is not a process of heaping up, because we can speak of addition of numbers or proofs or equations or ideas, in which case there is no question of 'heaping up'. Furthermore if 5+2=7 were an induction from observed physical fact then it ought to be one we hold to be true only for the most part, for if we pour 2 unit volumes of liquid into 5 unit volumes of liquid, the result is not in general 7 unit volumes of liquid, for chemical reactions may take place. This indeed is Mill's position, which he heroically maintains even in the case of 1 = 1: 'an actual pound weight is not exactly equal to another, nor are measured miles equal in length to another' (1936: 170). But the example merely makes it as clear as it could possibly be that, as Frege says, 'in order to be able to call arithmetical truths laws of nature, Mill attributes to them a sense which they do not bear' (1968: 13).

Frege concludes that arithmetical truths are known *a priori*, so the focus now returns to Kant and the real fundamental aim of *Foundations* – to expel intuition from arithmetic. In favour of his own view he cites two pieces of evidence. One is the universal applicability of arithmetic whose importance has already been stressed. He remarks: 'we are all too ready to invoke inner intuition, whenever we cannot produce any other ground of knowledge. But we have no business, in doing so, to lose altogether sight of the word "intuition"' (1968: 19). It is a thesis of Kant's that intuition is essentially connected with sensibility through which alone objects are given to us. But the universal applicability of arithmetic – its applicability beyond the sensible to everything thinkable – suggests that intuition so understood cannot be the basis of our knowledge of it.

The other argument for the independence of arithmetic from intuition which Frege gives at this point appeals to a difference between geometrical objects and numbers. One point cannot be distinguished in any way from another; the same applies to lines and places. Only when several geometrical objects are included in a single intuition do we distinguish them. Thus the geometrical points which we construct are not really particular at all, so they can stand as representatives of the whole of their kind. This makes it quite intelligible that general propositions of geometry should be derived from intuition. By contrast, each number has its own particularity and is different from all others, and so no advance can, in this case, be made from the particular to the general without the risk being taken that the generalization is ignoring some relevant particularity.

Frege now turns, in part II, to an examination of the concept of number. He takes it as established that the individual numbers must be defined in terms of one and increase by one, and that from these definitions (supplemented by definitions of one and increase by one) together with general laws, the correct numerical formulae must be derivable. But the general laws, precisely because of their generality, cannot be derived from definitions of the individual numbers but must, if they are analytic, be based on the general concept of number, which must, therefore, Frege argues, be the next subject of examination.

Frege's aim in this part of *Foundations* and its successor is 'to assign to Number its proper place among our concepts' (1968: 27). He notes that expressions for number appear in two roles. In arithmetical contexts numerals appear in the role of singular terms standing for objects, and descriptions of the form 'the number of F's' similarly appear to stand for objects. But number words also function adjectivally in the same sort of way as the words 'hard' and 'heavy' or 'red': we may speak of the Emperor's carriage being drawn by four horses as we may speak of it as being drawn by black horses; we conjoin number words with other adjectives in descriptions such as 'three wise men'. This suggests that numbers are properties of external things as colours are. There are, in fact, several possibilities to be considered, which we may set out, employing the terminology of Frege's mature ontology (prefigured in the notation of *Conceptual Notation*). First, numbers may themselves be objects (which, of course, is in the position Frege adopts). Secondly, they may be first-level concepts, properties themselves instantiated by objects. In either case their existence may be an objective matter or a subjective matter: they may exist (if they are objects) or be instantiated (if they are properties) independently of our mental processes or be the product of our mental processes. Thirdly, numbers may be second-level concepts, concepts themselves instantiated by first-level concepts, so that in a statement of number (a statement of the form 'there are n F's) a statement is made about a first-level concept and the property ascribed to the first-level concept is a number. In this case the concept of number will itself be a third-level concept instantiated by the second-level concepts which are the numbers.

First Frege argues that numbers are not properties of external things, that is, first-level concepts instantiated by physical objects.

There are two crucial considerations. The first is that if numbers are properties of external things they are not properties of them in the way in which colours are properties of them. If the leaves of a tree are green each leaf is green, but if the leaves are 1,000 that does not mean that each leaf is 1,000. If numbers are properties of external things they are more like shapes, sizes and weights than like colour; just as the leaves may number 1,000, though no single leaf numbers 1,000, so a pile of pebbles may be pyramidal in shape, have a volume of 108 cubic inches and weigh five pounds though no one pebble in the pile is pyramidal in shape, has a volume of 108 cubic inches or weighs five pounds.

However, this suggestion, too, is open to a fatal objection. For:

> If I give someone a stone with the words: find the weight of this, I have given him precisely the object he is to investigate. But if I place a pile of playing cards in his hand with the words: find the number of these, this does not tell him whether I wish to know the number of cards, or of complete packs of cards, or even, say, of honours cards at skat. To have given him the pile in his hands is not yet to have given him completely the object he is to investigate. I must add some further word – cards or points or honours. (1968: 28–9)

Frege hammers home the point with other examples: I am able to think of the *Iliad* as *one* poem, or as *twenty-four* books, or as some

large number of verses. *One* pair of boots may be the same visible
and tangible phenomenon as *two* boots. But, just as 'if I can call the
same object red and green with equal right, it is a sure sign that the
object named does not really have the colour green, so, an object to
which I can ascribe different numbers with equal right is not really
what has a number' (1968: 29).

These considerations suffice to refute the view that a number
is a property of any external object, and in particular, suffice to
refute Mill's view that a number is 'some property belonging to
the agglomeration of things which we call by the name: and that
property is the characteristic manner in which the agglomeration
is made up of, and may be separated into parts' (1968: 29–30). For
there is no such thing as '*the* characteristic manner': a bundle of
straw can be separated into parts by cutting all the straws in half,
or by splitting it up into single straws, or by dividing it into two
bundles. One straw is many cells and many more molecules. If 'an
agglomeration of things' is a physical object composed of parts, to
give someone an agglomeration is 'not yet to give him completely
the object he is to investigate' (1968: 28) when given the command:
'Find the number of these.'

Frege notes that Mill's view faces further difficulties. How are we
to account for ascription of the number 0? And how can we account
for the fact that we can count objects which do not make up an
agglomeration: 'Must we literally hold a rally of all the blind in
Germany before we can attach any sense to the expression "the
number of blind in Germany"? Are a thousand grains of wheat,
once they have been scattered by the sower, a thousand grains of
wheat no longer?' (1968: 30).

It is a further objection to Mill's position that number is applicable to everything thinkable: to events, ideas, concepts, proofs of theorems, figures of the syllogism. It hardly makes sense to speak of
agglomerations of such things. And if it is suggested that we derive
our concepts of the individual numbers from physical aggregates
and then apply them more generally then Frege suggests: 'The case
would be just like speaking of fusible events, or blue items, or salty
concepts, or tough judgements' (1968: 31).

These, however, are supplementary considerations. The crucial
point is the one made earlier: a number cannot be a property of an
external object because 'an object to which I can ascribe different
numbers with equal right is not what really has a number' (1968: 29).

The contrast here with the case of colour might be put like this:
'a colour such as blue belongs to a surface independently of any

decision of ours . . . our way of regarding it cannot make the slight-est difference. The Number 1, on the other hand . . . or any other number, cannot be said to belong to the pile of playing cards in its own right, but at most to belong to it in view of the way we have chosen to regard it' (1968: 29).

This suggests that number is a subjective phenomenon, a creation of our minds, something imposed on the world by our decision and not really existing in things themselves. Thus Frege quotes Berkeley:

'It ought to be considered that number . . . is nothing fixed and settled, really existing in things themselves. It is entirely the creature of the mind, considering either an idea by itself, or any combination of ideas to which it gives one name, and so makes it pass for a unit. According as the mind variously combines its ideas, the unit varies, and as the unit, so the number, which is only a collection of units, doth also vary. We call a window one, a chimney one, and yet a house in which there are many windows, and many chimneys, hath an equal right to be called one, and many houses go to the making of one unit.' (1968: 33)

But Frege is able to refute this suggestion easily. Number is no more a subjective 'creature of the mind' than the North Sea. It is our choice what we designate by 'the North Sea' and it is our choice what we designate by '10,000', but once the choice has been made, if we assert 'The North Sea is 10,000 square miles in extent' we assert something 'quite objective, which is independent of our ideas and everything of the sort' (1968: 34). Again: 'The botanist seems to assert something just as factual when he gives the Number of a flower's petals as when he gives their colour. The one depends on our arbitrary choice just as little as the other' (1968: 34).

This suffices to refute subjectivism, which, indeed, is only tempt-ing if we *start* from the preconception that numbers are properties of external objects; note the difficulty that 'if I place a [physical object] in [someone's] hands with the words: Find the Number of these . . . [I have not] given him completely the object he is to inves-tigate' (1968: 28–9); but persist in spite of it in the idea that Number *is* a property of the object, albeit one it only possesses 'in view of the way we have chosen to regard it' (1968: 39). The proper con-clusion to carry away, as Frege eventually explains, is rather that numbers are not properties of external objects at all.

At this point, however, Frege takes the opportunity to elaborate
on his view of the distinction between the objective and the subjective and to distinguish within the class of the objective the actual
from the non-actual. What is objective is what is subject to laws,
what can be conceived and judged, what is communicable. The
objective is what can be an object of common knowledge. But this
must be distinguished from the actual. 'The actual is that which
is causally efficacious, that which acts upon the senses, or at least
engages in actions which may have sense-perceptions as their immediate or remote consequences' (1968: 97). Examples of the non-
actual are the axis of the earth, the centre of mass of the solar system
and the Equator – these are not *products* of thought, but they are
not causally efficacious, and cannot, directly or indirectly, affect the
senses. This distinction is important for Frege, of course, because
he wishes to maintain *both* that Numbers are objectively existing
objects, *and* that they are not given in sensibility – we are not
affected by them and yet we recognize them in thought. Only by
acknowledging the existence of a third realm of the objective and
non-actual can Frege maintain this anti-Kantian position.

At this point, then, at the conclusion of section 27, Frege has
established that numbers are not properties of external things, nor
subjective like ideas, but non-sensible and objective. He is ready to
give his own account of numbers as non-actual but objectively existent objects. However, before he does so he interposes a refutation
of another view, which may be considered a rival view of number
as objects, the view that they are sets of units.

He introduces this view by first considering the cruder, indeed
evidently absurd view, that numbers are sets of things or objects,
that is, that the number of F's is the set of things which are F. The
reason that this latter view is absurd is that it implies that there is
no such object as *the* number 3, but as many number 3's as there
are sets of three things. Moreover, Frege notes, if by a set is meant
a plurality or multitude, then no account can be given on these lines
of the numbers 0 and 1. 'Set' may be understood as something like
'aggregate' or 'heap' or 'agglomeration', referring to a juxtaposition
in space, but then the view cannot account for the universal applicability of number already stressed in the critique of Mill.

Frege thus passes quickly on to the more sophisticated form
of the set theory of number: that numbers are sets of units. The
thought behind this view is that, as Frege puts it: 'the properties
which distinguish things from one another are, when we are considering their Number, immaterial and beside the point. That is why

we want to keep them out of it' (1968: 45). There is just one number 3, however many triples there are. But, according to the conception Frege opposes, we may arrive at this number by starting with any one triple and ignoring, or abstracting from, the properties which distinguish its elements from those of other triples. In this way we arrive at a set of three featureless *units* and since we would have arrived at the *same* sets of units by starting from any triple, this set of units may rightly be thought of as the number 3.

The fundamental idea here is that we may *create* new entities, 'units', by taking no account of, or *abstracting from*, the distinguishing features of old familiar objects. Frege is scornful of this idea. Quoting his Jena colleague, Thomae, as an advocate of it he writes:

> suppose that we do, as Thomae demands, 'abstract from the peculiarities of the individual number of a set of items' or 'disregard, in considering separate things, those characteristics which serve to distinguish them' . . . the things themselves do not in the process lose any of their special characteristics. If, for example, in considering a white cat and a black cat I disregard the properties which serve to distinguish them, then I presumably get the concept 'cat' . . . if I proceed to . . . call them . . . units, the white one still remains white just the same, and the black, black. I may not think about their colours . . . but for all that the cats do not become colourless and they remain precisely as before. (1968: 65)

However, Frege's objection to the abstraction theory is not merely that the creative process it postulates is a fiction; even if there were such a process, he argues, its products would be quite unsuited to be numbers. For units, so conceived, would have to account for plurality, but would have to be identical to account for the uniqueness of the individual numbers. The theory that numbers are sets of units is thus faced with an unanswerable dilemma.

Frege gives a lengthy and definitive presentation of this refutation, quoting extensively from authors who have adopted the abstractionist theory, and considering every possible response. Before this, however, he considers a tempting response to the question 'What are units?' which, if correct, might be thought to preclude the necessity of the appeal to abstractionism: namely, that units are *ones*, i.e. possessors of the property *being one*. This is, of course, just a particular application of the view of numbers as properties of external objects discussed in the preceding part of *Foundations*, so all the objections already brought to bear on the general

theory apply to the particular case. But, Frege argues, additional
objections apply to the particular case. Since every single thing
can be numbered everything must have the property of being one
but it 'is not easy to imagine how language could have come
to invent a word for a property which could not be of the slightest
use for adding to the description of any object whatever' (1968:
40).

Moreover, if 'one' signified a property of objects, like 'wise', we
should be able to infer from 'Socrates is one' and 'Plato is one',
'Socrates and Plato are one'. But we cannot. There is indeed
a general property of being individual, circumscribed and self-
contained. But we do not ascribe this property to anything when
we say that the earth has one moon; in respect of this property the
single moon of the earth is no better off than the moons of Venus
or Mars or Jupiter.

Using these and other arguments Frege soundly refutes the proposal that units, in the sense relevant to the set theory of number,
are individuals possessing the property of being one and turns
to the refutation of the abstractionist theory of number using the
dilemmatic argument sketched above (1968: 44ff.).

He drives his point home by asking how the symbolism of arithmetic might be adapted to conform to the abstractionist account.
Units cannot be identical for 'as Descartes says, the number (or
better, the plurality in things) arises from their diversity' (1968: 46).
But if they are different they should have different names. If 5 is a
set of five units then it is:

$$1 + 1 + 1 + 1 + 1$$

But if the units are different we should symbolize them differently.
So for 5 we should have:

$$1' + 1'' + 1''' + 1'''' + 1'''''$$

But then, as well as distinct 1's (units) we will have distinct 2's
($1' + 1''$, $1' + 1'''$, $1'' + 1''''$ and so on), distinct 3's ($1' + 1'' + 1'''$, $1' + 1''''$
$+ 1'''''$ ...) – in fact an infinite plurality of each number. How then
should addition and substraction be understood?

If we write the equation

$$3 - 2 = 1$$

as:

$$(1' + 1'' + 1''') - (1'' + 1''') = 1'$$

it seems that we get a satisfactory result. But what if we rewrite it, equally legitimately, if the abstractionist view is correct, as

$$(1' + 1' + 1''') - (1'''' + 1''''')$$

What can be the remainder now?

Thus Frege demonstrates that on the abstractionist account, which requires a plurality of distinct ones, twos, threes and the rest, 'arithmetic would come to a dead stop'. He considers a last bolt-hole for the abstractionist: an appeal to the properties of space and time to distinguish units. But this, he points out, is of no avail. For, apart from the fact that it ignores the universal applicability of number and implies that nothing would be numerable except what was spatio-temporal, it does not avoid the original dilemma. If units are distinct merely in virtue of their spatio-temporal positions, that is still enough for them to be distinct, and *that* is enough to generate the plurality of ones, twos, threes and so on, which brings arithmetic to a dead halt: 'supposing we do disregard all distinguishing marks except those of space and time, do we then really succeed in combining distinguishability with identity? Not at all. We are not one step nearer a solution. Whether the objects are so much more similar or so much less is beside the point, if they have still to be kept separate in the end' (1968: 53).

Finally, Frege considers the proposal of Jevons, that the difference between units consists merely in 'the empty form of difference' (1968: 56). That is to say, units differ, as required for plurality, but do not differ in respect of *any* particular features. Jevons explains his proposal in a passage Frege quotes:

> There will now be little difficulty in forming a clear notion of the nature of numerical abstraction. It counts in abstracting the character of the difference from which plurality arises, retaining merely the fact. Abstract number, then, is 'the empty form of difference'. (1968: 55-6)

Frege brings two objections to bear. First this account will not work for 0 and 1, since in the case of these numbers there is not even 'the empty form of *difference*', but 0 and 1 are numbers in the same sense as 2 and 3:

What answers the question How many? is a number, and, if we ask, for example, 'How many moons has this planet?' we are quite as much prepared for the answer 0 or 1 as for 2 or 3, and that without having to understand the question differently. (1968: 57)

Secondly, the mere fact of difference is already enough to produce the distinct ones and twos and threes which bring arithmetic to a standstill.

With his survey of untenable proposals completed, Frege now begins to develop his own positive account.

He has, he says, established that a number is not a property of external things, nor something subjective like an idea. It is not an aggregate of things nor a plurality of things. Nor is it a set of units (for units, to serve the purposes for which they are intended must combine, contradictorily, identity and distinguishability).

But these negative conclusions leave unanswered the question: 'When we make a statement of number, what is that of which we assert something?' (1968: 58). To throw light on the matter Frege suggests that we consider number in the context of a judgement which brings out its basic use. In fact, he reintroduces the type of example used to refute the suggestion that numbers are properties of external objects:

While looking at one and the same external phenomenon, I can say with equal truth both 'It is a copse' and 'It is five trees', or both 'there are four companies' and 'there are 500 men'. Now what changes here from one judgement to the other is neither any individual object, nor the whole, the agglomeration of them, but rather my terminology. But that is itself only a sign that one concept has been substituted for another. This suggests as the answer to the first of the questions left open in our last paragraph, that the content of a statement of number is an assertion about a concept. (1968: 59)

This, then, is how Frege arrives at his celebrated answer. Once stated it seems obvious: to make a statement of number, to say that there are n F's, is to make a statement about the concept F, or the property of being an F: it is to say that that concept is n-fold instantiated, that the property has n instances. But Frege's previous discussion (and passages he goes on to quote from other philosophers (Spinoza and Schroder) subsequently) illustrates very clearly how difficult this insight was to attain, and how close to the point other writers could come while still being unable to give it a precise formulation.

Frege immediately goes on to reinforce his contention by drawing attention to statements in which the number 0 is assigned to a concept:

> If I say 'Venus has 0 moons', there simply does not exist any moon or agglomeration of moons for anything to be asserted of; but what happens is that a property is assigned to the *concept* 'moon of Venus', namely that of including nothing under it. (1968: 59)

And, Frege goes on, assignments of other numbers should be understood in parallel fashion (here we see the importance for him of his contention that 0 and 1 are numbers in *just the same sense* in which this is true of 2, 3, 4, etc., namely answers to the question 'How many?'): 'If I say "the King's carriage is drawn by four horses", then I assign the number four to the concept "horse that draws the King's carriage"' (1968: 59).

Frege proceeds to show how this account resolves all the difficulties thrown up by his preceding critique.

First, it provides an answer to the question how number can be objective though numbers are neither external mind-independent objects, nor agglomerations of such, nor properties of such objects or agglomerations. Once concepts are distinguished from ideas, nothing stands in the way of accepting that statements about concepts express something factual and independent of our way of regarding things.

'All whales are mammals' expresses something objective, but it is a statement about concepts, expressing the subordination of the concept of a whale to that of a mammal, not a statement about objects (animals) 'for if we ask which animal, then, we are speaking of, we are unable to point to any one in particular' (1968: 60). Statements of number, understood as assertions about concepts, are similarly objectively true or false.

Secondly, the temptation to say that different numbers can be ascribed to the same object according to our way of regarding it is now explained. It is not the physical object which has the number but the concept under which it falls; as we think of the object as falling under different concepts different numbers seem to be available, but once we recognize that it is the concept which is the subject of predications of number 'numbers reveal themselves as no less mutually exclusive in their own sphere than colours in theirs' (1968: 62).

Thirdly, we can now see why there is a temptation to suggest that we get numbers by abstraction from things; what we do get by abstraction is the concept, and in this we then discover the number.

Fourthly, we can see why we do not need to assemble a gathering of all the blind in order to answer the question how many they are. The subject of a statement of number is not an aggregate or agglomeration, which requires the things numbered to be related in some spatio-temporal fashion, it is the concept which collects them in the only way that is relevant.

Fifthly, the wide applicability of number can now be understood. The subject of a statement of number is a concept, but any object of thought, not merely physical or spatio-temporal objects, falls under a concept – thus the numerable is coextensive with the thinkable, and the latter includes abstract objects as well as concrete objects, and even concepts themselves as well as objects, for they, too, fall under second-level (or second-order (1968: 65)) concepts.

Frege goes on to point out that in his account even the seemingly contradictory talk of 'units' can be given a kind of sense. For if we think of a concept as the unit relative to the number which belongs to it, 'we can achieve a sense for the assertions made about the unit, that it is isolated from its environment and indivisible. For it is the case that the concept, to which the number is assigned, does in general isolate in a definite manner what falls under it. The concept "letters in the word three" isolates the t from the h, the h from the r and so on' (1968: 44).

It is in this connection that Frege draws attention to a crucial restriction on those concepts that can serve as a unit relative to an assignment of number. The concept 'letters in the word three' isolates what falls under it in a definite manner, but the concept 'red' does not possess this feature: 'We can divide up something falling under the concept "red" into parts in a variety of ways, without the parts thereby ceasing to fall under the same concept "red". To a concept of this kind no finite number will belong' (1968: 66).

The distinction to which Frege here draws attention has come to be termed the distinction between 'sortal' and 'adjectival' concepts, and it is generally acknowledged that Frege's remarks are an inadequate acknowledgement of it. For Frege says only that no *finite* number can be assigned to the adjectival concept 'red', which, given his logic, is the correct thing to say, since if the concept is not vague, i.e. if *any* object is determinately red or not red, there must be *an* answer, albeit not finite, to the question how many red things there are. But the intuitive difficulty with counting red things is 'not that you cannot make an end of counting them, but that you cannot make a beginning, you can never know whether you have counted one already because "the same red thing" supplies no criterion of identity' (see Geach 1962: 63 for this statement of the difficulty, and others can be found in Dummett 1981 and 1991a, and Wright 1983). How best to characterize the difference between sortal terms, with which such a criterion of identity is associated, and adjectival terms, with which there is no such association, is a controversial matter, which there is no space to explore here.

We cannot take leave of this part of Frege's *Foundations* without noting his famous aside on the ontological argument for the existence of God:

> Affirmation of existence is in fact nothing but denial of the number nought. Because existence is a property of concepts the ontological argument for the existence of God breaks down. But oneness is not a component characteristic of the concept 'God' any more than existence is. Oneness cannot be used in the definition of this concept any more than the solidity of a house, or its commodiousness or desirability, can be used in building it along with the beams, bricks and mortar (1968: 65).

The thought here is often taken to be the same as that in Kant's earlier refutation: existence is not a predicate. Rather, it is 'merely the positing of a thing, or of certain determinates as existing in themselves'. When we say 'God is' or 'there is a God', we attach no new predicate to the concept of God, but only posit the subject in itself with all its predicates. And purely logical grounds never entitle anybody to assert the existence of anything: 'For if the existence of a thing is rejected we reject the thing itself with all its predicates, and no question of a contradiction can then arise' (1929 A595/B623: 502). But there is a difference between Kant's view and Frege's. For Frege *does* think that in certain cases, notably the case of number itself, rejection of existence does involve a contradiction. Hence he goes on:

> it would be wrong to conclude that it is in principle impossible ever to deduce from a concept, that is, from its component characteristics, anything which is a property of the concept. Under certain conditions this is possible, just as we can infer the durability of a building from the type of stone used in building it. It would therefore be going too far to assert that we can never infer from the component characteristics of a concept to oneness or to existence, what is true is, that

this can never be so direct a matter as to assign some component of
a concept as a property to an object falling under it. (1968: 65)

The form of indirect but valid 'ontological argument' whose
possibility is envisaged here is precisely what Frege now goes on
to provide in the remainder of *Foundations*, with the difference that
it is not the concept of *God* but that of number which he argues
on logical grounds must be necessarily instantiated.

The Development of Frege's Own Position

In part IV of *Foundations* Frege turns from a critique of other positions to the development of his own. He takes as his starting point
his fundamental result that the content of a statement of number is
an assertion about a concept. This immediately suggests an account
of what numbers are which has not so far been considered, namely
that they are properties of concepts, i.e. second-level (second-order)
concepts. Frege stresses the legitimacy of such concepts in the
remarks he makes immediately after his aside on the ontological
argument:

> If, for example, we collect under a single concept all concepts under
> which there falls only one object, then oneness is a component char-
> acteristic of this new concept. Under it would fall, for example, the
> concept 'moon of the Earth', though not the actual heavenly body
> called by that name. In this way we can make one concept fall under
> another higher, or, so to say, second-order concept. (1968: 65)

The immediately suggested thought is that we can understand
statements of number in terms of such concepts: for example, 'There
are n F's' asserts of the concept F that it is *n-fold instantiated* and
being n-fold instantiated is a second-level concept which may be identified with the number n. Of course, there are other uses of expressions for numbers apart from those in statements of number to be
accounted for; in particular the use of numerals in arithmetical
equations. And there is also the use of designations of numbers of
the form 'the number of F's' to be explained. But it is tempting to
suppose that we might be able to extend an account of numbers as
second-level concepts to such other uses by paraphrasing propositions in which numerical expressions occur in other contexts by
propositions in which they occur only in the context of statements

of number. For example we might attempt to explain the arithmetical identity '7 + 5 = 12' as meaning something like: it holds of every concept F and every concept G that there are exactly seven F's and exactly five G's and nothing is both an F and a G if and only if there are exactly twelve objects which are F or G.

Frege begins part IV with a vigorous attack on precisely this line of thought. His position is that a statement of number, 'There are n F's', can indeed be legitimately understood as saying of the concept F that it is n-fold instantiated, and thus as ascribing a property to the concept F, but it can *also* be legitimately understood as saying something of the number n, namely, that it is (identical with) the number of F's. Similarly, 'Socrates is wise' can be understood both as saying of Socrates that he falls under the concept *wise* and as saying of the concept *wise* that it itself, like, say, the concept *being snub-nosed* or the concept *being a teacher of Plato*, falls under the second-level concept *instantiated by Socrates*. Frege insists that we must not identify the object Cicero with the second-level concept *instantiated by Cicero*, and likewise that we must not identify the object which is the number n with the second-level numerical concept *being n-fold instantiated*. The analysis of statements of number as assertions about concepts is legitimate, but it is not the only legitimate analysis: for as well as the second-level numerical concepts there are *also* the individual numbers, each one of which is a self-subsistent object.

That is Frege's position. His argument for it is less easy to grasp.

He begins by formulating definitions which conform to the view that numbers should be identified as second-level concepts:

The number 0 belongs to a concept F if the proposition that a does not fall under F is true universally, no matter what a may be.

The number 1 belongs to a concept F if the proposition that a does not fall under F is not universally true, whatever a may be, and if from the propositions 'a falls under F' and 'b falls under F' it follows universally that a and b are the same.

The number (n + 1) belongs to the concept F if there is an object a falling under F and such that the number n belongs to the concept 'falling under F but not a'.

Expressed more briefly with Frege's jargon of 'belonging to a concept' and 'object falling under a concept' eliminated, what we have here are the following definitions:

'There are 0 F's' is to mean 'for all x, x is not F'.

'There is exactly 1 F' is to mean 'It is not the case that for all x, x is not F, and for all x and y, if x is F and y is F, x = y'.

'There are exactly n + 1 F's' is to mean 'for some x, x is an F and there are exactly n y's which are distinct from x which are F's'.

This seems both unobjectionable and a fulfilment of the programme the discussion of Leibniz suggested: to define the individual numbers 0 and 1 and increase by 1. However, Frege objects,

> strictly speaking we do not know the sense of the expression 'the number n belongs to the concept G' any more than we do that of the expression 'The number (n + 1) belongs to the concept F'. We can, of course, by using the last two definitions together, say what is meant by 'the number 1 + 1 belongs to the concept F' and then, using this, give the sense of the expression 'the number 1 + 1 + 1 belongs to the concept F', and so on, but we can never – to take a crude example – decide by means of our definitions whether any concept has the number Julius Caesar belonging to it, or whether that same familiar conqueror of Gaul is a number or not. Moreover, we cannot by the aid of our suggested definitions prove that, if the number a belongs to the concept F and the number b belongs to the same concept, then necessarily a = b. Thus we should be unable to justify the expression 'the number which belongs to the concept F', and therefore should find it impossible in general to prove a numerical identity, since we should be quite unable to achieve a determinate number. It is only an illusion that we have defined 0 and 1; in reality we have only fixed the senses of the phrases:

>> 'the number 0 belongs to'
>> 'the number 1 belongs to'

> but we have no authority to pick out the 0 and 1 here as self-subsistent objects that can be recognised as the same again. (1968: 68)

This is the first occurrence of 'the Caesar objection' (originally so dubbed by Wright in Wright 1983) in *Foundations*, and it must have been baffling to Frege's first readers. The objection is that a definition of number is inadequate if it does not give a sense to, and allow us to determine the truth-value (presumably false) of every statement of the form 'Julius Caesar is (identical with) the number n'. But the proponent of the position Frege is attacking maintains that numbers are second-level concepts not objects, so that no such identity proposition can be so much as formulated (since, as Frege himself repeatedly insists, identity is a relation between objects not concepts). Thus the Julius Caesar objection can only be brought to bear if it is taken to be *already* established that numbers are objects – in which case Frege's rejection of the definitions he criticizes as incomplete is, of course, completely correct.

In fact, it is plausible to read Frege as assuming, in the passage quoted, that he *has* established this. The defence of this assumption appears partly before and partly after it. Earlier in *Foundations*, as we have seen, he emphasizes the use of number words as proper names of objects in his criticism of the set-of-units accounts of numbers: 'when we speak of "the number one" we indicate by means of the definite article a definite and unique object of scientific study. There are not divers number ones, but only one. In 1 we have a proper name, which as such does not admit of a plural any more than "Frederick the Great" or "the chemical element gold"'. Again: 'only concept words can form a plural. If therefore we speak of "units", we must be using the word not as equivalent to the proper name "one" but as a concept word' (1968: 49–50). Following the passage quoted from part IV he goes on to remind the reader of these earlier contentions: 'I have already drawn attention above to the fact that we speak of "the number 1", where the definite article serves to class it as an object. In arithmetic this self-subsistence comes out at every turn, as for example in the identity $1 + 1 + 2$' (1968: 68–9).

The argument implicit in these passages has been explained and defended by Dummett (1973), Wright (1983) and Hale (1979, 1996). It begins from the premiss that the notions of a singular term (a 'proper name' in the wide sense Frege uses the latter expression) and an object go together: singular terms are just those linguistic expressions which (purport to) refer to objects, objects are just those entities capable of being referred to by singular terms. The next premiss is the crucial one, dubbed by Wright the 'syntactic priority thesis' and argued by him to be one aspect of Frege's context principle: the categorization of an expression as a singular term can be based on, broadly speaking, syntactic criteria whose application does not require *a prior* categorization of the entity it refers to or purports to refer to as an object. That is, one can identify expressions as functioning as singular terms *independently* of the assumption that these expressions refer – or purport reference – to objects. This second premiss is evidently just a special case of the more general claim that linguistic categories are prior to ontological categories: whether an expression is, for example, a singular term, first-level predicate or second-level predicate cannot be decided by investigating the entity which it stands for in order to determine whether it is an object, first-level concept or second-level concept. Rather, the answer to the linguistic question decides the answer to the ontological one.

Frege's reference to the presence of the definite article in 'the number one' and the inability of proper names to admit a plural are gestures towards criteria by which singular terms may be marked off from expressions of other linguistic categories without reference being required to the entities for which they stand. But, of course, these particular criteria are both parochial and inadequate. The second premiss of the argument, the syntactic priority thesis, thus requires a defence which Frege himself never gives. However, in the writings of Dummett, Wright and Hale this lack is plausibly supplied (Dummett 1973 and 1981, Wright 1983, Hale 1979 and 1996).

For now we can move on to the third premiss of the argument for the objecthood of number implicit in Frege's remarks. This is, as we might put it, the thesis of the priority of truth to existence, which is again argued by Wright to be an aspect of Frege's context principle. That is, no more is required for sub-sentential expressions of any given type to have reference, than that such expressions should occur – functioning as expressions of that type – in suitable true statements. In particular, if expressions function as singular terms in appropriate true statements, they have reference, and since they are singular terms, refer to objects. The existence of objects of a particular type requires no more than the truth of appropriate statements in which singular terms purporting to refer to such objects occur. (The qualification 'of appropriate statements' here is an acknowledgement of the plausibility of the unFregean view that non-referring singular terms can occur in *some* true statements (consider, for example, the negative existential statement 'Merlin never existed'): 'appropriate' statements will include at least affirmative existential statements and, much emphasized by Frege, identity statements.) The fourth premiss of Frege's implicit argument is then just that numerals and many other numerical expressions do function as singular terms in many appropriate true statements. The conclusion then immediately follows: there are entities which these expressions stand for, and these entities, the numbers, are objects.

Whatever may be thought of this argument there are, in fact, other criticisms to be made of the attempt to treat numbers as second-level concepts with which Frege begins part IV of *Foundations*. There are two that are most important. The first is that it provides only for counting objects, not concepts, and consequently, since it takes numbers themselves to be second-level concepts, it does not provide for counting numbers – and thus does not conform to the thesis of the universal applicability of arithmetic which Frege so stresses. The second criticism is that the treatment of numbers as second-level numerical concepts can only secure the infinity of the natural number series given the independent assumption of infinitely many *objects*. (If, for example, the 'natural number' *being n-fold instantiated* is said to be the successor of the 'natural number' *being m-fold instantiated* if and only if for every first-level concept F, F is n-fold instantiated if and only if there is an object y which is F and the concept *being an object x which is distinct from y and is F* is m-fold instantiated, the claim that each natural number has a successor distinct from all its predecessors will be false in a finite domain. For the second-level numerical concept *being m-fold instantiated* will possess a non-empty successor only if there exists an object y and there are exactly m objects other than y. And this will not be so if there are only m objects. If the successor relation over second-level numerical concepts is defined differently the requirement that an infinity of objects exists if the 'natural number' series is to be infinite will emerge somewhat differently. But the bulge in the carpet cannot be made to disappear. (See Dummett 1991a: 131–3, Wright 1983: 36–8, Heck 1997: 295, Rumfitt 1999: 152.)) But to make such an assumption would seem evidently to depart from Frege's aim of deriving arithmetic from logic alone.

Having established, to his own satisfaction at least, that numbers are objects, Frege next goes on to answer some objections that might be made (that we have no idea of number, that numbers are not spatially located), effectively employing the context principle in doing so. This section reinforces the attack on psychologism in the Introduction to *Foundations* and emphasizes the distinction between the objective and the actual, which Frege has previously drawn.

Frege acknowledges that we have no idea of number if an idea is something like a mental picture. The expression 'green field' will call up the very same picture as '*one* green field'. If we imagine the printed word 'gold' the picture does not change if we first ask 'How many letters?' and then 'How many words?' even though the two questions receive different answers. And in the case of the number zero the point is undeniable: 'we shall try in vain to form an idea of 0 visible stars' (1968: 70). But even when words *are* associated with ideas the idea does not determine the meaning of the word: different men may associate different ideas with a word they understand in exactly the same way. And in many cases we cannot associate anything but a manifestly inadequate idea with a word: 'Even so concrete a thing as the Earth we are unable to imagine as we know it to be; instead we content ourselves with a ball of moderate size . . . though we know quite well it is different from it' (1968: 71).

We are tempted to think that a word must have an idea associated with it if it is to be meaningful because we ask for its meaning in isolation and then we can find nothing else to be its meaning. But, Frege says, reaffirming the context principle

> We ought always to keep before our eyes a complete proposition. Only in a proposition have the words really a meaning. It may be that mental pictures float before us all the while, but these need not correspond to the logical elements in the judgement. It is enough if the proposition taken as a whole has a sense, it is this that confers on their parts also their content. (Frege 1968: 71)

The second objection to the contention that numbers are objects is that numbers have location: 'neither outside us nor within us' (1968: 71). But this Frege stresses, though quite correct, is no objection. Not every object has a place: an idea lies neither to the right nor left of another idea. Ideas are subjective, but it is not even the case that everything objective has a place. The number 4 is objective because it is exactly the same for everyone who deals with it; but such objectivity does not require spatiality: 'Not every objective object [*objektives Gegenstand*] has a place' (1968: 72).

These responses are entirely convincing, but, of course, they do not provide any further positive support for Frege's thesis that numbers are objects. That thesis rests on the linguistic facts already outlined and the considerations, which Frege does not make explicit, but could well have had in mind, that reveal the inability of the treatment of numbers as second-level concepts to accommodate the fact that we count numbers themselves and its incompatibility with the infinity of the natural number series unless an infinity of *objects* (entities, therefore, *distinct* from numbers) is assumed.

The next section of *Foundations* (section 62) is the most celebrated and most discussed in Frege's entire corpus. Dummett has called it 'arguably the most pregnant philosophical paragraph ever written' because it makes the very first example of what has come to be known as 'the linguistic turn' in philosophy. On the basis of this, Dummett claims, Frege's *Foundations* may justly be called 'the first work of analytical philosophy' (1991a: 111).

Frege begins section 62 with the Kantian question 'How, then, are numbers to be given to us, if we cannot have any ideas or intuitions of them' (1968: 73). Immediately he cites the context principle to justify reformulating his problem as: 'to define the sense of a proposition in which a number word occurs' (1968: 73). Then, appealing to the thesis that numbers are objects, he asserts that this is already enough to give us a class of propositions which must have a sense, merely those which express our recognition of a number as the same again. For:

> If we are to use the symbol *a* to signify an object, we must have a criterion for deciding in all cases whether *b* is the same as *a*, even if it is not in our power to apply this criterion. (1968: 73)

From this *general* claim about objects and criteria of identity Frege deduces that in the case of number what is required is a definition of the sense of propositions of the form

> the number which belongs to the concept F is the same as that which belongs to the concept G

a definition in which the content of this proposition will be reproduced in other terms, avoiding the use of the expression 'the number which belongs to concept F'.

Frege immediately offers such a definition, citing a passage in Hume as precedent:

> The number of F's is the same as the number of G's if and only if there is a one–one correlation between the F's and the G's

Because of his way of introducing it, this has come to be known as 'Hume's Principle'. Given, as Frege goes on to show later in sections 70–2, that a one–one correlation can be defined in purely logical terms (in second-order logic) without appeal to intuition, it looks as if this definition is, so far, in conformity with his logicist programme.

However, Frege insists, Hume's Principle 'raises at once certain logical doubts and difficulties, which ought not to be passed over without examination' (1968: 74).

The first doubt he considers is that identity is not to be found only among numbers: given objects of any kind we can ask whether they are identical or distinct. Thus we cannot define it especially for the case of numbers, but must rather use the general notion of identity, together with a definition of number, to define the notion of numerical identity.

Frege's response is that his intention is *not* to define identity especially for the case of number. Rather the purpose of Hume's Principle is to use the concept of identity, taken as already known, as a means of arriving at the concept of number.

To explain his intention he introduces another example, that of directions and parallelism, which he suggests is analogous to that of number, and proceeds from section 64 to discuss this example, with the intention that the reader should apply the results of the discussion, *mutatis mutandis*, to the case of number.

Just as Hume's Principle provides a criterion of identity for numbers, Frege says, parallelism provides a criterion of identity for directions. That is, the principle

(ED) The direction of line a is identical with the direction of line b if and only if a is parallel to b

stands in the same explanatory relation to the concept of direction as Hume's Principle stands to the concept of number. We obtain the concept of direction via our acceptance of (ED) 'by replacing the symbol [for parallelism] by the more general symbol =, through removing what is specific in the content of the former and dividing it between *a* and *b*' (1968: 74–5).

The immediate implication of this statement is that Frege intends both Hume's Principle and (ED) to be read as contextual definitions. A contextual definition is one in which complex expressions stand on both sides of the symbol for definitional equivalence, the expression being defined occurring only as a part of a complex expression, whose other parts already have established meanings. Later, in *Basic Laws*, Frege was to reject contextual directions. His explanation there of his reasons for doing so throw light on how he conceived this procedure in *Foundations*. He writes:

It is evident that the reference of an expression and that of one of its parts do not always determine the reference of the remaining parts. One therefore ought not to define a symbol or word by defining an expression in which it occurs and in which the remaining parts are already known. For . . . it would first be necessary to investigate whether it was possible to solve for the unknown, and whether the unknown was uniquely determined. (*Basic Laws*, vol. 2, section 66, translated in Frege 1997: 268–9)

In *Foundations* Hume's Principle and (ED) are conceived precisely as such equations, which are to be 'solved for the unknown' (the concepts of number and direction). Frege defends his procedure by appealing to the epistemological priority of the concept of parallelism to that of direction (and, by implication, to the epistemological priority of the concept of equinumerosity explained via one–one correlation to that of number). We cannot define parallel straight lines as those whose directions are identical because this removes 'the true order of things' (1968: 75.) We have intuitions of straight lines, but not of directions, and can only arrive at the concept of direction by a process of intellectual activity which takes its start from these intuitions.

Though the argument here given for epistemological priority appeals to features special to the geometrical case, the point is a general one. There is a class of objects, of which numbers and directions are examples, reference to and thought about which is parasitic on reference to and thought about other entities (objects or concepts), to which the former objects must be understood as related in a certain way.

Objects of which this is most clearly *not* true are concrete objects falling under count nouns. Reference to and thought about people, for example, does not require reference to and thought about objects other than people. A person can be identified demonstratively simply as 'that man', without any requirement that reference be made, or be possible, to objects of any other kind. The direction of the pointing finger, together with the stipulation that the referent falls under the sortal term 'person', can suffice to single out a unique object of reference. Colours are in the same category. Colours are possible objects of ostension. Since the coloured proper parts of anything that is uniformly coloured have necessarily the same colour as that of which they are proper parts, an utterance of 'that colour' and the ostension of a (uniformly) coloured region can be relied upon to single out a particular colour. Thus we can imagine a language in which names of colours are acquired prior to the acquisition of names for visual or material objects, and thus prior to learning of any functional expression with the meaning of 'the colour of'. By contrast there could not be a language in which it was possible to make reference to shapes but which did not contain any functional expression with the sense of 'the shape of'. This is because shapes, unlike colours, are not possible objects of ostension: even against the background of an appropriate criterion of identity, one cannot pick out a shape by pointing and saying 'this'. For an object or region which has just one shape (as every object or region has, of course) will also have proper parts which are of some shape or other, but not of the same shape as it is. So if I point to an object and say 'this shape', nothing is yet clear. I will be pointing to ever so many objects of different shapes. I must, then, further identify the shape I mean by saying *of* what object it is then the shape. Thus a language could not contain the means of making reference to shapes unless it also contained the functional expression 'the shape of' and names of objects and regions to serve as arguments of this function. There is a sense then in which shapes are necessarily 'of' objects in a way that colours are not.

Directions, of course, are, in this respect, in the same category as shapes. One could not conceive of a language in which directions were spoken of which did not contain a functional expression with the sense of 'the direction of' and the means of making reference to lines. And the same is true of numbers. It is conceivable that there should be a people whose language contained numerals where these were not explained as abbreviations for expressions of the form 'the number of F's'. They simply learn to apply their numerals without associating them with any counting procedure, simply recognizing straight off how many things of a given kind there are. However, it is inconceivable that the numerals in such a language should be used as names of objects unless it also contained a functional expression with the sense of 'the number of' and the users of the language were prepared to make identity statements in which the numerals are said to stand for particular values of this function. Thus numbers are 'of' concepts, in the same sense in which shapes are 'of' two-or-three-dimensional physical objects or regions, and directions are 'of' lines.

In putting forward Hume's Principle and (ED) as criteria of identity for, respectively, numbers and directions, Frege was, therefore, as he maintained, respecting the true epistemological position. Directions are 'of' lines and cannot be referred to or thought of by anyone whose language does not allow for the possibility of referring to them *as* directions of lines. Equally, questions of identity and difference of directions are not intelligible except as equivalent to questions about parallelism of lines: the possibility of thought about identity and difference of directions rests on the possibility of thought about parallelism or non-parallelism of lines. *Mutatis Mutandis*, numbers are 'of' concepts and cannot be referred to or thought of by anyone whose language does not allow for the possibility of reference to numbers *as* the numbers belonging to concepts (as 'the number of F's'). Equally, questions of identity and difference of numbers are not intelligible except as equivalent to questions about equinumerosity of concepts: the possibility of thought about identity and difference of numbers rests on the possibility of thought about equinumerosity or otherwise of concepts.

Frege now turns in section 65 to what he refers to as 'a second doubt'. Since identity is assumed to be already known, is it not possible that identity of direction (*mutatis mutandis*, of number) as defined by (ED) will conflict with the logical laws of identity? These laws are all derivable from one, Leibniz's Law:

Things are the same as each other, of which one can be substituted for the other without loss of truth.

Thus, in order to answer this second doubt, Frege points out, all he needs to ensure is that 'the direction of a' is substitutable for 'the direction of b' without loss of truth whenever line a is parallel to line b. But since the only context in which expressions of this form can occur, given his explanation so far of the concept of direction, are recognition statements of the form 'the direction of a = the direction of b', it suffices if substitution within such statements always preserves truth. Since parallelism is an equivalence relation, it does. Frege notes that if the language in which directions are spoken of is to be expanded, in order to preserve conformity with Leibniz's Law 'we can make it a rule always to see that it must remain possible to substitute for the direction of any line the direction of any line parallel to it' (1968: 77). That is, we may introduce a new stock of predicates applicable to directions by a stipulation of the form

The direction of line a is F* iff line a is F

– but only when for all lines a and b, if a is F and is parallel to b, b is F.

We now come, however, to the third objection to (ED) (and *mutatis mutandis* to Hume's Principle) which Frege considers. This is introduced in section 66 and by the end of section 67 he has convinced himself that it is insurmountable, and so abandons the project of defining numbers contextually and switches to his famous explicit definition in terms of extensions.

The objection is a rerun of the Julius Caesar objection already considered, but the aim is not now to prove that numbers (directions) are objects, which is now taken for granted:

> In the proposition 'the direction of a is identical with the direction of b' the direction of a plays the part of an object, and our definition affords us a means of recognising this object as the same again, in case it should happen to crop up in some other guise, say as the direction of b. But this means does not provide for all cases. It will not, for instance, decide for us whether England is the same as the direction of the Earth's axis – if I may be forgiven an example which looks nonsensical. Naturally no one is going to confuse England with the direction of the Earth's axis, but that is no thanks to our definition of direction. That says nothing as to whether the proposition 'the direction of a is identical with q' should be affirmed or denied, except for the one case where q is given in the form 'the direction of b'. (1968: 78)

The objection, if it is good, applies equally to Hume's Principle considered as a definition of the concept of number. No one is going to confuse Julius Caesar with say, 0 (the number of unicorns), but that is no thanks to Hume's Principle, for that says nothing as to whether the proposition 'the number of F's is identical with q' is to be affirmed or denied, except for the one case where q is given in the form 'the number of G's'.

The indisputable fact on which this objection rests is that Hume's Principle and (ED) do not determine unique functions as the referents of the functors 'the number of' and 'the direction of'. (ED) will be true, for example, if we read 'the direction of a' as standing for the shortest line parallel to a, or the longest line parallel to a, or the oldest line parallel to a (assuming that the lines we are referring to are particular token inscriptions). Equally we can understand 'the direction of' as standing for a function which for all lines except those parallel to a particular line l* (the Earth's axis) as argument yields the shortest line parallel to that line as value, but for any line parallel to l* as argument yields England as value. (ED) remains true.

Similarly we may understand 'the number of' as standing for a function which maps an n-fold instantiated concept as argument to the number n as value. But it is equally consistent with the truth of Hume's Principle that it be understood as standing for a function which maps any n-fold instantiated concept to n when n is not 0 or 1, but maps any empty concept to 1 and any singly instantiated concept to zero. It is equally consistent with Hume's Principle that 'the number of' be understood as standing for a function which maps any n-fold instantiated concept to n when n is not 0, but maps any empty concept to Julius Caesar.

Hume's Principle and (ED) do thus fail to determine unique references for the functors 'the directions of' and 'the number of' and do therefore fail to determine a truth-value for propositions of the form 'the number of F's (the direction of a) = q', where q is not explicitly given as a term for a direction (number). But why should that matter? Do we *need* an answer to the question whether England is identical with the Earth's axis or whether Caesar is the number zero? Can we not just treat these questions as answerable by further stipulation – *what* stipulation being a matter of indifference as long as *some* stipulation is made?

However, there are reasons to think that this response is inadequate, and that the Caesar problem goes deeper than it suggests (see also Heck 1997, to which the following is indebted).

First, it seems clear that Frege views the Caesar problem as presenting an *epistemological* challenge. It is not just that we regard the question whether the Earth is the direction of the Earth's axis as one which we cannot answer (as we may not be able to answer the question whether a particular patch of colour is red or orange, or whether a particular new-fangled type of amphibious vehicle is a ship or car). We *know* that the Earth is *not* identical with the direction of its axis. Similarly, we *know* that Julius Caesar is *not* the number zero. It seems evident that this knowledge can only have its source in our grasp of the concepts of direction and number. But then what the Caesar objection discloses is that there must be *more* to our grasp of these concepts than the knowledge that the criteria of identity for directions and numbers are given, respectively, by (ED) and Hume's Principle.

Secondly, the Caesar objection poses a semantic problem. (ED) and Hume's Principle could have been laid down simply as stipulative definitions of new simple symbols, possessing no semantic articulation. They would then have been totally unobjectionable. I can make any mark or sound which does not already have a meaning mean whatever I like. But this 'austere' (Wright 1983) interpretation of the LHS's (left-hand sides) of the contextual definitions is clearly not what Frege intends. He is considering (ED) and Hume's Principle as ways of introducing new first-level concepts – that of direction and number – and so it is essential that the LHS's of these equivalences can be legitimately read as semantically articulate; as, in fact, containing two singular terms flanking the sign of identity. But if so, in such an identity statement it must be possible to replace one of the singular terms by a *variable* to get an expression for a *condition* – 'q is the direction of the Earth's axis', say – which is satisfied by some (one) object and not others. However, if a condition is genuinely one which is satisfied (or not satisfied) by *an object*, it is satisfied (not satisfied) by it irrespective of how it is referred to. What the Caesar problem seems to show is that understood in this non-austere way (ED) and Hume's Principle fail of their purpose.

Frege notes that there is a temptation to respond to the problem with a supplementary stipulation such as:

q is a direction if there is a line b whose direction is q

But this is to go in a circle: to determine whether q is a direction by appeal to this stipulation one must first determine whether 'q is the direction of line b' is true for some line b. But when q is not given in the form 'the direction of a' this is precisely what (ED) leaves us unable to do.

If we were to say instead: q is a direction only if it is introduced by (ED), then we would be making the way q is introduced a property of it. But definitions assert nothing of objects; they only introduce symbols. Moreover, it is intrinsic to the concept of an object that any object can be presented to us in more than one way, otherwise identity statements could not be informative. So we cannot just presuppose that directions and numbers can only be given to us *as* directions and numbers.

These considerations are powerful, but it is not clear that we should draw the conclusion that we must *either* follow Frege in replacing (ED) and Hume's Principle by explicit definitions *or* find a solution to the Caesar problem, in the sense of attempting to argue that supplied with (ED) and Hume's Principle *alone* we are in a position to rule out the problematic identifications. For we are certainly not entitled to regard terms for directions and numbers, as introduced by (ED) and Hume's Principle, as *more* determinate in reference than everyday terms for concrete objects (see Rosen 1993: 169ff.). But consider the term 'Mont Blanc'. By every test that we could possibly devise this is a singular term. So, given the syntactic priority thesis, it will have reference if suitable statements containing it, such as 'Mont Blanc exists' or 'Mont Blanc is the mountain most often referred to by Frege', are true. But such statements *are* true, so 'Mont Blanc' has reference, that is, Mont Blanc exists. However, its reference is not determinate. For, as Rosen says, quoting Quine, 'it is inconceivable that our use of the term somehow determines a unique object – the contents of a unique space-time region – as its reference' (1993: 169). Any number of largely overlapping material objects differing slightly in their boundaries are equally good candidates for being the reference of 'Mont Blanc'. Thus there is no answer to the question whether Mont Blanc is identical with one of these precisely specified candidates for its reference. Nonetheless 'Mont Blanc' is a referential singular term in good standing. In this case indeterminate reference is reference enough. Perhaps the same is true of terms for directions and numbers.

The above line of argument suggests that, even in the absence of an answer to the Caesar problem, Frege need not have replaced (ED) and Hume's Principle by explicit definitions. (It requires, of course, that we maintain, for example, that the proposition 'England is identical with the direction of the Earth's axis' is not so much something we know to be *false*, but something we know we could never have reason to assert, as we could never have reason to assert 'Mont Blanc is identical with (precisely specified object) P'. This is to reject a presupposition of Frege's epistemological challenge, but that does not seem immediately objectionable.) However, the needlessness of Frege's abandonment of the method of contextual definition would, of course, be made more evident still if the Caesar problem could actually be solved.

Wright and Hale claim that this is the case (Wright 1983, 1998; Hale 1999). Their idea is that, notwithstanding that the *truth* of (ED) and Hume's Principle is consistent with the problematic identifications, *if* they are understood, as Frege intends, as *explanations* giving the *criteria of identity* associated with newly introduced concepts, *then* they rule these identifications out. Wright expresses this thought in the following passage:

> Consider a man who knows the reference of 'Caesar' and whose whole understanding of the meanings of the numerical singular terms is based on their introduction by Frege's account of numerical identity. Plainly he cannot reasonably suppose that any numerical

singular term has the same reference as 'Caesar'. The reason is that
Frege's account of numerical identity does at least make it plain that
numbers are things which are to be identified and distinguished
among themselves by appeal to facts that have to do with 1–1 correlation among concepts. Whereas questions of personal identity are
not decidable in this way. (1983: 114)

That numbers are things which *'are to* be identified and distinguished . . . by appeal to . . . 1–1 correlations' must mean here that
numbers *'can only be* identified and distinguished by . . .', for otherwise Wright's conclusion that the identification of Julius Caesar
with any number can be ruled out will not follow. And, indeed,
Wright is elsewhere quite explicit: 'For one who receives [Hume's
Principle] as [an explanation of a *kind* of thing] it will be understood
to be of the *essence* of cardinal numbers that facts about identity and
distinctness among them are constituted in fact about one one correspondence among concepts' (1998: 361, my italics).

Thus the thought is that (ED) and Hume's Principle are not just
truths constraining the interpretation of the functors 'the direction
of' and 'the number of'. They are explanations of the criteria of identity for directions and numbers, of what *constitutes* identity and distinctness for directions and numbers. If one receives (ED) in the
proper way one will understand that directions and numbers just
are (= are just) things for which parallelism and equinumerosity
constitute identity. As such they cannot be identical with things
whose identity is not so constituted.

There is a general principle here, to the effect that two sorts of
things cannot overlap if their constitutive criteria of identity are
different. Wright formulates this 'principle of sortal exclusion' as
follows:

> Gx is a sortal concept under which instances of Fx fall . . . only if there
> are or could be singular terms 'a' and 'b' purporting to denote
> instances of Gx, such that the truth-conditions of 'a = b' can be ad-
> equately explained by fixing its truth-conditions to be those of a
> statement which asserts that the given equivalence relation holds
> between a pair of objects in terms of which identity and distinctness
> under the concept Fx is explained. (1983: 114)

Given (ED), understood as an explanation of the sortal concept
direction in terms of parallelism of lines, this will rule out the identification of any line with a direction. For if 'l_1' and 'l_2' are singular
terms explicitly standing for lines (terms of the form 'the line

such that . . .') '$l_1 = l_2$' will not be capable of being adequately explained as equivalent in truth-conditions to a statement of the form 'l_m is parallel to l_n'; otherwise '$l_1 = l_2$' would be equivalent to the 'direction of l_m = the direction of l_n' and so 'l_1' would be equivalent to 'the direction of l_n' (or, 'the direction of l_m'). But no term explicitly standing for a line could be equivalent in this way to a term explicitly standing for a direction (see Rosen 1993 for further elaboration).

This is true enough, but what emerges from the reasoning is how strong a principle Wright's principle of sortal exclusion is: it implies that two sorts can overlap only if some identity statement in which the two terms flanking the sign of identity are explicitly terms for the two sorts (as 'the line which . . .' and 'the direction of . . .' are explicitly terms for a line and a direction respectively) is not merely true but conceptually true. This does indeed imply that no person is a number, and no line a direction. But it also seems to imply that no collection of molecules is a person (Rosen 1993: 173) and no lobster a meal (Sullivan and Potter 1997).

Debate about the adequacy of Wright's and Hale's solution to the Caesar problem is ongoing: the foregoing has merely scratched the surface. The importance of the question is, however, considerable. For if they are right Frege took an unnecessary step in replacing (ED) and Hume's Principle by explicit definitions, and if he had not done so his programme would not have become vulnerable to Russell's Paradox.

For it is only in his explicit definitions that he introduces references to extensions of concepts. In fact, once Frege gives his explicit definition of number (the explicit definition of direction being given merely as an illustrative example) in *Foundations* he uses it only to derive Hume's Principle and then proceeds in his informal sketches of his other results to appeal only to Hume's Principle, making no further use of extensions. Moreover, in *Basic Laws*, wherein Frege gives the formal derivations corresponding to the sketches in *Foundations*, he also makes no essential appeal to extensions – with the one exception of their use in the proof of Hume's Principle itself (Heck 1993: 579–601). Furthermore, it has been shown in recent years (Boolos 1998; Wright 1983) that arithmetic – more precisely the Dedekind–Peano axioms which are the standardly accepted axioms for arithmetic – can indeed be derived, within second-order logic, from Hume's Principle (this result has come to be known as 'Frege's Theorem'). Moreover Fregean arithmetic – second-order logic, with Hume's Principle as the sole non-logical axiom – is consistent (more precisely, is consistent if second-order arithmetic is).

All of this entails that Frege's work embodied a substantial mathematical result – that is, Frege's Theorem – which is unaffected by Russell's Paradox, and it suggests that something close to Frege's logicism may still be a viable programme. If Hume's Principle can be accepted as a non-derivative *explanation of the concept of number*, and hence in a good sense as a conceptual or analytic truth, then, Frege's Theorem can be interpreted as establishing that arithmetic is analytic after all. This is what Wright and Hale claim.

Their claim has generated much controversy and there is no space here to go into all the arguments on both sides. It will be useful, however, to mention two counter-arguments, both of which rest on a disanalogy between Hume's Principle and (ED) so far not mentioned.

Unlike (ED) Hume's Principle is second-level: it introduces a functor, 'the number of', whose reference is a function not from *objects* to objects but from *concepts* to objects – and moreover, from concepts under some of which numbers themselves fall. Although Frege never mentions this, it is vital to his subsequent proof sketches, because in order to establish the infinity of the number series he must allow numbers themselves to be counted, and so he must allow predicates applicable to numbers (like 'is a number less than or equal to 5,') to occupy the argument place of the functor 'the number of'.

What Hume's Principle does then is to partition all concepts into equivalence classes – two concepts being assigned to the same equivalence class if and only if they are equinumerous – and to stipulate a one–one correlation between these classes and certain objects, the numbers. But since given a domain with n objects, n + 1 such equivalence classes will be definable (the empty concepts, the singly instantiated concepts, the doubly instantiated concepts . . . the n-fold instantiated concepts), Hume's Principle is not satisfiable in any finite domain. In other words, Hume's Principle entails the existence of an infinity of objects (as it must do, of course, if it is to be adequate for arithmetic, since arithmetic requires an infinity of objects). Or to be more precise, Hume's Principle, together with a set of indisputable logical truths (e.g. that everything distinct from itself is distinct from itself), entails the existence of an infinity of objects. So it cannot be a logical truth in the standard sense of a formula true in *all* non-empty domains, and some of the opponents of Wright and Hale (Boolos 1998) have argued that, for the same reason, it cannot be an *analytic* truth. In response, Hale and Wright reply that they agree that Hume's Principle is not an analytic truth in *Kant's* sense, but that is, of course, not the relevant sense – otherwise Frege's contention that arithmetic is analytic could be rejected immediately.

In claiming that arithmetic was analytic Frege's fundamental contention was that the ultimate grounds of arithmetic were truths which could be known without any appeal to intuition. Since he rejected Kant's claim that objects could only be given in intuition, it was not, for him, something that could be ruled out by definition, that truths concerning the existence of objects, even truth concerning the existence of infinitely many objects, could be analytic. Thus, Wright and Hale contend, Hume's Principle is an analytic truth in the sense relevant to the discussion of Frege's logicism, since it can be known to be true without any appeal to intuition. This is so because it is analytic *of* our concept of number – it is an explanation of that concept and once one receives it as such, one is thereby put in a position to see, without any need to resort to intuition or anything else apart from logic, that an infinity of objects must exist.

The second consequence of the disanalogy between (ED) and Hume's Principle noted – that Hume's Principle is second-level – is that unlike (ED) Hume's Principle is not strictly speaking a contextual *definition*: it does not provide a rule for the elimination of the functor 'the number of' from all contexts in which it occurs. This means that it is irremediably impredicative, in the sense that as it introduces that functor its argument places can be filled by predicates defined over a domain that involves the natural numbers themselves, and, in particular, by predicates which themselves involve ineliminable occurrences of that very functor. Against Wright and Hale, Dummett (1991a, 1998) has argued that such impredicativity disqualifies Hume's Principle from functioning as an *explanation* of the concept of number because any such explanation must be viciously circular. In response Wright and Hale point out that Hume's Principle (unlike the similarly impredicative Basic Law (V), in whose bad company Dummett groups it) is consistent, and have attempted to show how our grasp of the concept of number can be derived from it by regarding the predicates to which 'the number of' can be attached as hierarchically ordered so that we can mount to a full grasp of the concept via a series of steps (Wright 1998; Hale 1999).

These are, of course, the merest indications of complex lines of argument, and I have not attempted to discuss a variety of other objections that have been made to the 'neo-Fregeanism' of Wright and Hale. The whole area is presently a centre of vigorous research activity.

However, it is all ultimately fruitless unless the Caesar objection can be answered, or at least finessed. Frege thought that it could not, and so thinking, moved on to his explicit definitions. To these we now turn.

As we have seen, equinumerosity partitions concepts into equivalence classes, each of which contains all and only those concepts equinumerous with one another. Similarly, parallelism partitions lines into equivalence classes, each of which contains all and only those lines which are parallel to one another. Now Frege's equivalent of the (naive) notion of a class is the notion of the extension of a concept. What extensions of concepts are, at the point in *Foundations* where Frege gives his explicit definitions, is left undiscussed (later, in the *Basic Laws*, when concepts are identified with functions whose values are truth-values, they emerge as a type of value range), but they possess three crucial features: (a) their identity conditions are extensional (as determined by Basic Law (V)): the extension of the concept F is identical with the extension of the concept G if and only if all F's are G's and conversely; (b) they are objects; and (c) they are *logical* objects, knowledge of which does not rest on intuition and with which we are assumed to be familiar.

Given that extensions possess these three features, Frege now proposes that the Caesar problem can be resolved by identifying directions and numbers with extensions. We can identify the direction of line a with the extension of the concept 'line parallel to line a', i.e. with the class of lines parallel to a, and we can identify the number of F's with the extension of the concept 'equinumerous with the concept F', that is, with the class of concepts equinumerous with the concept F. Thus the number attaching to an empty concept (say, *unicorn*) is identified with the class of *all* empty concepts. The number attaching to a singly instantiated concept is identified with the class of *all* singly instantiated concepts, and so on. Given that we know what extensions are, we know that Julius Caesar and the Earth are not extensions, and so the problematic identities can be rejected.

Of course, this response to the Caesar problem is wholly unconvincing because Frege gives no argument for his assumption that we have the kind of knowledge of extensions he assumes. The appeal to extensions merely postpones the difficulty, and Frege indicates some awareness of this in his last comment on his definition of numbers, at the end of section 107, where he writes:

> In this definition the sense of the expression 'extension of a concept' is assumed to be known. This way of getting over the difficulty cannot be expected to meet with universal approval, and many will prefer other methods of removing the doubt in question [i.e. resolving the Caesar objection]. I attach no decisive importance even to bringing in the extensions of concepts at all. (1968: 117)

By the time of *Basic Laws*, however, Frege is committed to the definition of numbers as extensions, apparently having convinced himself that no other 'method of removing the doubt' can work. He therefore needs a final resolution of the Caesar problem. He attempts such a resolution in section 10 of *Basic Laws*. Evidently just as the explicit definition of numbers as extensions merely pushes the Caesar problem back a stage, so an explicit definition of extensions as entities of some other, more basic kind, would merely be a further postponement of the inevitable confrontation. Frege does not offer such an explicit definition. Instead he rests content in the case of extensions with the contextual approach he rejects for numbers, defining the criterion of identity for extensions by Basic Law (V), in terms of coextensiveness of concepts. But as in the case of number, this leaves the reference of a term of the form 'the extension of the concept F' without a determinate reference (see Wright 1983: 125–6) and so the Caesar problem rears its ugly head once more.

In *Basic Laws* the only objects, apart from those explicitly given as extensions, that Frege has to acknowledge for his mathematical purposes, are the two truth-values, the True and the False. So the problematic identifications he is faced with are just those with a term for an extension on one side and a term for a truth-value on the other. He attempts to resolve the problem by making additional stipulations. Specifically, he stipulates that the True is to be identified with the extension of the concept 'identical with the True', and the False is to be identified with the extension of the concept 'identical with the False'. And he suggests that further stipulations of the same kind should be made whenever a type of object not already identified as a type of value range is introduced. But if this policy resolves the Caesar problem it could have been employed directly to supplement Hume's Principle, and the appeal to extensions would have been unnecessary, so either it is adequate and the

appeal to extensions is unnecessary or it is inadequate and the
appeal to extensions is insufficient. Either way, even setting aside
the fact that the appeal to extensions renders Frege's system vulnerable to Russell's Paradox, we have to conclude that it does not
solve the fundamental problem facing Frege's logicism.

The remainder of Frege's development of arithmetic in *Foundations*, however, does not rest on his explicit definition of number,
but only on Hume's Principle, so its worth remains so long as *some*
way of answering or finessing the Caesar problem is possible. And
it should be noted that in giving this explicit definition (and likewise the explicit definition of directions as classes of parallel lines),
Frege has not lost sight of the fundamental insight into the relative
epistemological priorities which motivated his contextual definitions. Since directions are identified with classes of *parallel* lines and
numbers with classes of *equinumerous* concepts it is assumed that
grasp of the concepts of parallelism and equinumerosity is prior to
grasp of the concepts of direction and number. In other words, the
contextual definitions are not rejected as *incorrect*, but merely as
insufficient.

That the concept of equinumerosity is epistemologically prior
to that of number is, however, something Frege has not *established*
before he gives his explicit definition, but merely assumed, appealing to the analogy with directions in support of the assumption. He
therefore takes this task up next in sections 70–3.

He illustrates the point with the famous example of the waiter:

> If a waiter wishes to be certain of laying exactly as many knives on
> a table as plates, he has no need to count either of them, all he has
> to do is lay immediately to the right of every plate a knife, taking
> care that every knife on the table lies immediately to the right of a
> plate. Plates and knives are thus correlated one to one, and that by
> the identical spatial relationship. (1968: 82)

This shows how knowledge of one–one correlation can be prior
to knowledge of number, and thus equinumerosity, defined in terms
of it, can serve without circularity in the definition of the concept
of number.

Frege now goes on to define a one–one correlation formally, gen-
eralizing from the example of the waiter.

His definition comes to this. The F's are correlated one–one with
the G's just in case there is a relation R such that: (a) every F bears
R to some G; (b) every G has the relation R borne to it by some F;

(c) for any x, y and z, if x stands in relation R to y and x stands in the relation R to z, z = y; and (d) for any x, y and z, if x stands in the relation R to y and z stands in the relation R to y, x = z.

With one–one correlation and, in terms of it, equinumerosity thus defined in purely logical terms, Frege is now able, assuming that extensions are logical objects, to put forward his definition of 'the number which belongs to the concept F' as 'the extension of the concept equinumerous with the concept F' as a definition in purely logical terms. He next defines

n is a number

to mean the same as

there exists a concept such that n is the number which belongs to it

And comments:

Thus the concept of number receives its definition, apparently, indeed, in terms of itself, but actually without any fallacy, since, the number which belongs to the concept F has already been defined. (1968: 85)

In the next section Frege goes on to derive Hume's Principle from his definition of numbers as classes of equinumerous concepts and then proceeds to define the individual numbers.

He first defines 0 as the number which belongs to the concept 'not identical with itself'; since every empty concept is equinumerous with this concept (as he shows) 0 is thus the number of F's whenever there are no F's.

He then defines the successor relation:

The proposition: 'there exists a concept F, and an object x falling under it, such that the number which belongs to the concept F is n and the number which belongs to the concept "falling under F but not identical with x" is m' is to mean the same as 'n follows in the natural series of numbers directly after m'. (1968: 89)

More briefly, this tells us that n is a direct successor of m (m immediately precedes n) if and only if for some F and some x, n is the number of F's and x is F and m is the number of F's distinct from x. Thus, on this definition 12 succeeds 11 since there is a concept F (*Apostle*) and an object x (*Judas*), such that 12 is the number of F's and x is an F and 11 is the number of F's distinct from x.

Next Frege defines 1 as the number belonging to the concept 'identical with 0'. Since every singly instantiated concept is equinumerous with this one, it follows that 1 is the number of F's if and only if there is exactly one F. He is then able to prove that 1 succeeds 0. This is so since there is a concept F (*identical with 0*) and an object x (0), such that 1 is the number of F's and x is an F and 0 is the number of F's distinct from x.

Frege's plan is to define each number except 0 in terms of its predecessor:

0 is the number of objects which are non-self identical
1 is the number of objects identical with 0
2 is the number of objects identical with 0 or 1

n + 1 is the number of objects which are members of the natural number series ending with n

But to do so legitimately he has to establish a variety of facts about the successor relation. Most importantly he must prove that every number has a successor, that is that the natural number series is infinite. Frege takes this task up in section 79. His aim is to show that the number of members of the number series ending in n (i.e. the number of natural numbers less than or equal to n) immediately succeeds the number n. But in conformity with his logicism he must first define the concept 'member of the natural number series ending in n' in purely logical terms.

At this point he appeals to the definition of the ancestral of a relation ('following in a series') he has defined in *Conceptual Notation* (see chapter 2 above). He insists that this definition makes the question whether one thing follows another in a series an objective matter: 'What I have provided is a criterion which decides in every case the question, Does it follow after?, whenever it can be put' (1968: 93). With the ancestral of a relation defined purely logically using the technique of *Conceptual Notation* Frege is now able to define purely logically what 'n follows m in the natural number series' means: n stands in the proper ancestral of the successor relation to m. 'n is a member of the natural number series beginning with m' can now be defined to mean: n stands in the ancestral proper of the successor relation to m. And this is equivalent to: 'm is a member of the natural number series ending with n', that is, m is less than or equal to n.

With the concept 'is a member of the natural number series ending with n' thus defined in purely logical terms, it remains only for Frege to prove that for every n, the number of members of the natural number series ending with n is a successor of n. He sketches a proof of this in *Foundations*, but does not give a full proof until *Basic Laws* (it is doubtful, in fact, whether the proof sketch in *Foundations* can be filled out into a formally correct proof, see Boolos 1998).

Finally, in the brief section 84, Frege introduces infinite numbers. Previously he defined a number as the number of a concept. The number that belongs to the concept 'finite number' is, therefore, unproblematic given his definitions. Usually it is symbolized by aleph-null. Unlike the finite numbers it follows itself in the natural series of numbers. Frege stresses that aleph-null is a perfectly legitimate number:

> About the infinite number [aleph-null], so defined there is nothing mysterious or wonderful. 'The number which belongs to the concept of F is [aleph-null]', means no more and no less than this: that there exists a relation which correlates one to one the objects falling under the concept F with the finite numbers. In terms of our definitions this has a perfectly clear and unambiguous sense: and that is enough to justify the use of the symbol [aleph-null] and to assure it of a meaning. That we cannot form any idea of an infinite number is of absolutely no importance, the same is equally true of finite numbers. (1968: 97)

He goes on to discuss Cantor's work on finite numbers, on the whole approvingly.

Frege opens the concluding part of *Foundations* with the statement: 'I hope I may claim in the present work to have made it probable that the laws of arithmetic are analytic judgements and consequently *a priori*' (1968: 99).

Only *probable*, of course, because to establish logicism with certainty it would be required to 'produce a chain of deductions with no links remaining' (1968: 102) to ensure that no appeal to intuition was ever made – only so could Kantianism be decisively refuted.

So Frege points forward here to the formal proofs of *Basic Laws* which was to be the definitive refutation of Kantianism. Unfortunately, as we know, Russell's Paradox can be derived in the formal system of *Basic Laws*.

Russell's brief statement of the paradox in his letter to Frege was quoted in chapter 1. Frege's own statement of the contradiction, given in the Appendix to volume 2 of *Basic Laws* is the following:

> Nobody will wish to assert of the class of men that it is a man. We have here a class that does not belong to itself. I say something belongs to a class when it falls under the concept whose extension the class is. Let us now fix our eye on the concept: *class that does not belong to itself*. The extension of this concept (if we may speak of its extension) is thus the class of classes that do not belong to themselves. For short we will call it the class C. Let us now ask whether this class belongs to itself as a class. First, let us suppose that it does. If anything belongs to a class it falls under the concept whose extension the class is.
>
> Thus if our class belongs to itself, it is a class that does not belong to itself. Our first support thus leads to self-contradiction. Secondly, let us suppose that our class C does not belong to itself, then it falls under the concept whose extension it itself is, and thus does belong to itself. Here, again, a contradiction. (1964: 128)

Frege traces the difficulty back to Basic Law (V), his general principle governing the identity criterion of value ranges, which, specialized to concepts, asserts that two concepts F and G have the same extension if and only if all and only the things falling under F fall under G. The inconsistency arises because Frege insists that extensions of concepts are themselves *objects* and are therefore admissible arguments for any first-level concepts whatsoever.

Basic Law (V) affirms the existence of a second-level function (the reference of the functor 'the extension of') that assigns to each first-level concept an object, its extension, and assigned *distinct* extensions to *distinct* concepts (concepts under which distinct objects fall) and the *same* extension to the *same* concept.

Thus Basic Law (V) splits into two halves:

(Va) If whatever falls under concept F falls under concept G and vice versa the extension of the concept F is identical to the extension of the concept G and

(Vb) If the extension of the concept F is identical with the extension of the concept G whatever falls under concept F falls under concept G and vice versa

(Va) is trivial, merely asserting the extensionality of concepts. Since it states only a sufficient condition for identity of extensions it will be satisfied if *every* concept is assigned the same extension.

(Vb) is the 'bad' half of (V): it says that if the concepts F and G are distinct then the extensions assigned to them must also be distinct. It thus requires that there be at least as many extensions as there are concepts. But as Cantor proved, the power set (set of all subsets) of a set with n members has 2^n members. Expressed in Fregean terminology this is to say that the set of all concepts defined over a given set is larger than the given set, since given a set with n members 2^n concepts can be defined over it, and $2^n > n$. If there are two objects, a and b, for example, there are four concepts definable over them: one satisfied by neither a nor b, one satisfied by both, one satisfied by a alone and one satisfied by b alone. There are thus more concepts than there are objects. (Vb), however, requires that there are *not* more concepts than there are extensions of concepts. If extensions are objects, (Vb) is refuted by Cantor's proof that there are more concepts than objects or equivalently that there can be no second-level function mapping concepts into objects which always maps distinct concepts into distinct objects. This is the conclusion Frege draws: 'for every second-level function of one argument of type 2 there are concepts which if taken as arguments of this function determine the same value, although not all objects falling under one of these concepts falls under the other' (1964: 136).

The problem the contradiction posed for Frege was acute, because by the time of *Basic Laws* he had become convinced that the recognition of extensions as logical objects and the identification of numbers with extensions provided the only way in which the analytic status of arithmetic could be assured. Thus he attempted a repair by modifying (Vb), which would allow him to retain the assumption that extensions were objects. But this repair only leads to new contradictions (see Quine 1955; Geach 1956; Resnik 1980: 215–20), and anyway blocks the proof of crucial theorems. The possibility that this might be so is clearly noted at the end of the Appendix: 'It would here take us too far to follow out further the result of replacing (V) by (V') [the repair]. We cannot but see that many propositions must have sub-clauses [conditions] added; but we need scarcely fear that this will raise essential difficulties for the course of the proofs. Anyhow, all propositions discovered up to now will need to be checked through' (1964: 143). Dummett plausibly suggests (1991a: 5–6) that whether or not Frege discovered the inconsistency in his repaired system, his abandonment of his logicism is sufficiently explained by his having found when he began on the necessary task of proof checking that, contrary to his expectations, 'essential difficulties' *were* raised for the course of the proofs – in fact, not even the proof of theorem (111), that 0 and 1 are distinct, goes through.

Frege eventually came to think that his resort to extensions as the foundation of his system was a consequence of his having been taken in by the deceptive features of language. In a diary he kept from 10 March to 9 May 1924 (the last year of his life) he wrote on 23 March: 'My efforts to become clear about what is meant by number have resulted in failure. We are only too easily misled by language and in this particular case the way we are misled is little short of disastrous' (1979: 263). And in a paper written the same year:

> One feature of language that threatens to undermine the reliability of thinking is its tendency to form proper names to which no objects correspond. If this happens in fiction, which everyone understands to be fiction, this has no detrimental effect. It's different if it happens in a statement which makes the claim to be properly scientific. A particularly noteworthy example of this is the formation of a proper name after the pattern of 'the extension of the concept a', e.g. 'the extension of the concept *star*'. Because of the definite article this expression appears to designate an object, but there is no object for which this phrase could be a linguistically appropriate designation. From this has arisen the paradoxes of set theory which have dealt the death blow to set theory itself. I myself was under this illusion when, in attempting to provide a logical foundation for numbers, I tried to construe numbers as sets. It is difficult to avoid an expression that has universal currency, before you learn of the mistakes it can give rise to. It is extremely difficult, perhaps impossible, to test every expression offered us by language to see whether it is logically innocuous. So a great part of the work of a philosopher consists – or at least ought to consist – in a struggle against language. (1979: 269–70)

4

Philosophical Logic

'Function and Concept'

In a letter to Husserl dated 24 May 1891, Frege included a diagram setting out the relations he thought to obtain between language and the extra-linguistic world.

sentence	proper name	concept word	
↓	↓	↓	
sense of the sentence (thought)	sense of the proper name	sense of the concept word	
↓	↓	↓	
reference of the sentence (truth-value)	reference of the proper name (object)	reference of the concept word (concept) →	object falling under the concept

In this chapter we shall mainly be concerned with the relations between the first and third levels of this diagram; the relation between the first level and the second, and that between the second level and the third, will be the concern of the next chapter.

In a fragment of August 1906 (1979: 184) entitled 'What May I Regard as the Result of my Work?' Frege wrote:

It is almost all tied up with the concept-script. a concept construed as a function. a relation as a function of two arguments. the extension of a concept or class is not the primary thing for me. unsaturatedness both in the case of concepts and functions. the true nature of concepts and functions recognised.

These ideas form the backbone of Frege's 1891 essay 'Function and Concept' (in 1969: 21–41), which is complemented by his 1904 essay 'What is a Function' (in 1969: 107–16). The problem of 'the concept *horse*' which they force him to confront is discussed in his reply to Benno Kerry (1969: 42–55).

As we have seen, already in *Conceptual Notation* the notion of a function was central to Frege's thought, his fundamental insight being the replacement of the distinction between subject and predicate by that between argument and function. But there the functions that he was concerned with were linguistic entities. In *Foundations* the notion of a concept is central – one of Frege's crucial tenets in that book being that there is a fundamental distinction between objects and concepts – and concepts are evidently non-linguistic entities, but they are never spoken of as functions.

In 'Function and Concept' Frege extends the notion of a function beyond the linguistic level, insists on a sharp distinction between functional sign and function, and identifies the concepts of *Foundations* with a special kind of function – 'concept words' thus being classified as a special type of functional sign. The incompleteness, unsaturatedness, or essentially predicative nature of concepts, which marks them off as fundamentally different from objects, now comes to be seen as a special case of the unsaturatedness of functions, which corresponds to an unsaturatedness in functional signs. As Frege puts it in 'What is a Function?': 'the sign for a function is "unsaturated"; it needs to be completed with a numeral. . . . The peculiarity of functional signs, which we here call "unsaturatedness", naturally has something answering to it in the functions themselves' (1969: 113–15).

'Function and Concept' begins with an analysis of the mathematician's notion of a function. Frege's first point is that a distinction must be drawn between a function and its name. A mathematician of his time would likely have answered the question 'What is a function?' by saying: 'A function of x is a mathematical expression containing x, a formula containing the letter x.' According to this proposal the expression '$2.x^3 + x$' would be a function of x, and the expression '$2.2^3 + 2$' would be a function of 2.

But, Frege says, this confuses sign and thing signified, form and content. The distinction is clear if we consider the latter expression. '$2.2^3 + 2$' is a complex arithmetical designation which stands for the same thing as '18' or '3.6': 'What is expressed in the equation "$2.2^3 + 2 = 18$" is that the right hand complex of signs has the same reference as the left hand one' (1969: 72). To think otherwise involves the same confusion as that involved in thinking that the sweet-smelling violet differs from *Viola adorata* because the names sound different. But if '$2.2^3 + 2$' and '18' stand for the same thing, this thing – the number 18 – cannot be identified with either expression.

It is now tempting to say that the function is the *reference* of the mathematical expression. But this will not do either. For the expressions: '$2.1^3 + 1$', '$2.2^3 + 2$' and '$2.4^3 + 4$' stand for numbers, viz. 3, 18, and 132. So if the function were really the reference of a mathematical expression, it would just be a number, and nothing new would have been gained for arithmetic by speaking of functions.

It is natural to respond here by saying that the mathematical expressions which stand for functions are ones in which a number is indicated indefinitely by a letter e.g. '$2.x^3 + x$'. But this, Frege says, makes no difference. For whatever x is, $2.x^3 + x$ is just a number; the only difference between '$2.x^3 + x$' and '$2.3^3 + 3$' is that the latter indicates a number definitely, the former indefinitely.

'Indicating a number indefinitely', he insists, must not be understood as 'indicating an indefinite number'; nor must we be misled by the mathematical custom of referring to indefinitely indicating letters such as the 'x' in '$2.x^3 + x$' as 'variables' into thinking that what is referred to by such an expression is a *variable* number. There are no variable numbers and no indefinite numbers.

This is a point that is of great importance to Frege and in 'What is a function?' he elaborates it. We might be tempted to say: 'When I say "the number that gives the length of this rod in millimetres" I am naming a number; and this is variable, because the rod does not always keep the same length, so by using this expression I have designated a variable number' (1969: 108). However, Frege says, we should compare 'the length of this rod' with 'the King of this realm'. We would not wish to say that the King of this realm is a variable man, one who was old ten years ago and young now. 'The King of this realm' does not designate anything at all unless a time indication is added and if one is added what is designated is then just a man, not a variable man. And if two different time indications are added, different men may be designated. Thus 'The King of this realm now is a young man' and 'the King of this realm ten years ago was an old man' may both be true, but this is simply because the subjects of predication in the two sentences are different, not because anyone has grown younger. Similarly 'the length of this rod in millimetres' does not designate any number at all if no time is mentioned. If mention of a time is supplied, then a number may be designated, e.g. 1,000, but this is an ordinary, invariable, number. A different time indication may result in the designation of a different number, say, 1,001, so it may be true both that the number in millimetres half an hour ago of the length of this rod was a cube and that the number in millimetres now of the length of this rod is not a cube. But this does not mean that any number has changed its properties. As in the example of 'The King of this realm', we simply have two different subjects of predication – the number in millimetres of the length of this rod half an hour ago, and the number in millimetres of the length of this rod now.

Nor should we think that numerical expressions containing indefinitely indicating letters designate indefinite numbers. There are no more indefinite numbers than there are indefinite men. Every object must be definite. The role of indefinitely indicating letters, such as the 'x' in '$2.x^3 + x$' or the 'n' in such a statement as 'If the number n is even, then cos $n\pi = 1$' cannot be explained by saying that such letters indicate indefinite numbers. Rather:

> Here only the whole has sense, not the antecedent by itself, nor the consequent by itself. The question whether the number n is even cannot be answered; no more can the question whether cos $n\pi = 1$. . . . We write the letter 'n' in order to achieve generality . . . of course we may speak of indefiniteness here: but the word 'indefinite' is not an adjective of 'number' but ['indefinitely'] is an adverb, e.g. of the verb, 'to indicate'. We cannot say that 'n' designates an indefinite number, but we can say that it indicates numbers indefinitely. And so it is always when letters are used in arithmetic, except for the few cases (π, e, i) where they occur as proper names. (1969: 110)

Nevertheless, Frege thinks, it is only by attending to the notation in which 'x' is used to indicate a number indefinitely that we can achieve a correct conception of the function.

In

$$2.x^3 + x$$

people call x the argument of the function and recognize the *same* function again in

2.1^3 + 1

2.4^3 + 4

2.5^3 + 5

with different arguments, viz. 1, 4, and 5.

Thus it is the *common element* of these expressions that is the sign for the function. This common element is what is left over if we remove the designation of the argument. We could write this as

2.( )^3 + ( )

But then we would have to indicate that the brackets must be filled with the same numeral each time to designate a value of the function. We might think that we could designate the function by '2.x^3 + x', or again, using Greek letters, as Frege later recommends, by '2.ξ^3 + ξ'. But a letter so used serves only to indicate where the argument sign is to be inserted and is in any case to be used only in the exceptional case in which we wish to symbolize the function in isolation (1969: 114); the function is *already* designated in '2.3^3 + 3' along with its argument. In his 'Logic and Mathematics' of 1914 Frege makes this absolutely clear:

when we say 'the function 1 + ξ − ξ', the letter 'ξ' is not part of the function sign; for the proper name '1 + 3 − 3' is composed of the function name and the proper name '3', and the letter 'ξ' does not occur in it at all. . . . the role of the 'ξ' is to enable us to recognise where the supplementing proper name is to be put. . . . If I write 'ξ − ξ', I indicate, by using the letter 'ξ' in both places, that the same proper name is to be put in both places, and so what I have is the name of a function of only one argument. When I call this the 'name of a function', this is to be taken *cum grano salis*. The proper name which we obtain by supplementing this function with a proper name, e.g '3 − 3', does not contain the letter 'ξ', although it contains the function name in question. This 'ξ' is therefore not a constituent of the function name but only enables us to recognise how the function sign is combined with the proper name supplementing it. This 'ξ' gives us a pointer for how to use the function name. (1979: 239–40)

The reader will recognize these considerations from the discussion in the second chapter of Frege's notion of a function as used in

Conceptual Notation. There we saw that we had to recognize that the sign for the function in such an expression as '$2.3^3 + 3$' had to be seen to be the common pattern it shares with '$2.4^3 + 4$', '$2.5^3 + 5$' and so on. In *Conceptual Notation* Frege shows himself to be aware of this by his use of the example 'Cato killed Cato'. In 'Function and Concept' his example is carefully chosen to make the point unmistakably clear.

The fact that signs for functions are patterns rather than quotable parts of expressions is what Frege means by calling them 'unsaturated' or 'incomplete'. We saw that such unsaturated signs, themselves called 'functions' in *Conceptual Notation*, could indeed be regarded as a type of linguistic function. In 'Function and Concept' he does not call them 'functions', but he does insist that the essence of the function itself is unsaturatedness. In 'What is a Function?' he makes it clear that this unsaturatedness of the function is to be explained in terms of the unsaturatedness of its sign. Functions are those entities which can be designated only by patterns exhibited in complex expressions. The function $2.x^3 + x$ is thus not designated by '$2.\ ^3 + $ ', nor by '$2.3^3 + 3$' nor indeed by '$2.x^3 + x$'. For although these expressions exhibit the pattern which designates the function, none *is* that pattern. Thus any attempt to say of the function that it *is* a function, by attaching the predicate 'is a function' to a name, must fail. For any completion would have to employ a quotable expression. But no quotable expression can name a function.

There is a paradox here, which we shall explore in some detail later (it is the paradox of the concept *horse*). But for now let us continue with Frege's exposition in 'Function and Concept'.

The result of completing a function with an argument, Frege says, is the value of the function for the argument. Thus 3 is the value of the function $2.x^3 + x$ for the argument 1. The value of the function for an argument is thus a number, and is to be distinguished from the function even when the value of the function is the same whatever the argument. Thus the function $2 + x - x$ is to be distinguished from the number 2 even though its value is always 2. The reason for this, Frege stresses, is the unsaturatedness of function names and therewith of functions: 'the expression of a function must always show one or more places that are intended to be filled up with the sign of the argument' (1969: 25).

Frege goes on to say that a function can be represented intuitively by a curve or a graph; if we plot the values of the functions for various arguments each such argument–value pair will correspond to a point on the curve. Two functions which have the same values for the same arguments will be represented by the same curve. This is true, for example, of the functions $x(x - 4)$ and $x^2 - 4x$. We can express this as follows:

$$x^2 - 4x = x(x - 4)$$

But here, Frege says, we have not put one function equal to another, but only the value of one equal to that of the other. The statement is to be understood as a universal generalization:

for any x, $x^2 - 4x = x(x - 4)$

The reason is that equality, or identity, is a relation that can only hold between *objects*, entities capable of being designated by saturated expressions. But functions are not objects. Nevertheless, Frege suggests, associated with functions there are certain objects, value-ranges, such that we can express the holding of such a universal generalization as an identity between objects.

Instead of

for any x, $x^2 - 4x = x(x - 4)$

we can write

the value-range of the function $x^2 - 4x$ = the value-range of the function $x(x - 4)$

This is an instance of Frege's Basic Law (V), by which, as he puts it, 'we may regard an equality holding generally between values of functions as a [particular] equality, viz. an equality between value-ranges' (1969: 26). The possibility of such a transformation, Frege says in 'Function and Concept', is indemonstrable; it must be regarded as a fundamental law of logic.

Here we see the main reason why the identification of concepts with functions is important for Frege. It allows him to identify the extensions of concepts, introduced in the *Grundlagen* as the 'logical objects' with which numbers are to be identified, with certain value-ranges, and thus to found arithmetic on what he thinks he is able to regard as a fundamental law of logic. Value-ranges, he thinks, are objects already well known to mathematicians, about which no anxiety need be felt, indeed 'in many phrases of ordinary mathematical terminology, the word "function" certainly corresponds to what I have here called the value-range of a function' (1969: 26). Thus the assimilation of concepts to functions and therewith the extensions of concepts to value-ranges provides a secure basis for his logicism.

Unfortunately for Frege, as we have seen, the security he thus thought he had found was illusory. Basic Law (V) is self-contradictory. Its restriction to concepts says that the extension of concept F is identical with the extension of concept G if and only if exactly the same objects fall under concept F and concept G, and the 'only if' part of this requires there to be more objects than there are (2^n if there are n). But until he received the letter from Russell Frege did not know this. Thus the rest of 'Function and Concept' is aimed at showing how concepts can be thought of as a kind of function and extensions of concepts as a kind of value-range. Hence, though the *value* of the assimilation of concepts to functions is independent of the logicist programme (as Frege in effect noted in his 1906 fragment 'What May I Regard as the Result of my Work?' quoted earlier), the *motivation* behind it is certainly not.

Frege attempts to make plausible his identification of concepts with functions by suggesting that it can be thought of as the culmination of a process of extension of the notion of a function already present in the writings of mathematicians. In the first place mathematicians extended the field of mathematical operations used for the construction of functions to include, as well as addition, multiplication and exponentiation, the various means of transition to the limit. Secondly, they extended the possible arguments and values of functions to include complex numbers.

Corresponding to the first direction of extension, Frege now suggests, we may add to the signs '+', '−', etc., which serve for the construction of functional expressions, also such signs as '=', '>', '<', so that we may speak, e.g. of the function $x^2 = 1$. What are the values of this function? Well, for the arguments −1, 0, 1, 2 we get:

$$(-1)^2 = 1$$
$$0^2 = 1$$
$$1^2 = 1$$
$$2^2 = 1$$

These are equations. The first and third are true, the second and fourth are false. Frege now proposes that we say 'the value of the function $x^2 = 1$ is the truth-value True, for the arguments (−1) and 1 and is the truth-value False for the arguments 0 and 2'. Consequently '$1^2 = 1$' stands for the True, as say, '2^2' stands for 4. And '$2^2 = 1$' stands for the False. The function $x^2 = 1$ can thus be thought of, Frege suggests, as mapping numbers onto truth-values. But, he goes on:

> If for a definite argument, e.g. –1, the value of the function is the True, we can express this as follows: 'the number –1 has the property that its square is 1'; or more briefly '–1 is a square root of 1' or '–1 falls under the concept: square root of 1'. If the value of the function $x^2 =$ 1 for an argument, e.g. for 2, is the False, we can express this as follows: '2 is not a square root of 1' or '2 does not fall under the concept: square root of 1'. We thus see how closely that which is called a concept in logic is connected with what we call a function. Indeed, we may say at once, a concept is a function whose value is always a truth-value. (1969: 30)

If we consider now adding '>' to the stock of signs by which functional expressions can be formed we can see also how relations may be assimilated to functions.

The function $x^2 + y^2$ is a function of two arguments, whose values are numbers. The function $x > y$ is a function of two arguments whose values are truth-values. In

$$3 > 2$$

we have the value of this function for the arguments 3 and 2. So, Frege says, just as we may say that a concept is a function of one argument whose values are always truth-values, so we may say that a relation is a function of two arguments whose values are always truth-values.

This identification of concepts with certain one-argument functions and relations with certain two-argument functions depends, of course, on what seems at first sight to be the extraordinary thesis that sentences are *proper names* of a certain type of *object*, truth-values. In fact this thesis has four components: (a) sentences have reference; (b) the reference of a sentence is a truth-value; (c) sentences are of the same logical type as proper names; (d) the reference of a sentence is an object. The fundamental contention here is that sentences have reference, and to understand Frege's attitude we have to understand why he regards not only sentences but also function signs (including expressions for concepts and relations) as unproblematically having reference. We shall come back to this question. For now, however, it is important to note that the very fact that Frege regards unsaturated expressions as having reference is enough to show that he was not misled into thinking of sentences as having reference because he thought of them as a kind of proper name. He did, indeed, maintain both theses, but the first is logically prior to and separable from the second.

In 'Function and Concept', taking it for granted that at least some sentences (mathematical equations and inequalities) have reference, the objection Frege considers is that it is unmotivated to regard their references as truth-values and thus to regard all of '$2^2 = 4$', '$2 > 1$' and '$2^4 = 4^2$' as standing for the same thing, the True. For, the objection goes, '$2^2 = 4$' and '$2 > 1$' make quite different assertions, express quite different thoughts.

Frege's response is to distinguish between sense and reference and to appeal to the fundamental *compositionality principle* governing the notion of reference:

> The reference of a complex expression is a function of, i.e. is wholly determined by, the references of its parts.

This implies that if an expression which is part of a larger expression is replaced by another having the same reference, the reference of the whole will remain unchanged.

Frege now argues as follows. '$2^4 = 4^2$' and '$4.4 = 4^2$' express quite different thoughts, but '2^4' and '4.4' have the same reference. Hence, given the compositionality principle for reference, so must '$2^4 = 4^2$' and '$4.4 = 4^2$', since they differ only in that the latter contains '4.4' where the former contains '2^4'. Hence the reference of a mathematical equation must be distinguished from the thought it expresses, and the objection is answered.

Frege drives home his point with a non-mathematical example: the famous case of the Morning Star and the Evening Star which occurs again in 'On Sense and Reference'. The sentence 'The Evening Star is a planet with a shorter period of revolution than the Earth' expresses a thought distinct from that expressed by the sentence 'The Morning Star is a planet with a shorter period of revolution than the Earth'; for someone who does not know that the Morning Star is the Evening Star might regard the one as true and the other as false. Nevertheless, if the two sentences are deemed to have a reference, the compositionality principle for reference requires that they must have the *same* reference; for it is just a matter of interchanging the words 'the Evening Star' and 'the Morning Star' which have the same reference, i.e. are names of the same heavenly body, the planet Venus.

Frege concludes:

> We must distinguish between sense and reference. '2^4' and '4.4' certainly have the same reference, i.e. they are proper names of the same number; but they have not the same sense, consequently, '$2^4 = 4^2$' and '4.4 = 4^2' have the same reference, but not the same sense (which means, in this case: they do not contain the same thought). (1969: 29)

It is important to be clear about what this argument achieves and what it does not achieve. Given (a) the compositionality principle for reference, (b) the assumption that sentences have reference, and (c) the assumption that the reference of a complex numerical designation is a number and the reference of a proper name of a concrete object is the concrete object it names, Frege is here able to establish that the reference of a sentence is *not* the thought it expresses (where two sentences express different thoughts if it is possible for someone who understands both to regard one as true and the other as false). This does not establish that the reference of a sentence is a truth-value, for it remains possible, as far as this argument goes, that the reference of a sentence is a type of entity less finely individuated than thoughts but more finely individuated than truth-values – in this connection philosophers have spoken of *facts* as structured entities corresponding to sentences in the way here envisaged. However, a plausible strengthening of Frege's argument, given originally by Alonzo Church, scuppers the attempt to defend the view that such entities could serve as the references of sentences.

Consider the four sentences:

(1) Sir Walter Scott is the author of *Waverley*.
(2) Sir Walter Scott is the man who wrote twenty-nine *Waverley* novels altogether.
(3) The number which is such that Sir Walter Scott is the man who wrote that number of *Waverley* novels is twenty-nine.
(4) The number of counties in Utah is twenty-nine.

(1) and (2) must have the same reference, if any, given Frege's compositionality principle for reference and the assumption that the reference of a definite description is the thing it describes, since the author of *Waverley* was the man who wrote twenty-nine *Waverley* novels altogether. The same is true of (3) and (4). While (2) and (3), if not synonymous, are so nearly so that it is plausible to think that they have the same reference if any two propositions ever do. It follows that (1) and (4) must have the same reference. But what do (1) and (4) have in common? They do not express the same thought, on Frege's criterion of identity for thoughts. Nor do they state the same fact, if facts are to be individuated in any way that corresponds to how we intuitively think of them, i.e. as structured entities composed of objects, properties and relations. In this case it seems hard to deny that all that is common to the four sentences is their truth-value. But if these sentences have to be regarded as having the same reference, the same conclusion can be drawn for all true sentences, and exactly parallel examples using false sentences can be used to argue that all false sentences have the same reference.

This argument shows how difficult it is to reject Frege's conclusion that the reference of a sentence is its truth-value, once one accepts the compositionality principle for reference, accepts that sentences have reference, and accepts the Fregean identification of the reference of a singular term with its designation (i.e. in the case of a proper name its bearer and in the case of a definite description the object it describes). However, it should be noted that Frege himself never argues in exactly this way: in fact, as we shall see later, once one understands why he regards it as unproblematic that sentences as well as singular terms have reference it requires only a small step to understand why he insists that the reference of a sentence is a truth-value.

At this point in 'Function and Concept', having given the arguments just discussed for his identification of the reference of a sentence with its truth-value, Frege goes on, in a passage already quoted, to make the identification of concepts with functions whose values are truth-values (1969: 30). He is quite explicit about the purpose of this identification. Immediately before giving it he writes:

It might further be asked: what, then, is the point of admitting the signs, =, >, <, into the list of those that build up a functional expression? Nowadays, it seems, more and more supporters are being won by the view that arithmetic is a further development of logic; that a more rigorous establishment of arithmetical laws reduces them to purely logical laws and to such laws alone. I too am of this opinion, and I base upon it the requirement that the symbolic language of arithmetic must be expanded into a logical symbolism. I shall now have to indicate how this is done in our present case. (1969: 30)

And immediately afterwards he points out that he is now in a position to identify extensions of concepts with value-ranges:

the functions

$$x^2 = 1 \text{ and } (x + 1)^2 = 2(x + 1)$$

always have the same value for the same argument, viz. the True for the arguments −1 and +1, and the False for all other arguments. According to our previous conventions we shall also say that these functions have the same ranges of values, and express this in symbols as follows:

$$\dot{\varepsilon}(\varepsilon^2 = 1) = \dot{\alpha}((\alpha + 1)^2 = 2(\alpha + 1)).$$

In logic this is called identity of the extension of concepts. Hence we can designate as an extension the value range of a function whose value for every argument is a truth-value. (1969: 30–1)

We have already discussed what Frege thought this achieved for his logicist project. It also helped him to make clear the distinction between the extension of a concept and the aggregate of things falling under the concept. If the extension of a concept is thought of as the class of items falling under it, and this, in turn, is thought of as in some way composed of its members, then the distinction between extension and aggregate becomes obscured, and the notion of the extension of an empty concept becomes doubtful. On Frege's conception of the extension of a concept as the value-range of a certain kind of function these difficulties disappear. As Frege indicates when he introduces the notion of a value-range, it is intuitive to think of a value-range as represented by a pairing of the arguments and values of the function of which it is the value-range; such a pairing may be shown by a curve on a graph. In the particular case of extensions then we should think of a pairing of arguments, e.g. numbers, with truth-values. So just as the pair $\langle 2,4 \rangle$ 'belongs to' the value-range of the function x^2 so *both* of the pairs $\langle 1, \text{True} \rangle$ and $\langle 2, \text{False} \rangle$ 'belong to' the extension of the concept $x^2 = 1$. The extension of the concept $x^2 = 1$ is no more to be thought of as composed of 1 and −1 (i.e. the arguments for which the value of the function is the True) than the value-range of the function x^2 is to be thought of as composed of those arguments for which that function has one particular value. Equally, then, the extension of an empty concept is not to be thought of as in any way problematic; it is simply the value-range of a constant function, i.e. a function which always yields the same value (the False) for every argument.

Having introduced functions whose values are always truth-values to analyse equations and inequalities, Frege has, of course, made the decisive step which he wished to take. He now extends his analysis to sentences in general. Thus, he says, we may:

> split up the sentence
>
> 'Caesar conquered Gaul'
>
> into 'Caesar' and 'conquered Gaul'. The second part is unsaturated – it contains an empty place; only when this place is filled up with a proper name, or with an expression that replaces a proper name, does a complete sense appear. Here too I give the name 'function' to what the 'unsaturated' part stands for. In this case the argument is Caesar. (1969: 31)

Thus we can speak of the concept *conquering Gaul* as we can speak of the concept *square root of 1*, and in the former case, as in the latter, we can regard this concept as a function mapping objects on to truth-values. The only difference is that we are now allowing ourselves to speak of 'functions' whose *arguments* are not numbers.

With this extension Frege has set out all the essentials of his functional theory of predication. And it is important to appreciate that it is not merely by analogy that he is entitled to speak of predicates, like functions symbols, as unsaturated. The example he uses, 'Caesar conquered Gaul', unfortunately, does not make the point clear, but his earlier example in *Conceptual Notation*, 'Cato killed Cato', does. Just as the function $2.x^3 + x$ is designated only by the common pattern in the designations of its various values so the concept *x killed x* is designated only by the common pattern in the sentences got by replacing the 'x' by different names of people.

The unsaturatedness of predicates thus has exactly the same standing as the unsaturatedness of function names. What stands in the way of recognizing unsaturatedness is in both cases the same:

the fact that in writing down the patterns exhibited by complex designations of numbers (like '2 + 3') or sentences (like 'Socrates is wise') we typically employ auxiliary expressions ('+', 'is wise') to construct the patterns thus exhibited. But we do not *always* do so (in mathematical symbolism the sign for the two-argument function *x raised to the power y* is 'x^y', and here there is no separable auxiliary expression which anyone could regard as the sign for the function) and we need *never* do so.

Having extended the notion of a function to allow objects generally as admissible arguments and truth-values as admissible values, Frege now goes further and allows objects without exception as values. Thus he allows himself to view 'the capital of the German Empire' as splittable into 'the capital of' and 'the German Empire'. The latter stands for the argument of the function, the former for the function itself.

Since objects without exception are now regarded as the values and arguments of functions, Frege says, the question now arises: what is an object? His answer is: 'an object is anything that is not a function, so an expression for it does not contain an empty place' (1969: 32).

Here we see indicated two important features of Frege's notion of an object: its generality and its derivative character. Since an object is whatever is not a function, and since, as we shall see when we consider the essay 'Concept and Object', it is impossible to *say*, either truly or falsely, of a function, that it *is* an object, the notion of an object for Frege is as general as any notion could possibly be: anything of which one can *say* that it is an object, is an object. Secondly, since objects are just those entities which are not functions, and functions are characterizable only as the references of unsaturated expressions, the ontological notion of an object is secondary to the linguistic notion of a saturated expression (one that does not contain any empty place).

Thus, Frege is able to conclude, since a sentence does not contains an empty place, we must regard what it stands for as an object. Since truth-values are what sentences stand for, truth-values are objects. By the same reasoning, since names of value-ranges contain no empty place, value-ranges are objects.

Having thus extended the field of things that may be taken as arguments, Frege now goes on, we must give more exact specifications of what signs already in use stand for. In particular, he says, we must specify the values of all functions for nonnumerical as well as numerical arguments. Thus we must define the sum function so that we know what the sum of the Sun and 1 are:

> It is thus necessary to lay down rules from which it follows, e.g. what 'O + 1' stands for if 'O' is to stand for the sun. What rules we lay down is a matter of comparative indifference, but it is essential that we should do so – that 'a + b' should always have a reference, whatever signs for definite objects may be inserted in place of 'a' and 'b'. (1969: 33)

If functions are to be defined for every possible argument, it must also be determinate for every object whether it falls under a given concept or not. But this requirement of 'sharp delimitation of concepts' is also used by Frege as the basis of an *argument* that all functions must be completely defined. If there is any argument x for which the addition function is undetermined, '$x + 1$' will lack reference. Hence

$$x + 1 = 10$$

will lack truth-value and the concept 'what gives the result 10 when increased by 1' will be incompletely defined. The requirement of sharp delimitation of concepts thus carries along with it this requirement for functions in general that they must be completely defined.

This argument relies on an implication of the compositionality principle for reference, namely:

> If a part of a complex expression lacks reference, the whole will lack reference.

Given that a mathematical equation of the form: '$x + 1 = 10$' has as its reference, if any, a truth-value, a truth-value gap, i.e. a sentence without any truth-value, must result if '$x + 1$' lacks reference.

Frege commits himself wholeheartedly to the compositionality principle for reference and thus concludes, implausibly, that ordinary language is radically defective for the purposes of science since it allows the formation of singular terms without reference and thus sentences without truth-value. Thus, in Frege's view, if France has no king,

> The King of France is bald

is neither true nor false, and the same is true of *any* sentence containing the description 'the King of France', e.g.

Either the King of France is bald or France is a republic.

He attempts to lessen the implausibility by insisting that such sentences, though truth-valueless, express thoughts. But actually, this only adds to the implausibility, for if 'the King of France is bald' expresses a determinate thought and that thought is not true, what stands in the way of saying that it is false?

We are now, however, in a position to locate the origin in Frege's thought of the thesis that the presence of an empty singular term in a sentence creates a truth-value gap. '9^3' designates a number, namely, 729, but if we replace '9' by an empty designation, for example, '$\sqrt{9}$' (which is empty because there are two square roots of 9, +3 and −3), the result '$(\sqrt{9})^3$' designates nothing – there is no saying whether it designates +27 or −27. If we now speak of what a complex numerical expression designates as its 'reference', we get the result that if in a complex numerical expression composed of a sign for an argument and a sign for a function the sign for the argument lacks reference, the same will be true of the whole complex designation. If we consider a non-mathematical function, e.g. *the capital of x*, we get the same result: the capital of England is London, the capital of France is Paris but what shall we say is the capital of the country of origin of the King of France if France is a republic? In this case, too, then, if we identify what a singular term designates with its reference, it is compelling that if in a complex expression composed of an argument sign and a function sign the sign of the argument has no reference, the same will be true of the whole expression.

But given Frege's functional theory of predication, sentences are such complex expressions composed of argument sign and function sign: 'The King of France is bald' is strictly analogous to 'the country of origin of the King of France'. Consequently, according to Fregean doctrine, if 'the King of France' has no reference because France is a republic, *both* of these complex completed functional expressions will lack reference.

But in the case of the sentence 'The King of France is bald', its reference, if it had one, would be a truth-value. Hence, that sentence, according to Frege, must be truth-valueless. And the same has got to be true of any sentence in which that empty description occurs. Thus 'The King of France is bald or France is a republic' must also be truth-valueless, just as 'the capital of the country of origin of the King of France' must lack reference.

We see, then, that there are three assumptions underpinning Frege's insistence that sentences containing empty singular terms are truth-valueless. The first is the functional theory of predication, the assimilation of sentences to complex numerical designations and the understanding of concepts as functions from objects to truth-values. The second is the identification of the reference of a sentence with its truth-value. The third is the identification of the reference of a singular term with the object it designates. Of these three assumptions the first is fundamental to Frege's thought – without it he simply does not have a theory of predication. The second Frege argues for explicitly and is hard to deny if the first and third are granted. What is left, then, is only the seemingly innocuous third assumption, that the reference of a singular term is the object it designates, i.e. the object in the world which we intend to speak of by its utterance. It is this that must be resisted if the implausible Fregean conclusion that sentences containing empty singular terms must be truth-valueless though expressing thoughts is to be rejected. It can still be allowed that two singular terms with the *same* designation have the *same* reference; what has to be denied is that when a singular term has no designation it has no reference. How this can be will seem puzzling; we shall return to the matter shortly.

First, however, we must complete the exposition of 'Function and Concept'.

By allowing truth-values to be arguments of functions as well as values Frege is now able to explain the symbolism for truth-functions introduced in *Conceptual Notation* in accordance with his general functional theory of predication.

Thus the content stroke of *Conceptual Notation* (now called simply 'the horizontal') is explained as designating that function whose value is the True if the True is its argument, and in all other cases, the False – i.e. both when the argument is the False and when it is not a truth-value at all. This function is thus a *concept*; we may think of it as the concept *identical with the True*.

Negation, symbolized by a little vertical stroke attached to the underside of the horizontal stroke is explained as that function (i.e. concept) whose value is the False for just those arguments for which the value of −x is the True, and, conversely, is the True for arguments for which the value of −x is the False.

allowed, and also unequal-levelled functions taking as arguments an object and a function. Again, second-level functions whose arguments are first-level functions of one argument must be distinguished from second-level functions whose arguments are functions of two arguments. As Frege notes, this results in a great multiplicity. But in all this multiplicity one thing remains constant: whatever arguments are allowed for functions, only objects can be allowed as values. Frege does not recognize functions whose values are functions. For functions are completed or saturated by their arguments, so that what results from the application of a function to its arguments must itself be complete and thus not a function.

Dummett has called this principle 'the principle of the completeness of the values of a function' (1993: 293) and has pointed out that the ground for it lies in a still deeper principle, Frege's principle of concept formation. An aspect of this principle is that judgements precede concepts. At the level of language what this requires is that a complex predicate is not to be thought of as put together out of simple components, but is to be thought of as formed from a sentence by omitting from it a name, perhaps at more than one occurrence, and analogously for names of functions of other types.

To see how the principle of the completeness of the values of a function now emerges an example will be useful. A function name is a pattern displayed by a complex completed functional expression, e.g. the pattern '$2.x^3 + x$' displayed by '$2.1^3 + 1$', '$2.4^3 + 4$' and so on, or the pattern 'x killed x' displayed by 'Cato killed Cato', 'Socrates killed Socrates' and so on. Thus the name of a function whose values are themselves functions would have to be the pattern displayed by various function names, e.g. by the function names 'x killed Plato', 'x killed Aristotle', 'x killed Socrates'. But the pattern here displayed is simply 'x killed y', which is the pattern common to the sentences 'Socrates killed Plato', 'Aristotle killed Socrates' and so on. If we start from these sentences, however, and remove the proper names in accordance with Frege's principle of concept formation, the pattern we thus discern can only be identified as the name of a first-level function of two arguments (in fact, a first-level relation) whose values are objects (truth-values). Thus we cannot distinguish the name of a second-level function of one argument whose value is a first-level function from the name of a first-level function of two arguments whose value is an object. And if we cannot distinguish these names, nor can we distinguish the func-

The condition stroke is explained as standing for that functi
two arguments (i.e. relation) whose value is the False if the Tr
its first argument and something other than the True is its se
argument.

The universal quantifier introduced in *Conceptual Notation* is
explained in accordance with the functional theory of predica
But to do so Frege has to introduce something essentially diffe
from what has gone before: second-level functions. So far the
arguments considered in 'Function and Concept' for functions l
been objects, but Frege now also allows functions which take f
tions as arguments. Such functions, he points out, have actu
long been used in Analysis; e.g. definite integrals (if we regard
function to be integrated as the argument) (1969: 38). And
example of a second-level function in mathematics is the limit f
tion: *the limit of $\phi(n)$ as n increases indefinitely*. Just as 'sin x' sta
for a first-level function so that replacement of 'x' by a num
results in a designation of a definite number, so replacemen
'$\phi(\ )$' in 'the limit of $\phi(n)$ as n increases indefinitely' by a name
particular first-level function results in a designation of a defi
number, e.g. if we replace '$\phi(\ )$' by a name of the function *th
power of $(x + 1)/x$* the result is a designation of the numb
(Anscombe and Geach 1961: 149).

The universal quantifier is now explained as a sign for a seco
level function mapping first-level functions onto truth-val
'$(\forall x)Fx$' has the True as its reference when the function Fx alw
has the True as its value whatever its argument; in all other cas
stands for the False. Such a second-level function is a concept
Frege draws explicit attention to the fact that his defined equival
of the existential quantifier, '$\neg(\forall x)\neg$' also stands for a second-le
concept. In this way he is able to bring together his functional the
of predication and his comments in *Foundations* about the mist
in the ontological argument. What were called in *Foundati
'second-order' concepts are now identified with second-le
concepts, understood in accordance with the functional theory
predication. The fallacy in the ontological argument is then s
to be that of treating existence as a first-level concept, which is
ignore the fact that 'just as functions are fundamentally differe
from objects, so also functions whose arguments are and must
functions are fundamentally different from functions whose arg
ments are objects and cannot be anything else' (1969: 38).

Once second-level functions of one argument have been intr
duced, second-level functions of two arguments must also

tions they name. Thus functions whose values are themselves functions cannot be recognized if we follow Frege's account, encapsulated in the principle of concept formation, of how the recognition of functions (and, in particular, concepts) must proceed.

Frege ends 'Function and Concept' by making explicit the generalization he has achieved: first people did calculations with individual numbers, then they dealt with individual first-level functions, next they achieved the general concept of a first-level function. The next step was the recognition of individual second-level functions, and finally, a step only taken by Frege himself, the achievement of the general concept of second-level functions. One might think that this would go on, but 'probably this last step is already not so rich in consequences as the earlier ones; for instead of second-level functions one can deal in further advances, with first-level functions – as shall be shown elsewhere' (1969: 41). Here Frege is alluding to the possibility, realized in *Basic Laws*, of making value-ranges do the work of functions in his philosophy of arithmetic. However, he insists, 'this does not banish from the world the difference between first-level and second-level functions, for it is not made arbitrarily, but founded deep in the nature of things' (1969: 41).

How deep it is is the purpose of the following year's 'On Concept and Object' to reveal.

We have noted that Frege explicitly argues for the identification of the reference of a sentence with its truth-value. But logically prior to the question *what* the reference of a sentence is is, of course, the question *whether* sentences have reference; equally, logically prior to the question whether the reference of a predicate is a function is the question whether predicates have reference at all. And, as Dummett has expressed the point:

> Anyone reading Frege for the first time will naturally take the notion of reference as modelled on the relation of name to bearer, since it is always as applied to proper names that it is first introduced. He will then be struck by the fact that Frege goes on to ask what constitutes the reference of a sentence and that of a predicate or of a relational or functional expression, almost always without stopping to justify the assumption that such a thing is to be ascribed to an expression of any of these types at all. The assumption that there is anything to which a sentence or predicate stands in a relation remotely analogous to that of a name to its bearer will seem at first sight absurd to him, and yet more puzzling Frege's apparent assurance that there is a unique correct way to draw the analogy. (1991b: 171)

The puzzle, as Dummett goes on to explain, can only be resolved by perceiving that the notion of reference for Frege is the notion of *semantic value*, or, a little more carefully, that the work the notion of reference does for Frege is that of the notion of semantic value.

The notion of semantic value may be understood as follows. The semantic *role* of any expression is that feature of it which goes to determine any sentence in which it occurs as true or otherwise. Such a semantic role may always be taken as an association between the expression and an entity, for even if no other suitable candidate can be found, the equivalence class of expressions having a given semantic role can always be assigned as the associated entity, and the entity so associated with an expression may be called its semantic *value*.

Given this notion of semantic value it is compelling that any expression whose occurrence in a sentence affects its truth-value, in the sense that its replacement by another expression may alter the truth-value of the whole sentence, must be ascribed a semantic value. Consequently, not only singular terms, but also functional signs, predicates and sentences themselves (since they can occur as components of more complex sentences) can be regarded unproblematically as having semantic values.

It is also unproblematic, given this conception of semantic value: (a) that the semantic value of a complex expression depends uniquely on the semantic values of its components; (b) that if a part lacks semantic value the whole lacks semantic value; and (c) that if a part of a sentence lacks a semantic value the whole sentence lacks truth-value.

Nothing follows, of course, so far, as to *what* the semantic value of any expressions are, for as Dummett expresses it, this conception of semantic value is 'wholly programmatic'. Nevertheless, as he observes (1981: 167), it is already determined by this conception at least what *type* of entity must be assigned to any incomplete expression, as its semantic value. For example, it is determined what type of entity must be assigned to a first-level one place predicate. For just what such a predicate does is to yield a sentence having a semantic value for each singular term having semantic value to which it is attached. The semantic value of a first-level one place predicate must then be represented as a one-argument function from the semantic values of singular terms to the semantic values of sentences. The same line of reasoning can be applied, *mutatis mutandis*, to each of the types of incomplete expression Frege recognizes.

We see, then, that if Frege's notion of a reference is understood in terms of the notion of semantic value, the *shape* of the resultant theory is precisely that of Frege's theory of reference: the compositionality principle for reference, the consequence that a complex expression containing a part without reference itself lacks reference, the truth-value gap thesis and the functional theory of predication all emerge straightforwardly from the identification. Furthermore, the identification explains how Frege could regard it as unproblematic to assign reference to incomplete expressions and to sentences.

However, as Dummett also makes clear, we cannot fully appreciate Frege's notion of reference if we think of it simply as the notion of semantic value. For this conception being purely programmatic, it leaves it undetermined what the semantic values of singular terms and sentences are. In fact, Frege took it for granted that the reference of a singular term was the object it designated – in the case of a proper name, ordinarily so called, its bearer, and in the case of a description the object described – and he argued, as we have seen, that the reference of a sentence must be its truth-value. But these two identifications are not required by the understanding of reference as semantic value. In fact, the opposite is rather the case. Starting simply from the conception of reference as semantic value we must regard two expressions as differing in reference if there is any sentence in which replacement of one by the other will result in a change in truth-value. But intensional contexts, of the type Frege considers in 'On Sense and Reference', e.g. belief contexts, provide examples of sentences in which replacement of one singular term by another with the same designation, or replacement of one embedded sentence by another with the same truth-value, will result in a change in truth-value. If John believes that the Evening Star is the Evening Star, but is ignorant of the identity of the Evening Star and the Morning Star, then the difference in truth-value of the two sentences

John believes that the Evening Star is the Evening Star

and

John believes that the Evening Star is the Morning Star

suffices, if we treat 'reference' as a mere synonym of 'semantic value' to show both that the two names 'the Evening Star' and 'the

Morning Star' and the two sentences 'the Evening Star is the Evening Star' and 'the Evening Star is the Morning Star' differ in reference.

Of course, Frege draws no such conclusion. His contention is rather that in such contexts there is a reference *shift*: singular terms and embedded sentences following 'believes that . . .' do not have their ordinary references – their designations and truth-values respectively – but different, indirect, references. We shall be explaining this theory of indirect reference in the next chapter. The point for now, however, is merely that the fact that Frege sets such contexts aside for special treatment, and retains his identification of the (direct) reference of a singular term with its designation and the (direct) reference of a sentence with its truth-value, shows that his notion of reference is not *merely* the notion of semantic value.

In fact, as Dummett explains (1981: 148ff.; see also Evans 1982: 8ff.), there is another ingredient in Frege's notion of reference, namely, the name/bearer relation as prototype. If we start from the conception of reference as semantic value, there is a plausible argument from the existence of intensional contexts that the reference of a proper name *cannot* be its bearer, but even if this argument is set aside, the identification is not *obvious* and stands in need of argument. Frege, however, never provides any argument. When he introduces the notion of reference he always begins with proper names and he always explains the reference of a proper name as its bearer; more generally, he explains the reference of a singular term as its designation. That the reference of a singular term is its designation is thus an assumption he makes at the outset and never questions. It is in this sense that the name/bearer relation is his prototype of reference. Intensional contexts (i.e. contexts in which singular terms with the same designation are not guaranteed to be substitutable without a change in truth-value, or *salva veritate*) are then set aside for special treatment precisely because their existence *is* otherwise in conflict with this assumption. And once they are set aside the conclusion that the reference of a sentence is its truth-value is easily derivable from the substitutability *salva veritate*, in the remaining *extensional* contexts, of sentences with the same truth-value.

Gareth Evans has called the two identifications – of the reference of a singular term with its designation and of the reference of a sentence with its truth-value – the 'two anchors' of Frege's semantic theory. And rightly, as we have seen, he has said that once these two 'anchors' are lowered, the type of entity that constitutes the semantic value (reference) of an expression of any other kind is determined. For example, if the reference of a singular term is what it designates, and the reference of a sentence is its truth-value, it follows that the semantic value of a one-place first-level predicate is a first-level concept – a function from the objects we designate with singular terms to truth-values. The references of expressions of other types are similarly determined, once the two Fregean anchors are lowered, as precisely the entities Frege assigns. However, it is important to appreciate that the two anchors are not independent; rather anchor two, the identification of the reference of a sentence with its truth-value, is secondary to anchor one, the identification of the reference of a singular term with the object it designates. Once anchor one is lowered intensional contexts must be set aside for special treatment, and then the interchangeability of sentences with the same truth-value in extensional contexts yields the conclusion that the reference of a sentence is its truth-value. So anchor one takes anchor two down with it. Moreover, the identification of the reference of a sentence with its truth-value is secondary in the sense that Frege does not assume it, but argues for it. We saw earlier how his argument, based on the compositionality principle for reference, proceeded. It should be clearer now how that argument relies also on the name/bearer prototype both for its assumption of coreferentiality of particular designations ('2⁴' and '4.4' and 'the Evening Star' and 'the Morning Star') and for its assumption that only substitutions in extensional contexts need be considered.

Once we see Frege's notion of reference as thus composed of two ingredients, the notion of semantic value and the name/bearer prototype, the puzzles it initially presents dissolve. But this is not to say that the notion thus understood is unproblematic. In fact, the contrary is the case. For it is precisely by combining the two ingredients that Frege commits himself to the conclusion that a sentence containing an empty singular term lacks truth-value. Since such a sentence, according to Frege, may express a perfectly determinate thought, this is deeply implausible, as we have already seen. Indeed, it is difficult even to understand what can be meant by a thought which is literally truth-valueless. As Evans puts the point:

here . . . we finally come to the great fault-line in Frege's mature philosophy of language. What can it mean on Frege's, or on anyone's, principles for there to be a perfectly determinate thought which simply has no truth-value? the notion of thought that Frege was intending to use had strong links with notions embedded in ordinary propositional attitude psychology – the notions of belief, knowledge, memory, information, judgement and so on. If someone understands and accepts a sentence containing an empty name, then, according to Frege, he thereby forms a belief; not a belief about language, but a belief about the world. But what sense can be made of a belief which literally has no truth-value – which is neither correct nor incorrect? (1982: 24)

Assuming the answer 'None' to Evans's final rhetorical question, we must conclude that Frege's admission of truth-valueless thoughts was mistaken. So long as it is allowed that there are singular terms which can occur in sentences which can be used to express thoughts even when they designate nothing, therefore, Frege's global identification of the semantic value of a singular term with the object it designates must be rejected. For such proper names or descriptions the most that can be said is that *when* they designate something their semantic value is determined by what they designate and when they designate nothing *that* constitutes their semantic value (so that in all cases two such singular terms will have the same semantic value just in case they have the same designation). Of course, it is open to a defender of Frege's identification to maintain that singular terms which can occur in sentences which can be used to express thoughts when they designate nothing are not expressions to which Frege's identification should be applied. Apparent counter-examples to this identification he can explain away as a result of misclassification. For example, he can say that definite descriptions, like 'Fred's wife' or 'the King of France' which Frege classified along with proper names, but for which it is utterly implausible to maintain that emptiness entails lack of semantic value, are incorrectly so classified; rather they must be grouped with quantifiers, as names of second-level concepts (this was in effect the conclusion of Russell's famous paper 'On Denoting' of 1905 (in Russell 1956)). And he can go on to say that Frege similarly misclassifies any proper names, ordinarily so called, whose occurrence in sentences which express thoughts does not require that they have a bearer. Whether any proper names, ordinarily so called, occurring in ordinary language are correctly classified by Frege will then, of course, be a matter for debate.

The point of the present discussion, however, has just been (a) to explain how it is the combination of Frege's assumption of the name/bearer relation as prototype together with his conception of reference as semantic value that leads him to the implausible conclusion that sentences containing empty singular terms must be truth-valueless, even when they express perfectly determinate thoughts; and (b) to make it clear that this conclusion can be avoided by a relatively small departure from the name/bearer prototype, namely by allowing that empty singular terms have a semantic value consisting precisely in the fact that they lack a designation. If this departure is made from Frege's position the compositionality principle for reference can still be maintained, and the identification of the reference of a non-empty singular term with the object it designates will still provide a reliable guide to what substitutions within a complex expression will leave the reference of the whole undisturbed; but from the non-existence of the *designation* of a part it will no longer be possible to infer the non-existence of a *reference* for the whole.

'On Concept and Object'

Frege ends 'Function and Concept' insisting that the difference between first-level and second-level functions 'is not made arbitrarily, but founded deep in the nature of things' (1969: 41). It is, of course, founded as deep as the difference between objects (the arguments of first-level functions) and first-level functions (the arguments of second-level functions) itself. And how deep that is it is the aim of Frege's subsequent essay 'On Concept and Object', in which he confronts the famous 'paradox of the concept *horse*', to explore.

'On Concept and Object' was written by Frege in response to Benno Kerry's criticisms of *Foundations*. Kerry had claimed, against Frege, that the distinction between concept and object was not absolute, that some entities were both concepts and objects. Frege emphatically denies this, arguing first that we must recognize a distinction between what can occur *only* as an object, and everything else, and secondly that, in fact, nothing could be both a concept and an object.

Frege argues for the first, weaker, claim by appealing to an analogy Kerry uses. Kerry had said that there was no more difficulty in the idea of an entity being simultaneously an object and a concept than there was in the idea of a man being both a father and a son. Frege retorts:

Let us fasten on this simile. If there were, or had been, things that were fathers but could not be sons, such beings would obviously be quite different in kind from men who are sons. Now it is something like this that happens here. (1969: 43)

The reason, Frege explains, is that the concept is predicative, in fact, it is the reference of a grammatical predicate. But a name of an object is quite incapable of being used as a grammatical predicate. Apparent counter-examples are statements in which one asserts that someone or something is Alexander the Great, or the planet Venus, or the number four. But Frege insists, such statements are identity statements, in which the 'is' is not the 'is' of predication, but has the sense of the relational expression 'is no other than'. Thus the proper name is not the *whole* predicate but merely part of it. In 'the Morning Star is Venus', for example, the predicate is not 'Venus' but 'is Venus', and what is predicated is not the object *Venus* but the concept *is no other than Venus*. Although this concept is one under which only one object can possibly fall, it is nevertheless still distinct from the object falling under it, i.e. the planet Venus, and this object can only ever occur as an object, never as a concept.

The distinction Frege makes here between the 'is' of identity and the 'is' of predication – which occurs in such statements as 'Venus is a planet' or 'Venus is large' – is a familiar one and widely accepted, and so far, as Frege notes, what he has argued is not particularly radical. It is part of the traditional doctrine of universals deriving from Aristotle that as well as universals, which can occur both as subjects and as predicates, there are also entities, particulars, which can occur only as subject, never as predicate.

However, Frege now goes further and denies that anything can be both a concept and an object. Immediately he runs headlong into the paradox of the concept *horse*:

Kerry ... gives the following example: 'the concept "horse" is a concept easily attained', and thinks that the concept 'horse' is an object, in fact one of the objects that fall under the concept 'concept easily attained'. Quite so; the three words 'the concept "horse"' do designate an object, but on that very account they do not designate a concept, as I am using the word. This is in full accord with the criterion I gave – that the singular definite article always indicates an object, whereas the indefinite article accompanies a concept-word. (1969: 45)

Despite the paradox, Frege defends the linguistic criterion of differentiation here indicated. As regards the indefinite article, he says, there are probably no exceptions to the rule except an obsolete formula for a Councillor ('Ein edler Rath'). In the case of the definite article, he says, the only possible exceptions are cases in which the definite article precedes a singular noun standing in the place of a plural. He considers two examples: 'The Turk besieged Vienna' and 'the horse is a four-legged animal'. In the case of the first, he says, 'the Turk' is indeed a proper name of an object – a people; in the case of the second an equivalent form is the universal judgement 'all horses are four-legged animals', which as he argues later, should be understood as asserting a relation between concepts (as is clear, of course, once the sentence is translated into Frege's conceptual notation or modern predicate logic symbolism). In fact, he goes on to say, the words 'all', 'any', 'no', 'some' are used to indicate the special kind of relation between concepts asserted in universal and particular affirmative and negative sentences. 'They are thus, logically speaking, not to be more closely associated with the concept words that follow them, but are to be related to the sentence as a whole' (1969: 48).

Thus Frege continues to insist on the absolute distinction between concept and object, recognizing only 'an awkwardness of language' if we say that the concept *horse* is not a concept. 'The concept *horse*', he here asserts, is a perfectly good proper name, but just for this reason, what it stands for is not a concept but an object. *What* object is suggested, rather coyly, in the following passage:

> If we keep it in mind that in my way of speaking expressions like 'the concept F' designate not concepts but objects, most of Kerry's objections already collapse. If he thinks . . . that I have identified concept and extension of concept, he is mistaken, I merely expressed my view that in the expression 'the number that applies to the concept F is the extension of the concept *like numbered to the concept F'* the words 'extension of the concept' could be replaced by 'concept'. Notice carefully that here the word 'concept' is combined with the definite article. (1969: 48)

Extension of concepts are objects, and thus not concepts, but if we form a phrase of the form 'the concept F', employing the definite article, the result is a proper name, a name of an object, and the object thus named is the very one named by the phrase 'the extension of the concept F'. And it is this *object* that is unintentionally spoken of when we aim to speak of the *concept* F. Thus as Frege puts it:

> I admit that there is a quite peculiar obstacle in the way of an understanding with my reader. By a kind of necessity of language, my expressions, taken literally, sometimes miss my thought: I mention an object, when what I intend is a concept. I fully realize that in such cases I was relying upon a reader who would be ready to meet me half-way – who does not begrudge a pinch of salt. (1969: 541)

Until this point in 'On Concept and Object', it must be said, Frege's insistence on accepting whatever consequences of the absolute divide between concept and object may be deduced – the paradox of the concept *horse*, the unavoidable 'awkwardness' of language, the predicament it is in whereby 'our expressions taken literally', must sometimes 'miss our thoughts' – seems more like a stubborn dogmatism than anything else. But, at last, at the end of the article Frege reveals what lies behind his insistence:

> not all the parts of a thought can be complete; at least one must be unsaturated; or predicative, otherwise they could not hold together. For example, the sense of the phrase 'the number 2' does not hold together with that of the phrase 'the concept *prime number*' without a link. We apply such a link in the sentence 'the number 2 falls under the concept *prime number*'; it is contained in the words 'falls under', which need to be completed in two ways – by a subject and an accusative, and only because this sense is thus 'unsaturated' are they capable of serving as a link. Only when they have been supplemented in this two-fold respect do we get a complete sense, a thought. I say that such words or phrases stand for a relation. We now get the same difficulty for the relation that we were trying to avoid for the concept. For the words 'the relation of an object to the concept it falls under' designate not a relation but an object; and the three proper names 'the number 2', 'the concept prime number', 'the relation of an object to a concept it falls under', hold aloof from one another just as much as the first two do by themselves; however we put them together we get no sentence. It is thus easy for us to see that the difficulty arising from the 'unsaturatedness' of one part of a thought can indeed be shifted but not avoided. 'Complete' and 'unsaturated' are, of course, only figures of speech, but all I wish or am able to do here is give hints. (1969: 55)

The problem here identified (at the level of sense because Frege's mind is full of the ideas in 'On Sense and Reference' which he has just written) is the traditional one of the unity of the proposition: what distinguishes a proposition, a sentence which expresses a thought, from a mere list of names? Frege's solution is that a sentence, unlike a list of names, exhibits patterns, which themselves have to be understood as having semantic values. Thus the sentence 'the number 2 is prime' exhibits the pattern: 'x is prime', the pattern exhibited by any sentence consisting of a proper name followed by the words 'is prime'. And it is this pattern which is the name of the concept *prime*, for it is only by recognizing a sentence as exhibiting it that we recognize it as a predication of the concept *prime* of an object. But, now, we cannot replace this pattern by the expression 'the concept *prime*' or any quotable part of a sentence. It simply makes no sense to speak of replacing a *pattern* exhibited by a sentence by a quotable *part* of a sentence. (We can replace the pattern by another, i.e. rearrange the parts, or preserving the pattern, replace some or all of the parts by other parts, but that is all.) *A fortiori* we cannot make such a replacement *salva veritate*. But it has no significance to speak of two expressions as having the same reference unless one can be substituted for the other *salva veritate*. Thus we cannot think of 'the concept *prime*', or any other quotable expression, as another (saturated) name of what is also named by the predicate 'x is prime'.

We might wish to insist that what is expressed in ordinary language by 'the number 2 is prime' is somehow more perspicuously expressed by 'the number 2 falls under the concept *prime number*'. But again, to recognize that as saying of the pair of objects, the number 2 and the concept *prime number*, that they are related by the relation *falling under* we have to recognize that sentence as exhibiting the pattern: 'x falls under y', that is, the pattern exhibited by any sentence consisting of a proper name followed by the words 'falls under' followed by a second proper name. And now we have to recognize that this pattern is not replaceable, *a fortiori* is not replaceable *salva veritate*, by 'the relation *falling under*' or any quotable part of a sentence.

The problem of the unity of the proposition is paralleled by (and for Frege is a special case of) the problem of the unity of the complex name. This explains the earlier explanatory footnote:

What I call here the predicative nature of the concept is just a special case of the need of supplementation, the 'unsaturatedness' that I gave as the essential feature of a function in my work *Funktion und Begriff*. It was then scarcely possible to avoid the expression 'the function f(x)', although here too the difficulty arose that what this expression stands for is not a function. (1969: 47)

And Frege returns to the point in the final paragraph in 'On Concept and Object':

> It may make it easier to come to an understanding if the reader compares my work *Funktion und Begriff*. For over the question what it is that is called a function in Analysis, we come up against the same obstacle; and on thorough investigation it will be found that the obstacle is essential, and founded on the nature of our language; that we cannot avoid a certain inappropriateness of linguistic expression; and there is nothing for it but to realize this and always take it into account. (1969: 55)

To see how general the problem is that Frege is concerned with let us consider again the example from 'Function and Concept': the function $2.x^3 + x$. Since we recognize

$2.1^3 + 1$

$2.4^3 + 4$

$2.5^3 + 5$

as three complex names designating the values of this function for the arguments, 1, 4, and 5 respectively, we must recognize as the function name the common element of these expressions, i.e. what is present in

$2.x^3 + x$

over and above the letter 'x', and this, of course, is the common pattern they exhibit. Thus neither '$2.x^3 + x$', nor 'the function $2.x^3 + x$', nor any quotable bit of language can be recognized as the name of the function, for no such quotable bit of language can be *substituted* for the pattern which is the function name and *a fortiori* no such quotable bit of language can be substituted for the function name leaving the reference of the whole unchanged (as identity of reference requires).

But now we can go further. 'The reference of the function-name "$2.x^3 + x$"' is itself a quotable bit of language and thus cannot have the same reference as the unsaturated function name we recognize in these complex names. If it has any reference at all, its reference must be an object, not a function. The same is true, *mutatis mutandis* of 'the reference of the predicate "x is a horse"'. These consequences follow from taking seriously the idea that function names generally and predicates, in particular, are unsaturated expressions. But if we now try to take account of the fact that it is such unsaturated expressions which refer to functions and concepts, again we must fail: the descriptions 'the reference of the function-name which is the pattern exhibited in "$2.x^3 + x$"' and 'the reference of the predicate which is the pattern exhibited in "x is a horse"' are themselves quotable bits of language and thus can only refer to objects if to anything.

Frege's 'paradox of the concept *horse*' is thus not easily dismissed. After 'Function and Concept' Frege came to think that it was a mistake to say that such expressions as 'the concept *horse*', and 'the function $2.x^3 + x$' had as their references objects which intruded whenever we wished to speak of the functions in question; rather such expressions and indeed the expressions 'concept' and 'function' themselves, are defective: 'the concept *horse*' would have to stand for a concept if it stood for anything: since it cannot, it stands for nothing. The predicates 'is a concept' and 'is a function', which are constrained by grammar to be first-level predicates, can similarly only be understood as standing for self-contradictory concepts (1979: 177–8). Nevertheless, Frege insists, the distinction between saturated and unsaturatedness remains, and with it the unbridgeable gap between objects and functions.

The conclusion we are driven to, as Dummett and Geach both explain (Dummett 1973: 245ff.; Geach 1976a), is that what Frege requires is the distinction made by Wittgenstein in the *Tractatus Logico-Philosophicus* (1961) between what can be *said*, and what can only be *shown*.

We can recognize as perfectly legitimate the first-level predicate 'x is an object'. Using this we can say of any object that it *is* an object using a sentence of the form

x is an object

in which 'x' is replaced by a proper name.

Similarly we can recognize as perfectly legitimate the second-level predicate expressible most conveniently in modern logical symbolism as: '$(\forall x)(\exists y)f(x) = y$', which is true of all and only first-level one-argument functions (given Frege's thesis that a function must be defined for all arguments). Using this second-level predicate we can say, for example, of the function $2x^3 + x$ that it is a first-level function:

$$(\forall x)(\exists y)(2x^3 + x = y)$$

Again we can recognize as perfectly legitimate the second-level function expressible as '$(\forall x)(f(x) =$ the True or $f(x) =$ the False)' true of all and only first-level concepts. Thus we can say, of the concept *horse*, for example, that it is a concept:

$$(\forall x)(x \text{ is a horse} = \text{the True or } x \text{ is a horse} = \text{the False})$$

We can proceed similarly to construct ways of saying all that can be legitimately meant by saying that a particular second-level function is a second-level function, or that a particular first-level relation is a first-level relation and so on.

But what we cannot do is to construct any legitimate way of saying that a particular object is *not* a first-level function, or that a particular first-level function is *not* an object – and so on.

'$(\forall x)(\exists y)(2x^3 + x = y)$' says, in the only way that it can be legitimately said, that the function $2x^3 + x$ is a function. '$\neg(\forall x)(\exists y)(2x^3 + x = y)$' says, falsely, that the function $2.x^3 + x$ is not a function. To say that Socrates, say, is not a function we must substitute a proper name of Socrates for the first-level function name occurring in '$\neg(\forall x)(\exists y)(2.x^3 + x = y)$' whereby we speak of the function $2x^3 + x$. But since the function name is unsaturated and any name of Socrates saturated such a substitution is impossible – that is, there is nothing which could *count* as such a substitution. So we cannot say, truly, of Socrates that he is not a function. *Mutatis mutandis* we cannot say, truly, of the function $2x^3 + x$ that it is not an object, for to do so we would have to substitute a name of the function for the name of Socrates in the false proposition 'Socrates is not an object', but this would be the impossible substitution of an unsaturated expression for a saturated expression.

Nevertheless, though we cannot *say* that Socrates is not a function and that the function $2x^3 + x$ is not an object, we can *recognize* that these things are so, and that they are so is something that, to use Wittgenstein's language, '*shows* forth and grasp of which will be manifested by proper use of a well-constructed formalized language such as that of the *Begriffsschrift*' (Geach 1976a: 55).

Paradoxical though this conclusion is, it appears that, as Frege puts it, it is founded 'deep in the nature of things'. But we must understand that this is *not* to say that it is grounded on something other than the nature of language; rather, it is precisely because the distinction between saturated and unsaturated *expressions* is the necessary origin of our grasp of the distinction between objects and functions that the Fregean paradox is unavoidable.

5
Theory of Meaning

The Distinction between Sense and Reference

In the last chapter we were concerned with Frege's notion of reference – the relation between the first and third levels in the diagram Frege sketched in his letter to Husserl (see p. 133). Now we must turn to his notion of sense and the relations between the first level and the second and the second level and the third. The need for an intermediate level, the need, that is, for the distinction between sense and reference, was not recognized by Frege when he wrote *Conceptual Notation* and *Foundations*, as we have seen. In that period he operated with an undifferentiated notion of 'content'. However, the distinction is present in 'Function and Concept' where it is employed in Frege's argument for the identification of the reference of a sentence with its truth-value, and it receives its fullest exposition and defence in 'On Sense and Reference', written simultaneously and published in the following year. Before turning to this, however, it is worthwhile to glance back at the diagram from the letter to Husserl and note several points, once controversial, which it makes clear. The first is that Frege intends the distinction between sense and reference to apply to predicates (and other incomplete expressions) as well as to singular terms and sentences. Secondly, the diagram makes it clear that Frege thought of the concepts as the references, not the senses, of predicates. Thirdly, it reveals, by their omission from it, the indirectness of the relation Frege thought of as obtaining between predicates and their extensions. And finally it indicates the precise parallelism Frege thought to obtain between the relations between a singular term, its sense and its reference and those between a predicate, its sense and its reference. Thus, while Frege's arguments for the necessity of the distinction between sense and reference usually relate to the case of singular terms rather than to that of predicates, his diagram makes it clear that they must be understood as applicable across the board.

A helpful summary of his notion of sense is given by Frege in a letter he wrote to Philip Jourdain around 1914:

Let us suppose an explorer travelling in an unexplained country sees a high snowcapped mountain on the northern horizon. By making inquiries among the natives he learns that its name is 'Afla'. By sighting it from different parts he determines its position as exactly as possible, enters it in a map, and writes in his diary: 'Afla is at least 5,000 metres high.' Another explorer sees a snowcapped mountain on the southern horizon and learns that it is called Ateb. He enters it on his map under that name. Later comparison shows that both explorers saw the same mountain. Now the content of the proposition 'Ateb is Afla' is far from being a mere consequence of the principle of identity, but contains a valuable piece of geographical knowledge. What is stated in the proposition 'Ateb is Afla' is certainly not the same thing as the content of the proposition 'Ateb is Ateb'. Now if what corresponded to the name 'Afla' as part of the thought was the reference of the name, and hence the mountain itself, then this would be the same in both thoughts. The thought expressed in the proposition 'Ateb is Afla' would have to coincide with the one in 'Ateb is Ateb', which is far from being the case. What corresponds to the name 'Ateb' as part of the thought must therefore be different from what corresponds to the name 'Afla' as part of the thought. This therefore cannot be the reference, which is the same for both names, but must be something which is different in the two cases, and I say accordingly that the sense of the name 'Ateb' is different from the sense of the name 'Afla'. Accordingly, the sense of the proposition 'Ateb is at least 5,000 metres high' is also different from the sense of the proposition 'Afla is at least 5,000 metres high'. Someone who takes the latter to be true need not therefore take the former to be true. An object can be determined in different ways. We find this in astronomy in the case of planetoids and comets. Now if the sense of a name was something subjective, then the sense of the proposition in which the name occurs, and hence the thought, would also be something subjective, and the thought one man connects with this proposition would be different from the thought another man connects with it; a common store of thoughts, a common science, would be impossible. It would be impossible for what one man said to contradict what another man said, because the two would not express the same thought at all but each his own. For these reasons I believe that the sense of a name is not something subjective [*crossed out*: in one's mental life], that it does not therefore belong to psychology and is indispensable. (1997: 320–1)

In the latter part of this passage Frege emphasizes an aspect of thoughts (and senses generally) which he regards as crucial, but which is also, as we shall see, problematic for him: thoughts are objective and shareable, and do not belong to psychology. Acts of thinking are, of course, psychological events. But two acts of thinking, by the same person at different times, or by different people, may have the same content: each may be a thinking *that p*. Thoughts are not acts of thinking but the contents of such acts, and, Frege insists, all such contents can be shared.

However, what is presently of most interest is the argument Frege gives here for the distinction between sense and reference. In short, the argument is that the distinction is necessary to resolve the *puzzle of identity*. The puzzle of identity is that a proposition asserting identity can be both true and informative, since it may be understood without being known to be true. The Fregean resolution of the puzzle, appealing to the sense/reference distinction, is that a proposition asserting identity will be *true* if the singular terms flanking the sign of identity have the same reference, but will be *informative* if the terms have different senses – different ways of 'determining' the common reference, or, as Frege alternatively expresses it in 'On Sense and Reference', two different 'modes of presentation' of the reference – so that it need not be known to be true by someone who understands it.

This argument for the sense/reference first appears in 'On Sense and Reference' where Frege recalls his earlier discussion in *Conceptual Notation*. There also Frege had spoken of different ways of 'determining' a 'content', and had operated with a tripartite distinction between (a) a sign, (b) its content, and (c) a way of determining that content. But he had at the same time regarded an identity proposition as being a proposition *about* the signs flanking the sign: one asserting *of* the signs that they had the same content. It is this feature of his earlier discussion which Frege now corrects. He writes:

EQUALITY gives rise to challenging questions which are not altogether easy to answer. Is it a relation? A relation between objects or between names or signs of objects? In my *Begriffsschrift* I assumed the latter. The reasons which seem to favour this are the following: a = a and a = b are obviously statements of different cognitive value: a = a holds *a priori* and, according to Kant is to be labelled analytic, while statements of the form a = b often contain very valuable extensions of our knowledge, and cannot always be established *a priori*. The discovery that the rising sun is not new every morning, but always the same, was one of the most fertile astronomical discoveries. Even today the identification of a small planet or a comet is not always a matter of course. Now if we were to regard equality as a relation between that which the names 'a' and 'b' designate [*bedeuten*], it would seem that a = b could not differ from a = a (i.e. provided a = b is true). A relation would thereby be expressed of a thing to itself, and indeed one in which each thing stands to itself but to no other thing. What is intended to be said by a = b seems to be that the signs or names 'a' and 'b' [*bedeuten*] designate the same thing, so that those signs themselves would be under discussion; a relation between them would be asserted. But this relation would hold between the names or signs only in so far as they named or designated something. It would be mediated by the connection of each of the two signs with the same designated thing. But this is arbitrary. Nobody can be forbidden to use an arbitrarily producible event or object as a sign for something. In that case the sentence a = b would no longer refer to the subject matter, but only to its mode of designation: we would express no proper knowledge by its means. But, in many cases, this is just what we want to do. If the sign 'a' is distinguished from the sign 'b' only as an object (here, by means of its shape), not as sign (i.e. not by the manner in which it designates something), the cognitive value of a = a becomes essentially equal to that of a = b, provided a = b is true. A difference can arise only if the difference between the signs corresponds to a difference in the mode of presentation of that which is designated. . . . It is natural, now, to think of there being connected with a sign (name, combination of words, letter), besides that to which the sign refers, which may be called the reference of the sign, also what I should like to call the *sense* of the sign, wherein the mode of presentation is contained. . . . The reference of 'Evening Star' would be the same as that of 'Morning Star', but not the sense. (1969: 57)

Frege's reasoning in this passage is somewhat obscure; but the general drift of the argument is evident enough. Frege takes the puzzle of identity to pose a problem for the view that identity is a relation. For if 'a = b' is true, a *is* b, so how can the two sides of the statement of identity differ in a way that is compatible with its informativeness? If identity is a relation between objects it seems that only the objects named by 'a' and 'b' can be relevant to the informativeness of the statement, but then if a *is* b how can it differ in 'cognitive value' from 'a = a'? Previously Frege took this as indicating that a statement of identity was not a statement of a relation between *objects* but a statement of a relation between *names* of objects. And at first sight it looks as if this might yield a solution to the puzzle, since *different* signs appear on the two sides of 'a = b', while the *same* sign appears on the two sides of 'a = a'. But now, Frege says, he no longer wishes to take this view, for if 'a = b' were merely a statement about the names 'a' and 'b' it would express no proper knowledge since 'nobody can be forbidden to use any arbitrarily producible event or object as a sign for something'. This is, perhaps, somewhat difficult to understand, but I think it is possible to see what Frege is getting at. If 'a = b' is a statement about the names 'a' and 'b' it can only mean that there is something which is named both 'a' and 'b'. But if this is not true one can *make* it true simply by stipulating that henceforth one will use 'b' as a name for a. Then it *will* be true that there is something named both 'a' and 'b'. But what was *originally* claimed, when it was first said that a = b, could not be made true by such a stipulation, since this was not merely that the signs 'a' and 'b' designated the same object, but, contrary to Frege's earlier view, a claim about the objects themselves. And so the puzzle as to how it can be both true and informative remains.

In fact, one can see independently of Frege's argument that the puzzle of identity could not possibly be explained by differences between the signs flanking the identity symbol considered, as Frege puts it, 'only as objects not as signs'. For such a difference is neither necessary nor sufficient for a true identity statement to be informative.

It is not sufficient because two singular terms with the same reference might have, in the ordinary English sense, the same meaning. Recalling that definite descriptions are singular terms makes this obvious. 'The oldest unmarried man in Britain' and 'the oldest bachelor in Britain' are synonymous. Hence the identity statement 'the oldest unmarried man in Britain is the oldest bachelor in Britain' is uninformative to anyone who understands it even though the signs flanking the symbol of identity differ 'as objects', i.e. have different spellings.

Furthermore, it is not necessary for the informativeness of a true identity statement that the signs flanking the symbol of identity be different. In Frege's example of the mountain Afla/Ateb it is quite inessential that the native communities the two explorers encounter have different names for the mountain. Suppose that quite coincidentally they do not, that both communities (the Northsiders and the Southsiders) call the mountain 'Ateb'. However, the communities have no contact or even any knowledge of one another. Then if the two explorers meet and converse about 'Ateb' there might be, but will at most be, an illusion of common understanding until they compare notes and realize that they visited quite different native communities. And when it is subsequently realized that the two explorers after all viewed the same mountain this new information will be reportable, in a suitable context, with the true identity statement 'Ateb is Ateb'. Again, suppose we are observing a ship, the middle of which is obscured by some tall building. You know that there is just one (very long) ship. I think that there are two ships of which only the stern of one and the prow of the other are observable. You can enlighten me by saying 'that ship' (pointing left) 'is that ship' (pointing right). Here again the informativeness of the identity statement is not due to any differences (considered as objects) in the signs flanking the symbol of identity (see also Perry 1977: 483; Evans 1982: 84; McCulloch 1989: 199ff.).

So an identity statement can be informative whether or not the sign on the left is the same as the sign on the right. Neither the sign nor the reference is crucial, but rather the *sense*, the mode of presentation of the reference, which must, therefore, be different in the case of two signs flanking the identity symbol in an informative identity statement.

We can expose more of the structure of this argument of Frege's by running through it once again using his example of the Morning Star/the Evening Star. The argument proceeds as follows:

(1) 'The Evening Star = The Evening Star' and 'The Evening Star = The Morning Star' differ in cognitive value (the puzzle of identity).

(2) The sense of 'The Evening Star = The Evening Star' is not the same as the sense of 'The Evening Star = The Morning Star'.

(3) The sense of 'The Evening Star' is not the same as the sense of 'The Morning Star'.

(4) The reference of 'The Evening Star' is the same as the reference of 'The Morning Star'.

(5) The sense of 'The Evening Star' is not the same as the reference of 'The Evening Star' (*mutatis mutandis* for 'The Morning Star').

(1) is the fundamental fact from which the argument proceeds. (2) follows from (1) given Frege's understanding of the notion of the sense of a sentence (a thought) as a cognitive notion, constrained by what Gareth Evans (1982: 18) has called 'The Intuitive Criterion of Difference' for thoughts: if it is possible for a thinker to assent to what is expressed (in a given context) by S and dissent from what is expressed (in the same context) by S', the sense of S (in the context) is different from the sense of S' (in the context). (3) follows from (2) given a compositionality principle for sense structurally identical with Frege's compositionality principle for reference: the sense of a complex expression is a function of (is wholly determined by) the senses of its parts. (4) follows from the fact that 'the Evening Star' and 'the Morning Star' are two designations of the planet Venus given that the notion of reference is constrained by the requirement that identity of designation entails identity of reference (which does not require, as we saw in the last chapter, that the reference of a singular term be *identified* with its designation). And (5), Frege's conclusion, follows from (3) and (4) (or rather, what strictly follows from (3) and (4) is the *disjunction* of (5) and the corresponding proposition about 'the Morning Star', but since there is no possible ground for regarding the two names differently, from (3) and (4) we must conclude that in the case of *each* name its sense differs from its reference).

An equivalent formulation of the argument for the distinction between sense and reference can be given by considering what, on Fregean principles, should be the result of substituting one codesignating singular term for another within the context of propositional attitude constructions. Such constructions, like '... believes that ...', '... knows that ...', '... wonders whether ...', take singular terms in their first slot and sentences in their second. The resultant sentences make psychological ascriptions. For example:

> John believes that snow is white
> Everyone knows that grass is green
> The Queen of England wonders whether the sky is blue

The embedded sentences in such ascriptions, may, of course, contain singular terms, as in the three examples above, or as in:

> All astronomers know that the Morning Star is the Evening Star

Now given the compositionality principle for reference, Frege is committed to holding that substitution of one coreferential singular term for another in a sentence cannot affect the truth-value of the whole sentence. So he appears to be committed to the universal validity of the inference schema (usually called Leibniz's Law)

> Fa
> a = b
> *Ergo* Fb

where 'Fa' contains one or more occurrences of a singular term 'a' and 'Fb' is the result of replacing one or all of these occurrences by 'b'.

However, substitution of codesignating names within propositional attitude constructions appears to yield counter-examples to this schema. In fact, this is an immediate consequence of Frege's observation that 'The Evening Star is the Evening Star' and 'The Evening Star is the Morning Star' differ in cognitive value. For this is just to say that someone can know that the Evening Star is the Evening Star without knowing that the Evening Star is the Morning Star, even though the Evening Star *is* the Morning Star. That is, it is just to say that the inference

> John knows that the Evening Star is the Evening Star
> The Evening Star is the Morning Star
> *Ergo* John knows that the Evening Star is the Morning Star

is invalid.

But using only the resources of his theory of reference, Frege cannot explain this invalidity. Since the names 'The Evening Star' and 'The Morning Star' are codesignative, as required by the truth of the identity statement which is the argument's second premiss, they are coreferential. Hence, given the compositionality principle for reference, either can replace the other in any sentence without changing the truth-value of the whole, or *salva veritate.* Thus substitution *must* preserve truth-value. To put the point another way. In 'John knows that the Evening Star is the Evening Star' we can discern a predicate 'John knows that the Evening Star is ( )', whose reference is a concept, i.e. a function from objects to truth-values. Using only the resources of his theory of reference Frege must say that 'John knows that the Evening Star is the Evening Star' is the result of completing this function name with the proper name 'the

Evening Star' whose reference is the Evening Star, i.e. the Morning Star. But since the value of a function for an argument does not depend on what the argument is called, 'John knows that the Evening Star is the Evening Star' and 'John knows that the Evening Star is the Morning Star', thought of in this way as completed function names, must have the same reference, i.e. the same truth-value.

The point can be argued still more directly by considering replacement of the whole sentence 'The Evening Star is the Evening Star' by 'The Morning Star is the Evening Star'. Given Frege's compositionality principle for reference, these two sentences must have the same reference. Therefore, appealing to the compositionality principle for reference a second time, substitution of the latter for the former in 'John knows that the Evening Star is the Evening Star' cannot change the truth-value of the whole. Once again, using only the resources of Frege's theory of reference, we are unable to explain the invalidity of what is, nonetheless, an evidently invalid form of argument.

The conclusion, then, must be that the resources of Frege's theory of reference are inadequate. There must be a feature over and above reference possessed by singular terms and sentences which accounts for the invalidity of these forms of argument. That feature, of course, is precisely what Frege means by 'sense'.

This argument for the distinction between sense and reference can be generalized to yield the conclusion that the distinction must be made for all expressions. Given *any* two sentences with the same truth-value differing in cognitive value but built up in the same way from corresponding components all of which have the same reference, the argument can be applied. Thus 'Socrates is a rational animal is true if and only if Socrates is a rational animal' differs in cognitive value from 'Socrates is a rational animal if and only if Socrates is a featherless biped' but (on the usual assumption that all and only rational animals are featherless bipeds) 'is a rational animal' has the same reference as 'is a featherless biped'. To explain the difference in cognitive values we must therefore postulate a difference between the sense and reference of the predicate 'is a rational animal'. The same form of argument can be applied to function names generally, whatever the type of their arguments and whatever the type of their values.

The argument starting from the puzzle of identity is Frege's main argument for the sense/reference distinction. However a subsidiary argument, which is at least implicit in 'On Sense and Reference', starts from the existence in natural languages of empty singular terms. Before drawing the distinction Frege was forced to maintain that an empty singular term occurring in a sentence rendered the whole meaningless:

> A sentence can be true or untrue only if it is an expression for a thought. The sentence 'Leo Sachse is a man' is the expression of a thought only if 'Leo Sachse' designates something. And so too the sentence 'this table is round' is the expression of a thought only if the words 'this table' are not empty sounds but designate something specific for me. (1979: 174)

Again:

> The rules of logic always presuppose that the words we use are not empty, that our sentences express judgements, that one is not playing a mere game with words. Once 'Sachse is a man' expresses an actual judgement, the word 'Sachse' must designate something, and in that case I do not need a further premiss in order to infer 'there are men' from it. (1969: 60)

However, this position is deeply implausible, as examples used by Frege himself in 'On Sense and Reference' make evident. 'The least rapidly convergent series' is a description which demonstrably has no designation, since for every convergent series another convergent but less rapidly convergent series can be found. But this is not a trivial mathematical fact. Hence, a mathematically uninformed person could certainly wonder whether there was such a thing as the least rapidly convergent series, or whether a particular series S was the least rapidly convergent, or whether the least rapidly convergent series had yet been discovered. But that is just to say that such a sentence as 'series S is the least rapidly convergent series' is not mere *noise* but has a meaning which cannot be accounted for using Frege's notion of reference alone. Moreover, unless I myself have just descended into error, sentences in which such empty definitions occur can have not only a meaning, but also a truth-value. For example, this is true of the sentence 'a mathematically uninformed reader could certainly wonder whether there was such a thing as the least rapidly convergent series', which has the truth-value True.

Even if we restrict our attention to proper names in the strict sense it seems plausible that such names can be empty without rendering any sentence in which they occur meaningless. To use another of Frege's examples, we do not know whether Homer's tales are woven out of whole cloth or based on distant historical fact (the same is true of the tales of King Arthur and Robin Hood). It is therefore at best doubtful whether the name 'Odysseus' has a reference. Suppose it does not. Nevertheless, the sentence 'Odysseus was set ashore on Ithaca while sound asleep' is not meaningless. We can understand it. Moreover, we can imagine a (no doubt somewhat eccentric) classical scholar who as a result of years of research arrived at the conclusion that Odysseus really existed and that, though very little reported of him was true, in fact he *was* set ashore on Ithaca while sound asleep.

To maintain that empty singular terms always render sentences in which they occur meaningless is thus not at all plausible. And so Frege has another argument for the distinction between sense and reference. Expressions without reference are not necessarily meaningless; they possess some feature, even in the absence of a reference, which enables sentences in which they occur to be used significantly and even (as we saw in the case of 'the least rapidly convergent series') to say something true. That feature is their sense.

But what is sense? So far we know only (a) that it is a cognitive notion, i.e. something postulated to explain differences in cognitive value in the absence of differences in reference; (b) that its presence is to yield an explanation of the invalidity of arguments proceeding by substituting codesignating names into propositional attitude contexts; (c) that it is governed by Evans's Intuitive Criterion of Difference for thoughts (the sense of sentences) and by a compositionality principle structurally identical to Frege's compositionality principle for reference; and (d) that it can be possessed in the absence of reference.

In the passage containing the discussion of Afla and Ateb Frege speaks of the sense of an expression as a 'mode of determination' of its reference. In 'On Sense and Reference' he speaks of it as a 'mode of presentation' of its reference, and elsewhere he speaks of different senses as illuminating the reference from different sides. Dispensing with these metaphors the easiest approach to the notion of sense (suggested and developed by Evans 1982: 14ff.) is to think of it as a *way of thinking of* something, a way of thinking of something *as* something. Thus I can think of the Evening Star *as* the Evening Star, or as the Morning Star, or as the planet Venus, or as the heavenly body most often referred to by philosophers writing about Frege. All these are different ways of thinking of one and the same object. In each case it is a matter of thinking of the object as the unique one satisfying a certain *condition*. If something satisfies the condition then it is determined as the reference associated with that sense, i.e. that way of thinking. Thus, when I think of an object as 'The Evening Star' I think of it as the object uniquely satisfying the condition 'occurring at such and such a place and time in the night sky'. Which object does satisfy that condition is in this case a matter of astronomical investigation to find out, and it may be open to doubt, before such an investigation has been carried out, whether *anything* (uniquely) satisfies it. In other cases the condition by way of which a thing is thought of may be one whose satisfaction is a matter of historical investigation: for example, if I think of a (possibly non-existent) person as 'the hero of Homer's *Odyssey* and the son of Laertes and Antikleia'. Or I may think of an object as the satisfier of a mathematical condition, e.g. as being the least convergent series, or the greatest prime, and then it will require a mathematical investigation to determine which object, if any, is the reference.

This way of identifying a sense – as a way of thinking of something *as* the satisfier of a certain condition – fits well with Frege's own infrequent specifications. Thus, in a footnote in 'On Sense and Reference', in which he is illustrating the imperfections of ordinary language, he writes:

> In the case of an actual proper name such as 'Aristotle' opinions as to the sense may differ. It might, for instance, be taken to be the following: the pupil of Plato and teacher of Alexander the Great. Anybody who does this will attach another sense to the sentence 'Aristotle was born in Stagira' than will a man who takes as the sense of the name: the teacher of Alexander the Great, who was born in Stagira. So long as the reference remains the same, such variations of sense may be tolerated, although they are to be avoided in the theoretic structure of a demonstrative science. (1969: 58)

In this passage Frege specifies by description the different conditions corresponding to the different senses associated with the name 'Aristotle' by different users. However, as has been stressed by Dummett (1973 and 1981) and Evans (1982) there is no need to assume that every way of thinking of an object must be via some descriptive condition, and there is not the slightest reason to think that Frege thought otherwise (as sometimes suggested, see Perry 1977, 1979). It is obvious that if anything can be thought of descriptively some things must be thought of non-descriptively if we are to have any reason to believe that any of our descriptions are uniquely satisfied. I can formulate a purely general condition like: being the first dog ever born at sea, but I can have no good reason to suppose that it is (uniquely) satisfied (Russell 1956; Strawson 1959). In fact, we identify things by relating them, directly or indirectly, to *ourselves*. We think of the Sun, for example, as the star nearest to *us* in the heavens, or as that which is the source of light and heat to the planet on which *we* live (Dummett 1981: 85). But we do not, and could not, without circularity identity *ourselves* descriptively. All this is completely evident and was doubtless so to Frege. Nevertheless, he applies the sense/reference distinction not just to proper names and descriptions, but also to pronouns, and, in particular, to 'I', in connection with which he says in his late paper 'Thoughts' (1984: 359), 'everyone is presented to himself in a special and primitive way, in which he is presented to no one else.' Thus, despite the fact that when he attempts to *specify* a sense Frege invariably does so via a *descriptively* identified condition, we must not suppose that he thought that sense *must* be descriptive, and in so far as modern critics assume this they are attacking a straw man.

Nevertheless, if Frege's notion of sense is explained via the notion of a way of thinking, as proposed by Evans, there is an assumption being made which can be questioned. This is the assumption that one cannot think of an object without thinking of it in a particular way, *as* the object presented in a particular way. That is to say, if one thinks of an object there must be an answer to the question *how* one thinks of it, an account of that in virtue of which one's thought is a thought about *that* object (Evans 1982: 20). The alternative, that one can think of an object without there being *any* answer to the question how one thinks of it, is precisely the thesis to which Frege is opposed; it is the thesis that we require no *cognitive* notion such as sense to explain reference. And as we shall see later, it is this contention which is at the heart of the most profound contemporary challenge to Fregean sense – that of Saul Kripke's 'Naming and Necessity' (1972).

With the understanding of the notion of sense now developed, we can reconsider the puzzles which motivated Frege's distinction, and assess how far we have travelled towards a resolution.

Intuitively, we now have a quite satisfying answer to the puzzle of identity. 'The Evening Star' is associated with a way of thinking of its reference as the satisfier of the condition: 'the object present at such and such a place and such and such a time in the night sky';

'The Morning Star' is associated with a way of thinking of its reference as: 'the object present at such and such a time and such and such a place in the morning sky'. Thus, when I think that the Evening Star is the Evening Star I merely think that the object satisfying the former condition is the object satisfying the former condition, but when I think that the Evening Star is the Morning Star, I do something very different, I think *of* the same object in two ways, *as* the object satisfying the former condition and as the object satisfying the latter condition, and I think that it is one and the same object which satisfies the two conditions.

Again, our present understanding of the notion of sense provides an intuitively quite satisfying account of the examples which were persuasive against Frege's proposal in *Conceptual Notation* that identity statements are statements about names. We saw that an identity statement might be uninformative even when the terms flanking the identity symbol were different, as in the example 'the oldest unmarried man in Britain is the oldest bachelor in Britain', and could be informative even if the terms were the same, as in the examples 'Ateb is Ateb' and 'that ship is that ship', in the context we imagined. The explanation of these facts can now be put as follows. The descriptions 'the oldest unmarried man in Britain' and 'the oldest bachelor in Britain', being synonymous, are associated with the same way of thinking of their reference. On the other hand, the name 'Ateb' as used by the first explorer is associated with a different way of thinking of its reference from that associated with the name 'Ateb' as used by the second explorer. The first explorer thinks of Ateb as: the mountain to be reached by a journey of such and such a length to the North; the second explorer thinks of Ateb as: the mountain to be reached by a journey of such and such a length to the South. Consequently the thought expressed by 'Ateb is Ateb' when the name is first used in the former sense and then in the latter, is the thought that these two distinct conditions are satisfied by one and the same object – something which is, indeed, a valuable extension of geographical knowledge. Again, when one learns that 'that ship' (pointing right) is 'that ship' (pointing left), what one learns is that the object one is thinking of in one way (as lying at a certain distance and direction) is the object one is thinking of in a second way (as lying in a different distance and direction).

The puzzle about the meaningfulness of empty singular terms can also now be given an initially intuitively satisfying answer. If the name 'Odysseus', say, has associated with it, as its sense, that way of thinking of an object which is thinking of it as the satisfier of the condition: the hero of Homer's *Odyssey* and the son of Laertes and Antikleia, then since one can grasp that condition, and appreciate what it would be for a person to satisfy it, even if no one does satisfy it, one can understand, via that appreciation, sentences containing the name 'Odysseus'. And ascriptions of propositional attitude such as 'That old professor thinks that Odysseus really existed and was set ashore on Ithaca while sound asleep' can even be true; for given that the embedded sentences 'about' Odysseus ('Odysseus really existed' and 'Odysseus was set ashore on Ithaca while sound asleep') have sense, i.e. express thoughts, such thoughts can be assented to or dissented from, and, therefore, an ascription of propositional attitude which records correctly that someone assents to them will be true.

However, as we have already noted in the last chapter, although by thus appealing to the distinction between sense and reference Frege is able to deny that empty singular terms render all sentences containing them meaningless, the position he achieves is still highly unsatisfactory. For since he never abandons the identification of the reference of a singular term with its designation, and continues to cleave to the compositionality principle for reference, he has to say that such a sentence as 'Odysseus was set ashore on Ithaca while sound asleep' (in which the name 'Odysseus' does not occur within a propositional attitude construction) has no truth-value at all, i.e. is incapable of semantic evaluation. And he must say the same of any truth-functionally complex sentence containing that sentence as a component. Again, though he can acknowledge that both 'Odysseus existed' and 'Odysseus never existed' have sense, he must say that neither sentence has a truth-value. And he is committed to saying the same of any sentence containing an empty description such as 'the least rapidly convergent series'.

That, despite his clear pronouncement in 'On Sense and Reference' that 'in grasping a sense, one is certainly not assured of referring to anything' (1969: 58), Frege remained uneasy about his (in reality untenable) position on empty singular terms is plausibly indicated, as Evans (1982: 28ff.) points out, by his way of speaking of such terms as 'mock' proper names, and of a sentence containing such a term as expressing a 'mock thought' ('Scheingedanke'):

> Names that fail to fulfil the usual role of a proper name, which is to name something, may be called mock proper names. Although the

tale of William Tell is a legend and not history, and the name 'William Tell' is a mock proper name, we cannot deny it a sense. But the sense of the sentence 'William Tell shot an apple off his son's head' is no more true than is that of the sentence 'William Tell did not shoot an apple off his son's head.' I do not say that this sense is false either, but I characterize it as fictitious . . . Instead of speaking about fiction we could speak of 'mock thoughts'. Thus, if the sense of an assertoric sentence is not true, it is either false or fictitious, and it will generally be the latter, if it contains a mock proper name. [*Footnote:* We have an exception where a mock proper name occurs within a clause in indirect speech.] Assertions in fiction are not to be taken seriously, they are only mock assertions. Even the thoughts are not to be taken seriously as in the sciences: they are only mock thoughts. If Schiller's *Don Carlos* were to be regarded as a piece of history, then to a large extent the drama would be false. But a work of fiction is not meant to be taken seriously in this way at all: it is all play. Even the proper names in the drama, though they correspond to names of historical personages, are mock proper names: they are not to be taken seriously in the work . . .

The logician does not have to bother with mock thoughts, just as a physicist, who sets out to investigate thunder, will not pay any attention to stage-thunder. When we speak of thoughts in what follows we mean thoughts proper, thoughts that are either true or false. (1979: 130)

However, too much cannot be made of this passage for the interpretation of Frege's views at the time of 'On Sense and Reference', both because of its probable date (1897) and because its translation (in particular, the translation of 'Scheingedanke' as 'mock thought') is disputable (Bell 1990). Frege's explicit position on empty singular terms in 'On Sense and Reference' is that they do have sense and sentences containing them do express thoughts, but that the possibility of constructing such expressions in natural language:

arises from an imperfection of language, from which even the symbolic language of mathematical analysis is not altogether free; even there combinations of symbols can occur that seem to stand for something but have (at least so far) no reference, e.g. divergent infinite series. (1969: 70)

No! this is the beauty of language

In a logically perfect language there must be no such possibility. Hence:

A logically perfect language (*Begriffsschrift*) should satisfy the conditions, that every expression grammatically well constructed as a proper name out of signs already introduced shall in fact designate an object, and that no new sign shall be introduced as a proper name without being secured a reference. (1969: 76)

In such a language: 'it could never depend upon the truth of a thought whether a proper name had reference' (1969: 70).

But how could this be guaranteed? Frege explains that it can be done by special stipulations – for example, the sign for the limit of a divergent infinite series can be stipulated to stand for the number 0, and similarly, compound proper names constructed from the expression for a concept with the help of the singular definite article can be stipulated to stand for 0 if there is not a unique thing falling under the concept. Now, stipulation of this kind can guarantee that Frege's condition on proper names in a logically perfect language is fulfilled (i.e. that their having reference does not depend on the truth of any thought) only if (to take the second example) it is *necessary* that *either* just one thing falls under the concept whose expression occurs in the compound proper name *or* something is (i.e. is identical with) the number 0. For if this disjunctive claim is not necessary then the stipulation's fixing a reference for the proper name will depend upon a certain possibility's not being the case, i.e. it will depend upon the truth of the thought which excludes that possibility. The form of the disjunctive claim in question here is the following: 'Either just one thing is F or just one thing is G.' And, in general, a stipulation of the kind Frege suggests will guarantee a reference for a name independently of the truth of any thought only if some disjunctive claim of this form is necessarily true. Now if there were no necessarily existent objects, that is, no objects whose existence does not depend on the truth of any thought (as presumably the existence of 0 does not) this would entail that yet another condition would have to be fulfilled if stipulations of the Fregean kind were to be sure to guarantee reference, namely that some disjunctive claim of *this* form be necessarily true: 'Either there is some unique, contingently existent object, which is F, or there is some unique, contingently existent object, which is G.' But it seems most implausible that any such claim could be necessarily true (it would entail, after all, that there *are* contingently existent objects, and this itself does not seem necessarily true), and it seems unlikely that Frege would have wished to argue to the contrary. But, if not, then the possibility of Fregean stipulations of reference guaranteeing reference independently of what thoughts are true depends upon the existence of necessarily existent objects. So if such stipulations are the only way reference can be guaranteed (and Frege never suggests another, even in *Basic Laws*) it follows that the possibility of a logically perfect language depends upon the existence of necessarily existent things (and a logically perfect language is just one, remember, none of whose sentences exhibit truth-value gaps or potential truth-value gaps – it is only because the possibility of empty names brings the latter with it that Frege regards it as an *imperfection* of natural language). It further follows that all the names in a logically perfect language have to be *capable* of naming necessarily existent objects, i.e. will name them if certain possibilities in fact obtain.

That Frege's position on empty names thus involves such a commitment (given that he thinks that a logically perfect language is not merely an unrealizable ideal) is surely further evidence, if any is needed, that his failure to distinguish the two ingredients in the notion of reference – the name/bearer paradigm and the concept of semantic value – is an error. The truth surely is that there can be (because there are) perfectly good proper names (i.e. ones whose presence in a language is not an indication of any imperfection or incoherence) which are names of contingently existent objects and, given their senses, could not be otherwise. The problem for a sympathizer with Frege is just how to accommodate this truth within a Fregean framework.

In summary, then, we have now seen how Frege's introduction of the sense/reference distinction provides an intuitively satisfying resolution of the puzzle with which he mainly motivates it – the puzzle of identity – and provides an initially intuitively satisfying, but ultimately unsatisfactory resolution of the subsidiary puzzle about empty singular terms.

Indirect Reference

However, we must now look more clearly at the puzzle of identity to see exactly *how* the appeal to the sense/reference distinction can resolve it. And in order to do so we must attend to the second formulation of the puzzle, in terms of the failure of substitutivity *salva veritate* in propositional attitude contexts of codesignating singular terms and sentences with the same truth-value.

As we saw, the inference from

(1) John knows that the Evening Star is the Evening Star

and

(2) The Evening Star is the Morning Star

to

(3) John knows that the Evening Star is the Morning Star

must be valid if (a) Frege's compositionality principle for reference is correct, (b) the reference of 'The Evening Star', is the reference of 'The Morning Star', and (c) the sentence 'John knows that the Evening Star is the Evening Star' can be analysed legitimately as containing the predicate 'John knows that the Evening Star is ( )'. And if this inference is valid 'The Evening Star is the Evening Star' and 'The Evening Star is the Morning Star' cannot, after all, differ in cognitive value, even if the names 'The Evening Star' and 'The Morning Star' *are* (somehow) associated with different ways of thinking of the planet Venus. So how exactly can the appeal to sense, intuitively satisfying though it is, provide a solution to Frege's puzzle of identity? Frege's answer is that it enables us to see how (b) above can be false. The truth of (b) was inferred from the truth of the identity statement 'The Evening Star is the Morning Star'. But the truth of that identity statement requires only that the two names have the same reference *in that context*. It is consistent with this that the two names do not have the same reference *in other contexts*, and, in particular, do not have the same reference in propositional attitude contexts.

And, indeed, Frege holds, this is the case (and is shown to be so by the invalidity of the inference from (1) and (2) to (3)). In fact, in 'John knows that the Evening Star is the Evening Star' the second occurrence of 'the Evening Star' (and, of course, the first also) has as its reference the *sense* that 'The Evening Star' has in the unembedded identity statement 'the Evening Star is the Morning Star', and likewise in 'John knows that the Evening Star is the Morning Star' the occurrence of 'the Morning Star' has as its reference the *sense* that that name has in the unembedded identity statement 'The Evening Star is the Morning Star'. Since these senses are different, the compositionality principle for reference does not require that substitution of one name for the other, *in this context*, should preserve truth-value and thus the invalidity of the inference can be accounted for, consistently both with the compositionality principle for reference and the legitimacy of the analysis of 'John knows that the Evening Star is the Evening Star' as containing the predicate 'John knows that the Evening Star is ( )' (we must just regard the sentence as designating the value of that function name for the sense of 'the Evening Star' as argument, rather than for the planet Venus as argument).

Frege proposes that we call the references the names 'the Evening Star' and 'the Morning Star' have in the unembedded identity statement 'The Evening Star is the Morning Star' their 'customary' reference and the references they have in propositional attitude contexts their 'indirect' reference. He likewise distinguishes between customary sense, which is the sense an expression has in a context in which its reference is its customary reference, and indirect sense, which is the sense an expression has when its reference is its indirect reference. His explanation of the failure of substitutivity can now be expressed as follows. The indirect references of the names 'The Evening Star' and 'The Morning Star' are their customary senses. But these are different. Consequently substitution of one for the other in propositional attitude contexts cannot be expected to preserve truth-value.

It is important to see that this theory of indirect reference is not merely an optional extra which can be grafted on to the distinction of sense and reference once that has been justified by an appeal to the possible difference in cognitive values of true identity statements of the form 'a = a' and 'a = b'. On the contrary, the distinction between sense and reference provides no resolution of the puzzle of identity *at all* unless supplemented by Frege's theory of indirect reference.

The theory of indirect reference can also be applied to the version of the puzzle in which we consider the substitution not of names but of sentences. Frege proposes that 'The Evening Star is the Evening Star' and 'The Evening Star is the Morning Star' do not stand for their customary references in the context 'John believes that . . .' In such a context they stand for their customary senses, and these are the *thoughts* they customarily express. Thus 'John believes that . . .' can be thought of as a predicate whose reference is a concept which maps thoughts onto truth-values. In asserting 'John believes that the Evening Star is the Morning Star', one is asserting a *relation* between a thinker (John) and a thought.

As Frege puts it:

> The case of an abstract noun clause, introduced by 'that', includes the case of indirect quotation, in which we have seen the words to have their indirect reference coinciding with what is customarily their sense. In this case, then, the subordinate clause has for its reference a thought, not a truth-value: as sense not a thought but the sense of the words 'the thought that . . .' which is only a part of the thought in the entire complex sentence. This happens after 'say', 'hear', 'be of the opinion', 'be convinced', 'include' and similar words. (1969: 66)

The theory of indirect reference also evidently yields a solution to the puzzle of how empty singular terms can occur, within the context of propositional attitude constructions, in sentences which have, not only a sense, but a truth-value, e.g. 'The old professor believes that Odysseus was set ashore on Ithaca while sound asleep', or 'That poor mathematician believes that series S is the least rapidly convergent series'. In such a context, according to Frege, the reference of the singular term is its customary sense, so it is *not*, in the context, an empty term at all.

Before exploring further the commitments and resources of Frege's theory of indirect reference it will be worthwhile first to note that for Frege it is just a particular case of a more general theory of the context-dependent character of reference. The example of direct quotation, he thinks, provides a particularly plausible illustration of this theory:

> If words are used in the ordinary way, what one intends to speak of is their reference. It can also happen, however, that one wishes to talk about the words themselves or their sense. This happens, for instance, when the words of another are quoted. One's own words then first designate words of the other speaker, and only the latter have their usual reference. We then have signs of signs. In writing, the words are in this case enclosed in quotation marks. Accordingly a word standing between quotation marks must not be taken as having its ordinary reference. (1969: 58–9)

According to this proposal, in the sentence

'The Evening Star' contains three words

'The Evening Star' is *used*, as it is in

The Evening Star is the Morning Star

but it is also *mentioned*, since it occurs as a name of itself. Thus the name of 'The Evening Star' in the former displayed sentence is not ' "The Evening Star" ', but merely 'The Evening Star'. Quotation marks provide a context within which expressions are used to refer to themselves rather than forming, together with the expressions occurring within them, designations of these expressions.

Given that the name 'The Evening Star' is thus *used* in

'The Evening Star' contains three words

i.e. given that it has a semantic value in that context, Frege's view that it is also *mentioned*, that is, that its reference is itself, can be justified by consideration of what substitutions will preserve truth-values since evidently any replacement will risk a change in truth-value. And it is the same type of consideration that allows Frege to conclude that in a propositional attitude context the reference of an expression is its ordinary sense. Thus we have to distinguish two components within Frege's theory of indirect reference: (a) the thesis that the reference of an expression is different in a propositional attitude context from its customary reference, and (b) the thesis that the reference of an expression within a propositional attitude context is its ordinary sense. The *general* view of reference as context-dependent might be accepted even if it is held that thesis (b) is mistaken and that Fregean senses are not to be countenanced. As Kaplan puts the point in an influential paper (1969: 213): 'My own view is that Frege's explanation . . . of what appears to be the logically deviant behaviour of terms in intermediate [i.e. propositional attitude] contexts is so theoretically satisfying that if we have not yet . . . satisfactorily grasped the peculiar intermediate objects in question, then we should simply continue looking.'

So far we have considered only occurrences of *singly* embedded sentences in propositional attitude contexts, as in

John believes that the Evening Star is the Morning Star

but such embeddings can be reiterated. Thus

Mary wonders whether John believes that the Evening Star is the Morning Star

makes perfect sense, and an indefinite number of further embeddings are possible ('Bill doubts that Mary wonders whether . . .', etc.).

Now according to Frege, just as within the context of a *single* occurrence of a propositional attitude verb, an expression refers to its customary sense and has as its sense its indirect sense, so an expression within a double embedding has a twice shifted reference, so that its reference is its indirect sense and its sense is a distinct, doubly indirect sense.

The reference of 'the Evening Star' in 'Mary wonders whether John believes that . . .' is thus its indirect sense in 'John believes that . . .' and its sense is one which is distinct from any expressed in the latter sentence, a doubly indirect sense.

Evidently this line of thought yields an infinite hierarchy of indirect references and keeping pace one behind, as it were, an infinite hierarchy of indirect senses, and Frege explicitly commits himself to this consequence of his thesis.

But this feature of Frege's theory has been thought to be at best implausible, and probably incoherent.

The argument for the incoherence is given by Dummett (1973: 266–7). According to Frege the name 'The Evening Star' has as its reference as it appears in 'John believes that . . .' its customary sense. But in general the same reference can be determined by indefinitely many senses (as Russell puts it in 'On Denoting' of 1905: 'there is no backward road from reference to sense' (in Russell 1956)). So knowing the reference of 'the Evening Star' in 'John believes that . . .' does not allow us to work out its sense in that sentence. We may speak of '*the* indirect sense' of 'the Evening Star' in 'John believes that . . .', but we cannot know what this is. But now, according to Frege's theory the indirect sense of 'the Evening Star' in 'John believes that . . .' is its indirect reference in 'Mary wonders whether John believes that . . .' So if we do not know what its indirect sense is in the former sentence, we do not even know what its indirect reference is in the latter. But given Frege's compositionality principle for reference, the reference, i.e. truth-value, of 'Mary wonders whether John believes that . . .' is determined by the references of its parts. It therefore seems to follow, given our ignorance of the reference of 'the Evening Star' in this sentence, that we cannot know how to appraise its truth-value – or that of any sentence containing such doubly embedded expressions. But, of course, we can and do make such appraisals, so this is a *reductio ad absurdum* of the theory.

Dummett's response to this argument is to suggest that Frege need not distinguish customary sense and indirect sense in the first place. If this distinction is not made, the generation of the infinite hierarchy is stopped at stage one and no worries about ignorance of indirect senses, and hence, one further embedding on, indirect references, can arise. However, Frege cannot accept the identification of indirect sense with customary sense given his thesis that sense determines reference, for he must distinguish customary reference and indirect reference, as we have seen, to resolve the puzzle of identity, and if sense determines reference non-identity of reference entails non-identity of sense. Dummett's suggestion is that Frege's mistake is to think that sense determines reference (given how things are) *independently* of context. Rather, we should conceive of reference as determined jointly by sense and context:

> The sense of a word may thus be such as to determine it to stand for one thing in one kind of context and for a different thing in some other kind of context. We may therefore regard an expression occurring in an indirect context as having the same sense as in a direct context, though a different reference. (Dummett 1973: 26–7)

As Dummett explains, this modification of Frege's position is compelling if we equate the sense of an expression with its meaning, its conventional significance in the language to which it belongs, since there is no *ambiguity* in 'the Evening Star'. However, as he also notes, the equation of sense with linguistic meaning is only one strand in Frege's notion, and in some tension with the notion of sense as a mode of presentation or, as Evans explains it, a way of thinking of a reference. This tension is clearly visible when we consider sentences containing indexical expressions ('I', 'now', 'here') which have a context-dependent reference. For such an expression, say 'I', is not ambiguous (in the way in which, say, the word 'bank' is ambiguous). On the other hand the thoughts expressed by different utterances of type identical sentences containing the pronoun 'I' will not all be the same – the thought I express when I say 'I have a headache' must be different from the thought you express with that sentence since what I say may differ in truth-value from what you say. Thus we must say that the sense of 'I', conceived as a component of the thought I express with sentences containing it, and as a way of thinking of its reference, is not identical with its linguistic significance and varies from user to user.

If, however, we think of sense as mode of presentation we cannot abandon, as Dummett proposes, Frege's thesis that sense, independently of context, determines reference. However, a more modest revision of Fregean theory may be all that is required to save it from

Dummett's *reductio*. On the basis of the substitutions which preserve the truth-value of singly embedded sentences in propositional attitude context we must say that in such contexts expressions stand for their customary senses, and so, given the thesis that sense determines reference, we must distinguish the (singly) indirect sense of an expression from its customary sense. But consideration of what substitutions are possible *salva veritate* within doubly embedded sentences gives no reason to think that the reference of an expression in such a context is anything other than its customary sense. On the contrary, exactly the same substitutions for 'the Evening Star' would appear to be truth-preserving in

Mary wonders whether John believes that the Evening Star is the Morning Star

as in

John believes that the Evening Star is the Morning Star

We therefore have reason *both* to distinguish *singly* indirect reference from ordinary reference and hence, given Frege's principle that sense determines reference, singly indirect sense from customary sense, *and* to identify doubly indirect reference with singly indirect reference. Stopping the climb up the hierarchy at this point, however, does block Dummett's *reductio*, since we know what the singly indirect reference of an expression is, namely, its customary sense. On this proposal we must still distinguish an expression's sense from its conventional significance, since we will still have to ascribe multiple (two) senses to any expression which can occur both within and without propositional attitude constructions even if it has a single conventional significance, but we have seen that this distinction is forced on Frege anyway, once the application of the sense/reference distinction to indexical expressions is considered.

The Objectivity of Sense

The distinction between sense and conventional significance and the possibility of sense varying from speaker to speaker are relevant also to the assessment of one of Frege's most frequently stressed contentions – that sense is objective.

That sense is objective means for Frege that it is not subjective, i.e. not psychological, and the contrast here is with ideas. We have already noted this thesis in the *Foundations*, where, indeed, Frege lays it down as the first of his three fundamental principles: 'Always to separate sharply the psychological from the logical, the subjective from the objective', and it recurs in 'On Sense and Reference'. Frege writes:

> The reference and sense of a sign are to be distinguished from the associated idea . . . The same sense is not always connected, even in the same man, with the same idea. The idea is subjective: one man's idea is not that of another. . . . This constitutes an essential difference between the ideas and the sign's sense, which may be the common property of many and therefore is not a part or a mode of the individual mind. For one can hardly deny that mankind has a common store of thoughts which is transmitted from one generation to another. (1969: 59)

The emphasis here is on the *shareability* or *intersubjectivity* of thoughts, and senses generally, in contrast with ideas: the same sense can be grasped by different thinkers, it is therefore not, like an idea, a mode or part of any one mind.

Frege reinforces the point in the two succeeding paragraphs. It is not excluded that different men may associate different senses with a particular word. However, they are not

> prevented from grasping the same sense; but they cannot have the same idea. *Si duo idem faciunt, non est idem.* If two persons picture the same thing, each still has his own idea. It is indeed sometimes possible to establish differences in the ideas, or even in the sensations of different men; but an exact comparison is not possible, because we cannot have both ideas together in the same consciousness. (1969: 60)

Frege gives an analogy to clarify his position:

> Somebody observes the moon through a telescope. I compare the Moon itself to the reference; it is the object of observation, mediated by the real image projected by the object glass in the interior of the telescope, and by the retinal image of the observer. The former I compare to the sense, the latter is like the idea or experience. The optical image in the telescope is indeed one-sided and dependent upon the standpoint of observation; but it is still objective, inasmuch as it can be used by several observers . . . But each would have his own retinal image. (1969: 60)

Shareability is the feature of sense Frege stresses most often when discussing its objectivity, but there is another feature of the objectivity he thinks belongs to sense, which emerges particularly in 'Thoughts' (1984: 351–72). Senses, he thinks, are *mind-independent*. They are not created by thinking and exist regardless of whether anyone has apprehended them. Senses are in this sense like physical objects; though they are not perceived, but grasped. Again, the contrast is with ideas.

Frege states four theses about ideas, which characterize them, he says, as belonging to an 'inner world' distinct from the 'outer world' of physical objects:

(1)   Ideas are not perceptible. I do not *see* my visual impressions: I have them. --

(2)   Ideas belong to somebody: there could not be a pain or a mood or a wish going round the world which was nobody's pain or mood or wish. The inner world presupposes someone whose inner world it is.

(3)   Ideas need an owner: it is so much of the essence of any one of my ideas to be a content of my consciousness, that any idea someone else has, is, just as such, different from mine.

(4)   Every idea has only one owner; no two men have the same idea.

Thoughts, and senses generally, are distinct from physical objects because, like ideas, they are not perceptible (thesis (1)). But they are also distinct from ideas: they are shareable as ideas are not (theses (3) and (4)), and they are mind-independent, as ideas are not (thesis (2)). Thus they must be recognized as belonging to a 'third realm'. One inhabitant of this third realm is the Pythagorean theorem. This 'is timelessly true, true independently of whether anyone takes it to be true. It needs no owner. It is not true only from the time when it is discovered; just as a planet, even before anyone saw it, was in interaction with other planets.' And Frege adds in a footnote: 'When [a person] thinks a thought he does not create it, but only comes to stand in a certain relation to what already existed – a different relation from seeing a thing or having an idea' (1984: 363). The two ways in which thoughts are mind-independent recognized here are distinguished by Frege in his 'Logic' of 1897 and both explicitly endorsed 'what is true is true independently of our recognising it as such . . . We can go a step further. In order to be true thoughts . . . not only do not need to be recognised by us as true: they do not have to have been thought by us at all . . . they are independent of our thinking as such' (1979: 133), consequently 'they are not the product of our thinking, but only grasped by thinking' (1979: 148).

Since thoughts and senses generally are eternal and unchangeable, they are not affected by anything that takes place in the outer world or by our psychological activities. If I think a thought today which I did not think yesterday the relational properties of the thought change but not its essential properties. However, though we cannot affect thoughts, they can affect us, and thereby the outer world:

> How does a thought act? By being grasped and taken to be true. This is a process in the inner world of a thinker which may have further consequences in this inner world and . . . which may make itself noticeable in the outer world as well. If, for example, I grasp the thought we express by the theorem of Pythagoras, the consequence may be that I recognise it to be true, and further that I apply it in making a decision which brings about the acceleration of masses. . . . And yet we are inclined to regard thoughts as unactual, because they appear to do nothing in relation to events . . . How very different the actuality of a hammer appears, compared with that of a thought. . . . When a thought is grasped, it at first only brings about changes in the inner world of the one who grasps it; yet it remains unchanged in the core of its essence, for the changes it undergoes affect only inessential properties. There is lacking here something we observe everywhere in physical processes – reciprocal action. Thoughts are not wholly unactual but their actuality is quite different from the actuality of things. And their action is brought about by the performance of a thinker, without this they would be inactive at least as far as we can see. And yet the thinker does not create them but must take them as they are. (1984: 371)

Belonging as they do to a third realm, distinct from the outer realm of physical objects and the inner realm of ideas, thoughts are also governed by their own laws, which are the laws of logic, the laws of truth. The laws of logic are *descriptive* of this realm, as the laws of nature, such as Newton's First Law of Motion, are descriptive of the physical realm. But they lead to *prescriptions* about how one should think and infer. However, human beings do not always think as they ought, just as they do not always obey the moral or civil laws. Thus the laws of logic, understood in this way as prescriptive, must be distinguished from the psychological laws, the laws of thinking, which are *descriptive* of our actual thought processes, errors and all. For 'error and superstition have causes just as much as correct cognition. Whether what you take for true is false or true, your taking it comes about in accordance with psychological laws' (1984: 351).

This story about thoughts is often referred to as Frege's 'myth of the third realm' (for example, Dummett 1991b: 241ff.). For it is hard to take seriously the picture of thoughts as mind-independent, shareable, eternally changeless entities, which can, however, affect indirectly the physical world by being 'grasped' by thinkers and taken to be true and which are governed by laws which, somehow, are simultaneously descriptive of one realm and prescriptive for another. On the other hand, Frege's distinction between thoughts and ideas is generally applauded, and indeed is recognized as the inspiration of Wittgenstein's definitive attack on 'ideational' theories of meaning. Wittgenstein's attack, however, is directed against the position that understanding is a mental process (Wittgenstein 1968), or as it could be expressed in Fregean language, that *grasp* of sense is a psychological occurrence. What Wittgenstein shows is that nothing that occurs in the mind of a thinker at a particular time can constitute his thinking a thought with a particular content. For whatever occurs is open to more than one interpretation and cannot compel its interpretation in a particular way. Thus I may be thinking of an old man walking up a hill and it may be that the vehicle of this thought in my mind is a mental image of an old man on a hillside leaning on a stick (Wittgenstein 1968: 54). But this image does not compel its interpretation in this way; it could equally well represent someone sliding downhill in that position. Perhaps a Martian would naturally interpret it in this way. In general thoughts are not contents of consciousness and hence, even if God were to look into our minds, he could not see *there* what we were thinking (1968: 217).

Frege would agree with this, of course, since for him to know what someone is thinking is to know what thought he is grasping and one could no more know that by inspecting the contents of a person's mind than one could know what physical object someone is grasping in his hand just by examining the contents (the muscles, bones, tendons, etc.) of his hand. Nevertheless, for Frege, grasping a thought is a psychological occurrence. It is 'a process in the inner world of a thinker' (1984: 371), which 'presupposes someone who grasps it, who thinks' (1984: 369). It should not be confused with the thought itself: 'Similarly Algol itself is different from the idea someone has of Algol' (1984: 369). However, this comparison must be mistaken: when I think of Algol I do so by employing a way of thinking, a sense, which is not determined by any idea which happens to be present in my mind; but my grasp of a thought cannot simply be an accompaniment to my thinking, in a certain way, *of* the thought. Thus either Frege provides no account of what grasping a thought is, or he provides an inappropriate account. Either way, his conception of thoughts as mind-independent but not perceptible inhabitants of a third realm explains nothing.

What is wrong with this conception is illuminated by a comparison Dummett suggests between language and chess.

> There are sentences which no one has framed, and such sentences have senses just as do those which are uttered; these are legitimate grounds for saying with Frege that a thought does not depend for its existence upon our grasping or expressing it. [Equally] there are many different moves which pieces have had in obsolete or still-practised variations of chess, such as those of the pieces called Camel and Giraffe in Tamerlane's 'great chess'; and there must be countless other possible moves that might be assigned to pieces in versions of chess that have never been played or thought of. It is harmless to say that 'there are' such moves . . . [and they] are objects by Frege's criteria, for they can be named and have predicates applied to them. (1991b: 249)

Nevertheless, it would be insane to think of chess moves as inhabiting a 'third realm' which we cannot affect, but only come into relation to when playing chess, and which can (indirectly) thereby affect the 'outer world' via its effects on our 'inner world'. It would be insane because chess moves are not self-subsistent objects, but are 'of' chess pieces in the sense that they cannot be conceived of *except* as the moves of certain pieces. Consequently chess pieces are not logically independent objects, reference to which does not in principle depend upon reference to objects of any other kind; rather, reference to any chess move must identify it as the move had by some chess piece (1991b: 249–50). Similarly, Dummett suggests, thoughts and senses generally, though perfectly rightly thought of by Frege as objects, are not self-subsistent. To conceive of any sense is to conceive of it as the sense had by some possible expression. Frege's mistake was not to recognize this. Languageless thought might indeed be possible, and may even be possible for human beings, but, because thoughts are not contents of consciousness, in the sense established by Wittgenstein, all thought must have a vehicle; 'it is not possible for someone to have a thought at a particular time without there being some event, overt in his actions, or interior to his mental life that embodies it' (1991b: 322). Hence the phenomenon of languageless thought does not impugn the 'conclusion that senses are always *of* something, namely whatever serves as the medium [vehicle] of their expression, in communication or in soliloquy' (Dummett 1991b: 262).

We began this section by noticing that the distinction between sense and conventional significance, which Frege is forced to make when he applies the sense/reference distinction to indexical expressions, is relevant to his contention that sense is objective. Frege is well aware of this. The problem he thinks that indexicals pose for him he expresses in the following passage:

> A sentence like 'I am old' may seem to be a counter-example to our thesis that a thought is independent of the person thinking it, insofar as it can be true for one person and false for another, and thus not true in itself. (1979: 134)

indexicality

His response to this problem is to insist that the *same* thought cannot be 'true for one person and false for another':

> The reason for this is that the sentence expresses a different thought in the mouth of one person from what it expresses in the mouth of another. In this case the mere words do not contain the entire sense: we have in addition to take into account who utters it. There are many cases like this in which the spoken word has to be supplemented by the speaker's gesture and expression, and the accompanying circumstance. The word 'I' simply designates a different person in the mouths of different people . . . words like 'here' and 'now' only acquire their full sense from the circumstances in which they are used. If someone says 'it is raining' the time and place of utterance has to be supplied . . . so the explanation of all these apparent exceptions is that the same sentence does not always express the same thought, because the words need to be supplemented in order to get a complete sense, and how this is to be done can vary according to the circumstances. (1979: 134–5)

However, there is a further problem, which Frege does not recognize here, and which only emerges in 'Thoughts'. For as we have seen, at the heart of Frege's notion of the objective is the shareable or intersubjective. But in 'Thoughts' he recognizes a sense for 'I' which can only be grasped by one thinker:

Everyone is presented to himself in a special and primitive way in which he is presented to no one else. So, when Dr. Lauben has the thought that he was wounded, he will probably be basing it on this primitive way in which he is presented to himself. And only Dr. Lauben himself can grasp thoughts specified in this way. (1984: 359)

Whether indexicals in general pose the same difficulty is another matter. One might think that it was so. For one might think that the thoughts expressed by a thinker using 'here' and 'now' are ones that could not be thought elsewhere and elsewhen and so (even if strictly speaking still *shareable* since another thinker *could* have been at that place and time, even if no one was) cannot belong to the 'common store of mankind's thoughts' of which Frege speaks as being capable of being passed on from one generation to another. However, Frege allows that the same thought can be expressed using different indexicals in different contexts: 'If someone wants to say today what he expressed yesterday using the word "today", he will replace this word with "yesterday". Although the thought is the same, its verbal expression must be different in order that the change of sense which would otherwise be affected by the different times of utterance may be cancelled out. It is the same with words like "here" and "there"' (1984: 358). This position is compatible with the Intuitive Criterion of Difference for thoughts, which requires only that sentences S and S' (as uttered in a content C) must express different thoughts if it is possible for someone *in* C to assent to the thought expressed by S while dissenting from the thought expressed by S'. Moreover, it is an entirely reasonable position, as Gareth Evans has made beautifully clear (1982: 192–6). For we want to allow that a belief may *persist*, i.e. that a thinker may continue to think the same thing, even though what is required for him to express his belief changes. If today I think that it is sunny I can express that thought by saying 'It is sunny today'. If I retain this belief tomorrow I can only express it by saying 'It was sunny yesterday'. But it is surely unreasonable, and not required by any Fregean doctrine, to regard this as a different thought, somehow *inferred* by me from my earlier thought via the (at no time thinkable) thought 'today is yesterday'. Thus Evans speaks helpfully of 'dynamic' Fregean thoughts, which can be the contents of such persisting but only indexically expressible beliefs, and whose expression necessarily changes from time to time and place to place.

'I'-thoughts, however, are a special case and Frege's view that there is 'a special way in which each one is presented to himself in which no one is presented to anyone else' seems defensible. For if my 'I'-thoughts could be thought by you – as I can think tomorrow what I thought today – you could express them, presumably using 'You'. But from *your* point of view my existence is a contingent feature of the external world and so none of your thoughts can be dependent on it for their thinkability (this is a generalization of the point, which we have seen to be problematic for Frege, but nonetheless an integral part of his position, that sense does not *require* reference). Thus the thoughts you express, addressing me, using 'You', could be thought and expressed by you even if I did not exist. However, my 'I'-thoughts could not be thought if I did not exist. For they could only be thought if they could be expressed. But if I did not exist they could not be expressed using 'I', of course. Suppose, however, that someone attempted to express them using 'You' or 'He'. Then if he was talking to, or of, someone existing in his world, he would be giving expression to his 'I'-thought, if any, not mine. If he was confronting a mere hallucination of an HN-lookalike this would not be so, but there would then be no reason to say that he was expressing *my* 'I'-thoughts rather than those of any of my innumerable possible doubles. And if he was neither hallucinating nor confronting anyone actually existing in his world, then, whatever he was doing, it could not possibly count as expressing one of my 'I'-thoughts. Hence none of the thoughts you express using 'you' can be identical with any of my 'I'-thoughts, and so, as Frege says, we are indeed driven to the conclusion that each of us is presented to himself in a way in which he is presented to no one else.

Frege is unhappy with this conclusion, however, because it conflicts with what he conceives to be necessary for communication – the transmission of thoughts. Thus he distinguishes the 'I' of soliloquy, whose sense is the special and primitive way one is presented to oneself, from the 'I' of communication, whose sense is shareable. So Frege continues the passage last quoted about Dr Lauben's 'I'-thoughts as follows:

But now he may want to communicate with others. He cannot communicate a thought he alone can grasp. Therefore, if he now says 'I was wounded', he must use 'I' in a sense which can be grasped by others, perhaps in the sense of 'he who is speaking to you at this moment', by doing so he makes the conditions accompanying his utterance serve towards the expression of a thought. (1984: 359–60)

However, this proposal is unsatisfactory. For I can entertain the thought 'I am he who is speaking to you at this moment' and not know that it is true: 'I' cannot therefore have the same sense as 'he who is speaking to you at this moment'. Apart from this, the suggestion that we habitually use 'I' in different senses when we attempt to communicate and when we soliloquize is utterly implausible – it would imply that you, overhearing my soliloquy, could only have an illusion of understanding, but that if I, unbeknown to you, became aware of your presence, and decided to communicate, your understanding would henceforth be genuine.

What lies behind Frege's insistence on the distinction between the 'I' of soliloquy and the 'I' of communication is the assumption that communication requires the transmission and hence the sharing of thoughts, and what lies behind this assumption, in turn, is Frege's belief that what cannot be shared cannot be mutually known, cannot be *conveyed*, as George (1997) puts it. This belief emerges whenever Frege argues from the unshareability of ideas to our necessary ignorance about the ideas of others. Thus in 'On Sense and Reference':

> If two persons picture the same thing, each still has his own idea. It is indeed sometimes possible to establish difference in the ideas, or even in the sensations of different men; but an exact comparison is not possible, because we cannot have both ideas together in the same consciousness. (1969: 60)

And in 'Thoughts':

> when the word 'red' is meant not to state a property of things, but to characterise sense-impressions belonging to my consciousness, it is only applicable within the realm of my consciousness. For it is impossible to compare my sense-impression with someone else's. In order to do that it would be necessary to bring together in one consciousness a sense-impression belonging to one consciousness and a sense-impression belonging to another consciousness. (1984: 361)

This inference from unshareability to unconveyability commits Frege to the position, which he does not regard as contentious, that ideas are *private objects* in precisely the sense that Wittgenstein (1968: 88) attacked items belonging to the individual consciousness and, because only introspectable by one, only knowable by one. (Here, then, we see another reason why Wittgenstein's philosophy should be considered an advance on Frege's.) But 'I'-thoughts need not be thought of in this way. They are indeed in one sense private and incommunicable; but not in any objectionable sense. They are private and incommunicable in that only their subject can *think* them; but other people can know precisely what she is thinking when she does so, so they are not private objects in the sense spoken of by Wittgenstein (cf. Dummett 1993: 140). When I say, for example, using the 'I' of soliloquy, 'I have a headache', I thereby give expression to a thought you cannot think; but you can say exactly *what* thought it is which I thus express and you cannot think, namely, the thought (there is only one) expressible by me using the sentence 'I have a headache'. And in identifying my thought in this way you are not picking it out by a merely *accidental* property of it (as a 'private sensation' might be identified as the one contingently connected with a certain type of behaviour); given the meaning (conventional significance) of the sentence 'I have a headache' it is *essential* to my thought that it be thus expressible, and no other thought could be expressed by me in those words.

Challenges to Sense

The two most important and influential challenges to Frege's distinction between sense and reference in this century have been mounted by Bertrand Russell and Saul Kripke. We shall first look at Russell's attack and then at (some aspects of) Kripke's.

Russell's attack on Fregean sense is most famously presented in 'On Denoting' (1956: 41–56). 'On Denoting' is a classic of twentieth-century analytic philosophy, but also deeply obscure in parts. It is clear that Russell's main aim in the article is to give reasons for rejecting an earlier theory of 'denoting' which he had expounded in his book *The Principles of Mathematics* (1903) and long struggled to defend. However, that theory involved a distinction between 'meaning' and 'denoting' which Russell takes to be more or less the same as Frege's distinction between sense and reference (at least in the case of the category of expressions Russell called 'denoting phrases'). Thus he regards himself as simultaneously arguing in 'On Denoting' against Frege as well as against his own earlier self.

The easiest approach to Russell's criticisms of Frege is via the problem of empty singular terms. Such terms pose a problem for

Frege because of his adherence to the name/bearer prototype as an ingredient in his notion of reference. Because of this he identifies the semantic value of a singular term with its designation and is then led to conclude that sentences containing such terms must be truth-valueless (except in cases where the terms have their indirect reference); a conclusion he thought tenable because given the sense/reference distinction he was able nonetheless to ascribe such terms senses and regard sentences containing them as expressing thoughts. However, as we have seen, this position is deeply implausible, particularly in the case of empty definite descriptions, like 'the least rapidly convergent series'. It is this implausibility that Russell points out in his first criticism of Frege (in which for 'meaning' read 'sense', and for 'denotation' read 'reference'):

> If we say, 'the King of England is bald', that is, it would seem, not a statement about the complex meaning 'the King of England', but about the actual term denoted by the meaning. But now consider 'the King of France is bald'. By parity of form, this also ought to be about the denotation of the phrase 'the King of France'. But this phrase, though it has a meaning, provided 'the King of England' has a meaning, has certainly no denotation, at least in any obvious sense. Hence one would suppose that 'the King of France is bald' ought to be nonsense; but it is not nonsense, since it is plainly false. Or again, consider such a proposition as the following: 'If u is a class with only one member, then that one member is a member of u' . . . This proposition *ought* to be always true. But 'the u' or 'that one member' is a denoting phrase, and it is the denotation, not the meaning, that is said to be a u. Now if u is not a unit class, 'the u' seems to denote nothing, hence our proposition would seem to become mere nonsense as soon as u is not a unit class. (1956: 46)

This is not as clear as one might like (it is not, of course, a consequence of Frege's position that 'the King of France is bald' is *nonsense*), but the general point is clear: Frege is committed to saying both of subject-predicate sentences like 'the King of France is bald' and of truth-functionally complex sentences like 'If u is a class with only one member, then that one member is a member of u', containing empty definite descriptions, that they are neither true nor false. However, that is unacceptable, for such sentences can be *false* (the former case), and even *true* (the latter).

The problem arises for Frege because he groups definite descriptions with proper names, ordinarily so called, and regards both types of expression as having objects as their semantic values. By contrast he treats quantifying expressions as having as their references second-level functions from first-level concepts to truth-values. Thus Frege would regard, say

Some King of France is bald

as analysable as saying of the first-level concept which is the reference of the predicate 'is bald' that it falls under (or, strictly, falls within) the second-level concept which is the reference of the quantifying expression 'some King of France' and he would say that the word 'some', as it occurs in this sentence, indicates a relation between concepts, i.e. has as its reference a second-level relation between the first-level concepts which are the references of the predicates 'is a King of France' and 'is wise' (1969: 48).

Russell's solution to the problem of empty definite descriptions, if we gloss over many differences in terminology and ontology, is essentially that definite descriptions should be treated, like 'some King of France' in Frege's theory, as quantifying expressions. This at first sight seems counter-intuitive. Grammar suggests that 'the King of France is bald' and 'the King of England is bald' are analogous to 'Edward is bald'. But, Russell suggests, grammar in this case is not a good guide, it disguises the true 'logical form' of sentences containing definite descriptions. We can see what 'the King of France is bald' actually says, and what its true logical form is, if we split it up into three components:

(1) There is at least one King of France
(2) There is at most one King of France
(3) Anything which is King of France is bald

Each of these three sentences is quantificational in form, that is, in Frege's terminology, says of a first level concept that it falls within a second-level concept (Russell would have phrased this point by saying that the sentences make assertions about *propositional functions* which are his analogues of Frege's concepts), but their conjunction is equivalent to 'the King of France is bald'. Putting the pieces together, introducing modern logical symbolism and the abbreviations 'is F' for 'is a king of France' and 'is G' for 'is bald', we arrive at

$$(\exists x)(Fx \land Gx \land (\forall y)(Fy \rightarrow x = y))$$

as the perspicuous representation of the logical form of 'the King of France is bald'. And this came to represent for Russell the logical form of any sentence of the grammatical form 'the F is G'.

But now we can see that this simply says of the first-level concept which is the reference of

'. . . is G'

that it falls within the second-level concept which is the reference of

'$(\exists x)(Fx \wedge \ldots x \wedge (\forall y)(Fy \rightarrow x = y))$'

(or, in Russellian terminology, that the propositional function *is G* has an instance which is also an instance of the propositional function *is uniquely F*). We can therefore regard the definite description 'the King of France' as just another way of writing the displayed second-level predicate and hence as having as its semantic value not an object but a second-level concept (in Russell's own terminology, a function from propositional functions to propositions).

To see the parallelism with 'Some King of France is bald' it suffices to note that the latter has, according to both Frege and Russell, the logical form

$(\exists x)(Fx \wedge Gx)$

which differs from that of 'the King of France is bald' by the omission merely of the final conjunct '$(\forall y)(Fy \rightarrow y = x)$' asserting uniqueness. This says of the first-level concept which is the reference of ' is G' that it falls within the second-level concept which is the reference of

'$(\exists X)(Fx \wedge \ldots x)$'

The difference between 'the King of France is bald' and 'Some King of France is bald' is thus merely that the former makes a more complicated assertion about the reference of the predicate 'is bald' than the latter.

We can, if we like, go further (Russell did not) and propose that 'the', like 'some' on Frege's proposal, be itself regarded as standing for a second-level relation between concepts, i.e. a function mapping a pair of concepts onto the truth-value True if and only if the first concept is instantiated by just one object and that object falls under the second concept.

In essence, then, this is Russell's theory of definite descriptions; it is simply an extension of the Fregean treatment of quantifying expressions to a class of expressions to which Frege had not thought of applying it.

The power of the theory is nevertheless undeniable. The problem that empty definite descriptions pose for Frege is completely resolved, and in an intuitively satisfactory way, using only resources already available within the Fregean approach. Since definite descriptions are now not thought of as having objects as their semantic values, the non-existence of a designated object does not imply that 'the King of France' has no semantic value, and hence does not imply that sentences containing it must be truth-valueless. 'The King of France is bald' in particular, can now be seen as plainly false, as Russell requires, since it entails $(\exists x)(x$ is a King of France), which is false (since there is no King of France). As for the truth-functionally complex sentence 'if u is a class with only one member that one member is a member of u', it comes out, as he requires, as true if u is not a unit class (having no, or more than one, member). For then 'that one member' designates nothing, so 'that one member is a member of u' is false according to the theory of descriptions (like 'the King of France is a King of France' or 'the inhabitant of London is an inhabitant of London'), as is 'u is a class with only one member', and with false consequent and false antecedent the whole conditional (read truth-functionally) is true.

As we saw, for Frege not just descriptions but also proper names, ordinarily so called, can have sense without reference – 'Odysseus', for example, is probably such a name he thinks, and he would have said the same, if he had been writing for an English readership, of such proper names as 'King Arthur' and 'Robin Hood'. Thus, according to Frege, sentences containing such proper names, like sentences containing empty definite descriptions, express thoughts, but are truth-valueless.

In this case, also, Frege's position is implausible, and once again Russell has a solution. In short his solution is to extend his treatment of descriptions to proper names by treating names as abbreviated descriptions.

Frege says of the sentence 'Odysseus was set ashore at Ithaca while sound asleep' that it expresses a thought but is truth-valueless since the name 'Odysseus' does not have a bearer and so the function referred to by 'was set ashore at Ithaca while sound asleep' is not presented with any argument. Russell, on the other hand, proposes that whenever someone utters this sentence he must have in mind a description by which he would identify Odysseus. This description might vary from speaker to speaker and might even be different for the same speaker from time to time, but there always will be *some* description of Odysseus which a competent utterer of the sentence could provide, and this description will be what he means by the name. Thus, as Russell puts it, using a different example:

> The names that we commonly use, like 'Socrates', are really abbreviations for descriptions . . . When we use the word 'Socrates' we are really using a description. Our thought may be rendered by some such phrase as 'the master of Plato', or 'the philosopher who drank the hemlock', or 'the person whom logicians assert to be mortal'. (1956: 201)

But if proper names abbreviate descriptions and descriptions are quantifying expressions then the problem of bearerless proper names goes the way of the problem of empty descriptions. *[Russell's solution]*

At a stroke, then, Russell appears to have completely resolved the puzzle of empty singular terms which causes so much trouble within the Fregean framework, and consequently has shown that, at least as regards *this* puzzle, no appeal to the notion of sense is necessary.

Moreover, as Russell goes on in 'On Denoting' to explain, his approach has other advantages. Within the Fregean framework quantifying expressions have *scope*: we can distinguish between

Some King of France is not bald

and

It is not the case that some King of France is bald

representing the former as

$(\exists x)(Fx \wedge \neg Gx)$

and the latter as

$\neg(\exists x)(Fx \land Gx)$

The difference between the two is that in the former the quantifier has wide scope relative to the negation operator and in the latter it has narrow scope relative to the negation operator.

Now treating descriptions as quantifiers allows us to extend the notion of scope to descriptions, and so we can discern an ambiguity in

The King of France is not bald

which can be read either as having the logical form

$(\exists x)(Fx \ \& \ \neg Gx \ \& \ (\forall y)(Fy \rightarrow x = y))$

– and so as being false, or as having the logical form

$\neg(\exists x)(Fx \ \& \ Gx \ \& \ (\forall y)(Fy \rightarrow x = y))$ ˙

– and so as being true. (Russell speaks of 'the King of France' as having 'primary occurrence' when the sentence is read in the first way and as having 'secondary occurrence' when the sentence is read in the second way.) Thus Russell is able to claim for his theory that it can account for the logical truth of the Law of Excluded Middle. By that law either 'the King of France is bald' or 'the King of France is not bald' must be true. According to the theory of descriptions the former is false, and one might think the same is true of the latter, since if we enumerated the things that are not bald we should not find the King of France in the list (1956: 48). But, in fact, Russell says, the latter is ambiguous, and if we read the description as having secondary occurrence, it is true, as the Law of Excluded Middle requires.

In so far as the scope ambiguity Russell discusses here is a genuine one, as it seems to be, Russell's theory of descriptions is to be preferred to Frege's theory, for that cannot account for such ambiguities. Moreover, it should be noted, even if, as suggested earlier, we follow Evans (1982) and modify Frege's theory by distinguishing the semantic value of a singular term from its designation, thus allowing an empty singular term to have a semantic value, the scope ambiguities Russell's theory predicts still cannot be accounted for within a Fregean framework so long as the semantic value assigned to a singular term is an *object* and not a *function*. In the modified theory we will be able to regard 'the King of France is bald' as false, and so we will be able to regard 'It is not the case that the King of France is bald' as true, but we will not be able to account for the reading of 'the King of France is not bald' on which it is *false* (the reading Russell would explain as involving a primary occurrence of the description). To do so within the Fregean framework it would be necessary to regard the negation symbol as standing for a function mapping concepts (e.g. the concept *is bald*) onto concepts (the concept *is not bald*), but as we saw in the last chapter, Frege's principle of concept formation does not allow functions whose values are concepts. To recognize the reading of 'the King of France is not bald' on which it is false, therefore, we must treat the sentence as of the form 'for some x, x is the King of France and x is not bald' and regard the description as of the same type as a quantifier.

That it allows the possibility of treating names and descriptions as having scope is therefore an important advantage of Russell's theory and Russell argues that this possibility can also be used to resolve the Fregean puzzle of identity.

Russell uses his own example to illustrate how his theory of descriptions can solve this puzzle:

> If a is identical with b, whatever is true of the one is true of the other, and either may be substituted for the other in any proposition without altering the truth or falsehood of the proposition. Now George IV wished to know whether Scott was the author of *Waverley*, and in fact Scott *was* the author of *Waverley*. Hence we may substitute *Scott* for *the author of Waverley*, and thereby prove that George IV wished to know whether Scott was Scott. Yet an interest in the law of identity can hardly be attributed to the first gentleman in Europe. (1956: 49)

The problem is to explain the invalidity of the inference from

(1) George IV wished to know whether Scott was the author of *Waverley*

and

(2) Scott was the author of *Waverley*

to

(3) George IV wished to know whether Scott was Scott

Russell's response is to appeal to the distinction between the primary and secondary occurrence of a definite description and to discern an ambiguity in the argument. If we read the description 'the author of *Waverley*' in (1) as having a primary occurrence, its logical form (using 'Wx' to mean 'x wrote *Waverley*') is:

(∃x)(Wx ∧ (∀y)(Wy → y = x) & George IV wished to know whether Scott = x)

This says that one and only one man wrote *Waverley* and George IV wished to know whether Scott was that man, that is, that George IV wished to know *of* the man who, in fact, wrote *Waverley* whether Scott was he. This would have been true, for example, as Russell says, if George IV had seen Scott at a distance and asked 'Is that Scott?'

From (1), so interpreted, it does follow, given that Scott was the author of *Waverley*, that, in a sense, George IV wished to know whether Scott was Scott. That is, it follows that George IV wished to know *of* Scott whether Scott was he, i.e.

(∃x)(x = Scott ∧ George IV wished to know whether Scott = x)

However, (1) is naturally read in a way that gives the description 'the author of *Waverley*' a secondary occurrence, as having the logical form:

George IV wished to know whether (∃x)(Wx ∧ (∀y)(Wy → y = x) ∧ Scott = x)

But from (1) so understood and (2), Russell says, we cannot infer that George IV wondered whether Scott was Scott, where this was the logical form:

George IV wished to know whether Scott = Scott

This is so because there is no *constituent*, 'the author of *Waverley*', in (1) understood in this way, for which we could substitute 'Scott' (1956: 52).

But this is obscure. The question we are interested in, recall, is whether by appeal to the theory of descriptions Russell can resolve

Frege's puzzle of identity. Russell shows that the argument about George IV and the author of *Waverley* can be read in two ways, according as the description 'the author of *Waverley*' is interpreted as having a primary or secondary occurrence (wide or narrow scope) in (1), and he points out that when the description is read as having wide scope (and the second occurrence of the name 'Scott' in (3) read in parallel fashion) the argument is valid. But what needs explaining is how the argument can be *invalid* when the description is read as having narrow scope in (1). It is only if Russell's theory can explain this that it can be said to show how an appeal to sense is unnecessary to resolve the puzzle of identity. But it is precisely at this point that Russell lapses into his obscure talk of the non-existence of a constituent, 'the author of *Waverley*', in (1), for which 'Scott' can be substituted.

To get clearer about this matter it is convenient at this point to replace Russell's example by a simpler one. Let us suppose that George IV believed that the author of *Waverley* was a Scot, but did not believe that the author of *Ivanhoe* was a Scot, although, in fact, the author of *Waverley* was, of course, the author of *Ivanhoe*. The challenge to Russell is now to explain the informativeness for George IV of the identity statement

The author of *Waverley* is the author of *Ivanhoe*

or, equivalently, to explain the invalidity of the inference from

George IV believed that the author of *Waverley* was a Scot

and

The author of *Waverley* was the author of *Ivanhoe*

to

George IV believed that the author of *Ivanhoe* was a Scot

when the descriptions are read as having secondary occurrences in the first premiss and the conclusion. That is, the challenge is to explain the invalidity of the inference (using obvious abbreviations) from

George IV believed that $(\exists x)(Wx \wedge (\forall y)(Wy \rightarrow y = x) \wedge Sx)$

and

$$(\exists x)(Wx \wedge Ix \wedge (\forall y)(Wy \to y = x) \wedge (\forall y)(Iy \to = x))$$

to

George IV believed that $(\exists x)(Ix \wedge (\forall y)(Iy \to y = x) \wedge Sx)$

However, as we have so far understood Russell's theory of descriptions, it provides no explanation of the invalidity of this inference. For the theory of descriptions, as so far understood, is simply the contention that definite descriptions are quantifiers, i.e. in Fregean terms, expressions whose semantic values are second-level concepts, functions from first-level concepts to truth-values. But the second-level concept which is the semantic value of the description 'the author of *Waverley*', i.e. of '$(\exists x)(Wx \wedge (\forall y)(Wy \to y = x) \wedge \ldots$ x)', *is* the second-level concept which is the semantic value of the description 'the author of *Ivanhoe*', i.e.'$(\exists x)(Ix \wedge (\forall y)(Iy \to y = x) \wedge \ldots x)$' (every first-level concept the first concept maps onto the True the second maps onto the True and *vice versa*). For Frege himself this presents no problem since he regards quantifiers, like proper names, as having sense as well as reference and having indirect reference in propositional attitude contexts like 'George IV believes that . . .' But Russell's aim is to get by without sense, and without sense the semantic value of 'the author of *Waverley*' in 'George IV believed that the author of *Waverley* was a Scot' must be the same as its semantic value in the identity statement 'the author of *Waverley* is the author of *Ivanhoe*'. If this is the same as that of 'the author of *Ivanhoe*', 'George IV believed that the author of *Waverley* was a Scot' must in turn have the same semantic value as 'George IV believed that the author of *Ivanhoe* was a Scot' and these two sentences cannot differ in truth-value.

The reason Russell thought otherwise is that he did not, in fact, regard the semantic values of descriptions as second-level Fregean functions from Fregean concepts to Fregean objects, for he did not regard the semantic values of descriptions as having *extensional* identity conditions. We noted parenthetically that Russell's analogue of a Fregean concept was a 'propositional function', a function from objects to propositions. But, whereas for Frege the concept *featherless biped*, say, is identical with the concept *human being* (given that all and only human beings are featherless bipeds), Russell would here recognize two distinct propositional functions defining the same class of entities. Similarly Russell would distinguish the semantic value of 'the author of *Ivanhoe*' from that of 'the author of *Waverley*'. However, this means that Russell's theory of descriptions does not, after all, by itself provide a way of resolving the Fregean puzzle of identity *without invoking any notion akin to sense,* for in so far as propositional functions are individuated non-extensionally they are sense-like entities.

In sum, then, the conclusion of our assessment of Russell's challenge to Frege must be that it fails: his theory of descriptions brilliantly resolves the puzzle of empty singular terms, and by allowing the application of the notion of scope to definite descriptions answers to a real need that a Fregean account can only ignore, but he is only able to present the appearance of resolving the Fregean puzzle of identity by smuggling in (under the title of 'propositional functions') a notion in crucial respects akin to Fregean sense.

But now we must turn to the challenge to Fregean sense put forward by Saul Kripke in his highly important and influential 'Naming and Necessity' (1972). (Related and overlapping arguments have been put forward by Donnellan (1972) and Putnam (1975) and both externalism in the philosophy of mind and 'causal' and 'direct reference' theories of reference in the philosophy of language owe their inspiration to these arguments. The extent to which these developments constitute an advance on Frege is one of the most important questions for contemporary philosophy of mind and language in the analytic tradition. Here we shall have space only to examine Kripke's explicit challenge to Frege.)

'Naming and Necessity' is a remarkable work of philosophy, a gold mine of thought-provoking contentions and arguments on issues relating to meaning, necessity, the *a priori* and *a posteriori*, identity, essentialism, natural kinds, the mind–brain identity theory and the necessary non-existence of unicorns. We shall be concerned only with the main argument of the book, which is intended to refute a theory of proper names which Kripke rightly took to be the orthodoxy at the time he was writing and controversially took to be the appropriate synthesis of the views of Frege and Russell. This theory of proper names is often referred to as the 'description theory of proper names', or, reflecting its supposed origin, the 'Frege–Russell theory'. In essence, and very roughly (Kripke gives a much more precise statement) it is the theory that every ordinary proper name is equivalent to a description, or cluster of descriptions, of its bearer, and that it is only in virtue of using a proper name with the intention of speaking of a certain descriptively identified individual that one can refer using proper names at all.

Since our interest is in the question of the extent, if any, to which Kripke's arguments are effective against Frege's theory of sense, the first thing we must get clear about is the relation of this 'Frege–Russell theory' to Frege's actual views.

As we have seen, Frege and Russell in fact disagreed considerably about the correct account of proper names in ordinary language. Frege viewed them as in a distinct semantic category from quantifiers, but in the same semantic category as definite descriptions, as having sense and, if the world obliged, reference. Russell took them to be abbreviations of definite descriptions, though differing from speaker to speaker and time to time in the descriptions they abbreviated, and therefore, like descriptions, in the same semantic category as quantifiers, and without sense (a notion he claimed he had no need for given his theory of descriptions). However, despite these differences Russell and Frege were agreed on one very important point. This is the contention Gareth Evans (1982) has called 'Russell's Principle' (it could equally well have been called 'Frege's Principle'). According to this contention one cannot speak or even think about a thing unless one knows *which* thing one is speaking or thinking about. In order for an object to be the object of one's reference in speech or thought one must know of some condition satisfied uniquely by it and thus be able, in thought, to discriminate it from every other possible object of reference. This entails that the link between word and world is made by the word user's knowledge and intentions, and hence that one cannot refer to an object of which one lacks identifying knowledge.

To reject Russell's Principle is to claim that ignorance and error are no bars to reference, and it is this that Kripke's arguments are intended to establish. It is for this reason that he regards himself as in opposition both to Russell and Frege.

However, the question still remains: whatever Kripke's intentions, is the theory of proper names he attacks one appropriately thought of as Fregean, or does the assumption that a name user's knowledge of its bearer must be descriptive render his argument irrelevant to Frege's position? This is a much-debated question. To get clearer about it let us first note that we can distinguish three types of knowledge to which a defender of Russell's Principle can appeal. First, there is, indeed, descriptive knowledge, knowledge of some specifiable condition which an object has to satisfy to be the object to which reference is being made. Secondly, there

[handwritten marginal note: Sounds logical but it's not true]

is recognitional knowledge: knowledge which consists in the ability to pick out the object of reference when presented with it in suitable circumstances. And finally, there is what Russell calls 'knowledge by acquaintance', that knowledge one has of an object which does not consist in knowledge of any specifiable condition it satisfies, nor, necessarily, requires any ability to recognize it in other circumstances, but is simply knowledge of it *as given*.

Both Frege and Russell employ the first and third of these notions in their discussions of reference. This is explicit in Russell, who makes a great point of the distinction between knowledge by acquaintance and knowledge by description, and holds that what backs up the use of an ordinary proper name is knowledge by description while knowledge by acquaintance is what backs up the use of what he thinks of as genuine, or logically proper names. However, as we have seen, Frege also employs the same notion of non-descriptive knowledge (primitive and irreducible modes of presentation) in his discussion of indexicals: for these expressions then it is quite clear that Frege does not equate knowledge of sense with knowledge of an abbreviating description, which in this case (with indexical expressions eliminated) could only be, absurdly, a description in purely general terms. And it is also clear that Frege is in no way committed to the equally absurd view that the senses of ordinary proper names can be given by descriptions formed in purely general terms. Nor is Frege committed to the contention that the sense of any proper name must be equivalent to that of a description at all, even one containing indexicals. Although whenever he *gives* the sense of a proper name he does so by giving an equivalent description, it is entirely open to him, given his notion of sense (as a mode of presentation of a reference), to hold that in some cases grasp of the sense of a name can consist solely in a capacity to *recognize* its bearer, suitably presented. Such a recognitional capacity will involve a sensitivity to features the object has which could, of course, be described, but it need be no part of the name user's grasp of the sense of a name that *he* can describe the features in question. We recognize people, for example, by their facial appearance, but how we do so we need have no idea. Thus it is entirely open to Frege, consistently with his views on sense, to hold that a person's grasp of the sense of a name of one of his acquaintances might consist of a combination of *non-individuating* descriptive knowledge and an ability to pick him out, in suitable circumstances, when asked.

However, just as it is not a requirement of Frege's position that he think of proper names as having (wholly) descriptive senses, so it is not a requirement of his position that he _deny_ that names can have descriptive senses. And, in fact, it is plausible to suppose that this is how he did think of the sense of such names as 'Aristotle' or 'Odysseus'. For, in the case of such names of (putatively) long-dead historical figures, the appeal to recognitional capacity as constitutive of grasp of sense is highly far-fetched.

We can conclude that despite his mistaken assumption that Frege had to hold the sense of proper names to be descriptive, Kripke's arguments against the 'Frege–Russell' theory of names cannot be dismissed from the outset as merely irrelevant to Frege's position. For Frege is committed to holding at least that the sense of a proper name _can be_ that of a description, and probably further holds that this _is_ so, at least in the case of some ordinary proper names. But Kripke's arguments are intended to show that _no_ proper name has the sense of any description and that no proper name could be equivalent in sense to a description.

Kripke employs two main lines of argument against the description theory of names: the rigidity argument, and the argument from ignorance and error.

The rigidity argument starts from the observation that proper names are what Kripke calls rigid designators. An expression is a rigid designator according to Kripke if it designates the same individual in every possible world in which it designates at all. We can see what this comes to by considering Kripke's example of Benjamin Franklin, who was the first Postmaster General of the United States and the inventor of bifocals.

The sentences

(1) the inventor of bifocals might not have been the inventor of bifocals

and

(2) Someone other than the inventor of bifocals might have been the inventor of bifocals

are ambiguous. (1) can mean either

(1′) Concerning the man who in fact invented bifocals: he might not have been the inventor of bifocals or

(1″) The following might have been the case: the inventor of bifocals was not the inventor of bifocals

This is a scope ambiguity, comparable to the scope ambiguity present in Russell's example 'George IV wondered whether Scott was the author of *Waverley*'. (1′) is true because the inventor of bifocals, i.e. Benjamin Franklin, might never have got round to inventing bifocals, given the busy life he led. But (1″) is absurd since it says that the proposition *the inventor of bifocals was not the inventor of bifocals* is a possible truth.

Similarly, (2) is ambiguous between the true

(2′) Concerning the inventor of bifocals: someone other than he might have been the inventor of bifocals

and the absurd

(2″) The following might have been the case: someone other than the inventor of bifocals was the inventor of bifocals

However, if we replace 'the inventor of bifocals' in (1) and (2) by 'Benjamin Franklin' these ambiguities disappear:

(3) Benjamin Franklin might not have been Benjamin Franklin

can only be heard in one way, as saying of the man Benjamin Franklin that he might not have been Benjamin Franklin. And this is absurd. Benjamin Franklin might not have been called 'Benjamin Franklin', he might have had a wholly different career and done none of the things we in fact know him by, but he would still have been Benjamin Franklin.

Similarly

(4) Someone other than Benjamin Franklin might have been Benjamin Franklin

can only be heard as saying of the man Benjamin Franklin that someone other than he might have been Benjamin Franklin, and this is also absurd. For although someone other than Benjamin Franklin might have been called 'Benjamin Franklin' and might have done the things which make Benjamin Franklin a famous figure in American history, no one other than Benjamin Franklin could have *been* Benjamin Franklin.

That (3) and (4), unlike (1) and (2), are not ambiguous, Kripke says, shows that the name 'Benjamin Franklin' is a rigid designator, whose designation in any possible world is its *actual* designation, whereas 'the inventor of bifocals' is a non-rigid, or flexible designator, whose designation in any possible world is whoever, in that world, satisfies the condition of being the inventor of bifocals. But now, because the name and the description behave differently in modal contexts, the name cannot be equivalent in meaning to the description (for synonymous expressions behave the same in all linguistic contexts). But in general names behave like 'Benjamin Franklin', that is, are rigid designators, and descriptions behave like 'the inventor of bifocals', that is, are flexible designators, so no name can be synonymous with any description.

Defenders of the description theory have responded to this argument in two main ways: (a) they have appealed to the idea of a *scope convention*, and (b) they have appealed to the possibility of *rigidifying* descriptions.

The ploy of using the notion of a scope convention to respond to Kripke's argument was first proposed by Michael Dummett (1973). It cannot be denied that ordinary proper names are rigid designators, i.e. display the scope indifference in modal contexts that Kripke points out, but a possible explanation of this, Dummett suggests, is that names *are* abbreviations of descriptions but are used subject to the convention that in modal contexts they are to be read as having maximal scope relative to the modal operators. Certainly, one *can* introduce an expression which is stipulated to be synonymous with another except that, unlike the latter, it is to have a wide scope relative to a certain class of operator. Thus, as McCulloch points out (1989: 108ff.), one might introduce an expression '*' by the stipulation that it is to be synonymous with the multiplication symbol '×', but is to be read as having wide scope relative to other arithmetical operators. Then '2 × 3' and '2*3' will mean the same, but '2 × 3 – 5' will be ambiguous, while '2*3 – 5' will unambiguously denote the same as '2 × (3 – 5)', i.e. –4.

Similarly, it might be, for all that has so far been said, that 'Benjamin Franklin' *does* mean the same as 'the inventor of bifocals', but is to be read, as a matter of convention, as having wider scope than modal operators. The absence of ambiguity in (3) and (4) will then be explained.

The second possible response available to the description theorist is to acknowledge that names are not synonymous with non-rigid descriptions like 'the inventor of bifocals', but to point out that any such description can be paired with a rigidified description like 'the actual inventor of bifocals', with which the name can be regarded as synonymous. 'The actual inventor of bifocals' behaves, in modal contexts, like 'Benjamin Franklin'; its reference with respect to every possible world is the man who in the actual world invented bifocals, so if we replace 'the inventor of bifocals' in (1) and (2) by 'the actual inventor of bifocals' the ambiguity is eliminated, just as if we replace it by 'Benjamin Franklin'. But 'the actual inventor of bifocals' is nonetheless a *description*, so its availability provides a second way in which descriptions theorists of names might be able to maintain their position against Kripke's rigidity argument.

The debate about the adequacy or otherwise of these possible descriptivist responses to Kripke's rigidity argument is still ongoing, and the foregoing sketch has omitted complexities with which a further discussion would have to deal (in particular Kripke's distinction between *de facto* and *de jure* rigidity and his contention that rigidity is a feature of proper names which can be recognized independently of their behaviour in modal contexts (see the Introduction to Kripke 1980)). But what I wish to do now is rather to consider how the rigidity of proper names might be accounted for within an explicitly Fregean framework.

Frege never explicitly discusses modal contexts, but how he would have thought of them is nevertheless fairly evident. For modal contexts are like propositional attitude contexts in blocking substitutivity of codesignating singular terms. For example,

(5) It is a necessary truth that the inventor of bifocals, if he existed, invented bifocals

is true, but

(6) It is a necessary truth that the first Postmaster General of the United States, if he existed, invented bifocals

is false.

Within a Fregean framework this failure of substitutivity can be accommodated only by regarding 'the inventor of bifocals' and 'the first Postmaster General of the United States' as having indirect reference in these sentences. In general, a Fregean account of modal operators must treat them, like propositional attitude verbs, as creating contexts in which reference shifts occur.

Now the ambiguities which are present in such modal sentences as

(1) The inventor of bifocals might not have invented bifocals

are also present in ascriptions of propositional attitude such as

George IV wondered whether the author of *Waverley* was a Scot

A Russellian account of the latter ambiguity employs the notion of scope and we have so far characterized the ambiguity in (1) in the same way. But from a Fregean viewpoint this cannot be the full explanation of the matter (we saw in the last section of this chapter that this is true also from a Russellian viewpoint, though Russell himself did not acknowledge the fact). The ambiguity in the sentence about George IV has to be explained from a Fregean point of view in something like the following way. On one reading of the sentence it asserts that a relation (of *wondering whether*) holds between George IV and the thought identified in the that-clause, the thought that the author of *Waverley* was a Scot. On this reading of the sentence, 'the author of *Waverley*' has indirect reference after 'George IV wondered whether'. On the other reading of the sentence (the one a Russellian would describe as that in which the description has primary occurrence) 'the author of *Waverley*' retains its direct reference after 'George IV wondered whether'. The sentence, therefore, does not assert that the relation of *wondering whether* holds between George IV and an identified thought. Rather it merely asserts *of* the author of *Waverley* that George IV wondered whether he was a Scot, that is, that thinking of the author of *Waverley* in a certain way, i.e. under a certain mode of presentation, George IV wondered whether the man *so presented* was a Scot.

We can bring out this ambiguity by using some convenient terminology and notation from a paper by Peter Geach (1976b: 36ff.). Geach uses the term 'aspect' to mean the Fregean sense of an (actual or possible) proper name, and speaks of an aspect α as an 'aspect of' an object x when, in Fregean terminology, α is a mode of presentation of x, a way of latching onto x in thought. However, as well as aspects which are not embodied in the use of any actual proper names, there are aspects which are not aspects of anything, as there are actual, but bearerless proper names. Next he writes '[α is F]' to stand for the thought composed of the aspect α and the sense of the predicate 'is F'. As Geach says, this puts together a dodge belonging to Quine's theory of quasi-quotes and his use of square brackets to put a ringfence round intentional contexts. In '[α is F]' the Greek letter does not belong to the intentional context: the thought that [α is F] is the thought you would express in language by attaching the predicate 'is F' to a subject term whose sense is the aspect α.

Now the two readings of the sentence about George IV can be brought out as follows. The reading which Russell would describe as giving the description secondary occurrence is

George IV wondered whether [the author of *Waverley* was a Scot]

– this *needs* no special notation. The reading which Russell would describe as giving the description primary occurrence is:

(∃α)(α is an aspect of the author of *Waverley* and George IV wondered whether: [α was a Scot])

Using this notational apparatus we can express in a parallel way the ambiguity in:

(1) The inventor of bifocals might not have invented bifocals

This may be read as

(1′) It might have been the case that [the inventor of bifocals did not invent bifocals]

or as

(1″) (∃α)(α is an aspect of the inventor of bifocals and it might have been the case that [α did not invent bifocals])

(1′) is false, (1″) evidently true (a suitable instantiation of the variable would be the sense of 'the first Postmaster General of the United States').

Now we are in a position to give a Fregean account of what the rigidity of proper names comes to which is consistent with the description theory: namely, that there is a convention in force whereby a proper name – as opposed to a description – must not be used in a modal context to refer to its indirect reference. Evidently this proposal is very similar to the proposal that proper names are abbreviations of descriptions conventionally read as having wide scope. It explains the same phenomena and makes urgent the same question: what could the rationale of such a convention be? But within a Fregean framework it is possible to answer this question. For as we have noted, it is Frege's view that ordinary proper names vary in sense from speaker to speaker. But we aim, in conversing with people, to speak about the same things as they do. If we fail to do this, if we lack a common subject matter, we fail to communicate at all. But if the senses of proper names vary from speaker to speaker we *will* lack a common subject matter if we use proper names with their indirect references, to speak about the senses *we* associate with them. A convention whereby we must refrain from doing so is thus evidently sensible against this Fregean background (see further Noonan 1979; Burge 1979).

Of course, this suggestion appeals to a feature of the ordinary use of proper names that Frege regards as a *defect* of ordinary language; whether Frege is right to think of it in this way is a question we will return to shortly.

In sum, we have so far seen that Kripke's rigidity argument is at least not conclusive against the description theory of proper names, and *a fortiori* is not conclusive against the Fregean thesis that names have sense as well as reference, and we have seen that one possible response can be developed within a Fregean framework.

But now we must turn to Kripke's second argument against the description theory of names, the argument from ignorance and error. In fact, this is a much greater challenge to Fregean sense than the rigidity argument. For if it is correct it refutes not merely any version of the description theory, but also Russell's Principle, and therewith any theory, like Frege's, which requires that our capacity to refer is epistemically constrained.

The starting point of the argument from ignorance and error is the observation that most people use names of such famous people as Cicero (the Roman orator) on the basis of the scantiest information about them. Defenders of the description theory, when asked what sorts of descriptions determine the reference of such a name, normally offer descriptions of the famous deeds of the individual. But, as Kripke points out, it is a tribute to the education of philosophers that this thesis was held for so long in this form. In fact, most people do not have such a detailed general and historical knowledge. Most people, for example, when they think of Cicero, just think of *a* famous Roman orator. Or, to take another example, when they think of Richard Feynman, they just think of a famous contemporary physicist without being able to give any details which distinguish him from Murray Gell-Mann. 'The man in the street may . . . use the name "Feynman". When asked he will say: well he's a physicist or something. He may not think that this picks out anyone uniquely. I still think he uses the name "Feynman" as a name for Feynman' (Kripke 1972: 292). (This was before Feynman won popular fame for his role in the *Challenger* disaster enquiry.)

Moreover, Kripke goes on to argue, even when a user of a name *seems* to be in a position to give an identifying description of its bearer, it will often be the case that there is an unacceptable circularity. For example, any student of philosophy, whatever his classical education, will be able to provide an identifying designation of Cicero if he has read Quine (1960), namely the man who denounced Catiline. But if such a student only knows from reading Quine that Cicero denounced Catiline it is probable that all he will know of Catiline is that he was denounced by Cicero. But if his only way of identifying Cicero is as the denouncer of Catiline and his only way of identifying Catiline is as the man denounced by Cicero then his apparently identifying knowledge simply runs in a circle and leaves both names without reference, according to the description theory. Kripke illustrates the same point with another example: Einstein. Everyone, of course, knows who Einstein was: the man who discovered the theory of relativity. And almost everyone is ready with an answer to the question what the theory of relativity is: Einstein's theory. But a person whose knowledge is exhausted by these identifications does not have knowledge which fixes the reference of the name 'Einstein' non-circularly.

These arguments are designed to show that successful reference with proper names is compatible with ignorance of any identifying information about the bearers of the names. Kripke uses another example to show that successful reference is compatible with error. Suppose someone says that Gödel proved the incompleteness of arithmetic and is able to specify exactly what this means (so he is not in the position of the man who can only 'identify' the theory of relativity as 'Einstein's theory'). Then he has identifying knowledge capable of determining an object as the reference of his use of the name 'Gödel' in accordance with the description theory, and a descriptivist must say that if this is the only identifying knowledge

he associates with the name he must, when using the name 'Gödel',
be referring to and thinking of the man who proved the incompleteness of arithmetic. But Kripke argues, it need not be the case
that his reference is determined by this description. For if Gödel was
not, in fact, the author of the incompleteness theorem (unbeknown
to anyone), which was, in fact, proved by Schmidt, a friend of
Gödel's who disappeared in mysterious circumstances, after which
Gödel passed off the proof as his own, nevertheless the reference of
'Gödel' as used by the person in question will still be the famous
public figure and not the long-dead unknown Viennese. This
example is fictional but there are others which are not. Thus
someone might think of Peano as the discoverer of Peano's axiom,
and might be able to write Peano's axioms down, but in using the
name 'Peano' he will not be referring to Dedekind (who did, in fact,
discover 'Peano's axioms' – Peano credited him in a footnote), but,
despite his error, to Peano.

In this way, and with a wealth of other examples, Kripke argues
that ignorance and error are no impediment to successful reference
with proper names, and, as will now be apparent, if these examples
succeed, they refute not merely any description theory of proper
names, but also any sense theory, at least if a speaker's grasp of the
sense of a name must be thought of as providing him with identifying knowledge of its reference which is of one of the three
categories distinguished earlier: descriptive, recognitional or by
acquaintance.

A plausible first response to these arguments is to say that, in fact,
they do not refute the description theory since if the speakers imagined really did associate *just* the descriptions Kripke supposes with
the names used, then their references would indeed be determined
by those descriptions. For example, if someone really did know
nothing about the bearer of the name 'Cicero' save that he was a
famous Roman orator then he could not use the name 'Cicero' to
refer to Cicero. If someone really did associate *only* the description
'the man who proved the incompleteness of arithmetic' with the
name 'Gödel', then in the situation imagined by Kripke he would
be referring to the long-dead Viennese and not the famous public
figure.

However, the response continues, realistic cases of the kind
Kripke is attempting to describe do not occur. What do occur are
cases in which the speaker is ignorant of, or badly in error about,
the *biography* of the bearer of the name he is using. But such cases
are not cases in which he is incapable of associating *any* definite

descriptions, or only incorrect ones, with the name. The classically uneducated philosophy student who learns about 'Cicero' from Quine associates with the name 'Cicero' not only the description 'the denouncer of Catiline', but also the description 'the man Quine refers to by the name "Cicero"'; the man who thinks of Gödel as the discoverer of the incompleteness of arithmetic also thinks of him as the man to whom the incompleteness of arithmetic is commonly attributed. Kripke is aware of this possibility and quotes Strawson on it:

> The identifying description, though it must not include a reference to the speaker's own reference to the particular in question, may include a reference to another's reference to that particular. If a putatively identifying description is of this kind, then, indeed, the question whether it is a genuinely identifying description turns on the question, whether the reference may borrow its reference, as a genuinely identifying reference, from another; and that from another, but this regress is not infinite. (Strawson 1959: 181n)

Kripke makes three main points in response to this kind of counter-argument. First, he points out that the use of such a description as 'the man to whom the incompleteness of arithmetic is commonly attributed' will succeed in securing a reference for a name only if *not* everyone relies on it. Secondly, he points out that if I defer to Joe, in the sense of associating such a description as 'the man Joe thinks proved the incompleteness of arithmetic' with the name 'Gödel' I cannot be sure that there is no circle involved. I cannot therefore use such a putatively identifying description with any confidence. Kripke's third point is that if you use such a description as 'the man whom Joe *called* "Gödel"' in order to determine the reference of a name, you need to remember from whom you got the name, but often you do not. This shows, he says, that the view he advocates has consequences which can actually *diverge* from those suggested by Strawson's footnote. Suppose that the speaker has heard the name 'Cicero' from Smith and others, who use the name to refer to a famous Roman orator. He later thinks, however, that he picked it up from Jones who, unbeknown to him, uses 'Cicero' as a name of a notorious German spy and has never heard of any orators in the ancient world. Then according to Strawson's paradigm, the speaker must determine his reference by the resolution 'I shall use "Cicero" to refer to the man whom Jones calls by that name', while on the view that Kripke advocates (according to which the reference of a use of a proper name is determined by a chain of causal links leading back from that use to an initial baptism) the reference will be the orator in spite of the speaker's false impression about where he picked up the name. Kripke takes this to show that his own view is preferable, because it conforms to the principle that it is the *actual* chain of communication, and not what the speaker *thinks* is the chain of communication, which is relevant.

This, in essence, is Kripke's response to the proposal (offered on behalf of the description theorist) that a speaker may use a name *deferentially* to others, relying on his membership of a linguistic community and the knowledge present in it for his reference to succeed, but nevertheless referring only because *he himself* has identifying knowledge of his reference in the form of descriptions which relate to it via the knowledge and activities of the other members of his community. I have presented Kripke's response to this 'socialized' version of the description theory largely in his own words, so as not to state it unfairly, but I do not think that it is persuasive.

While there is a great deal more to be said, the essential point is that the constraint against circularity to which a description theory of reference must conform is much weaker than Kripke presents it as being in the course of his arguments. The description theorist is thus not restricted in the way Kripke thinks in the sort of descriptions to which he can appeal.

What Kripke has to show is that one can refer to a thing by a name, know and assert things about it, even when one knows of *no* descriptions which determine the reference of the name, *not even one which involves a first-person reference to oneself*. But none of his examples show this. It is true that someone, say Jones, may use 'Feynman', to refer to Feynman, knowing little more than that he is a famous physicist. But this will not be *all* that Jones knows. He will also know that there is just one person such that (a) he is named Feynman, and (b) his (Jones's) familiarity with the name 'Feynman' as a name of a physicist derives from having encountered references to that person by that name. Suppose Jones believes this to be so, but it is not so: there are two physicists named 'Feynman' and Jones has encountered references to both of them under that name, without realizing that there are two. Then, evidently enough, Jones is not referring to anyone when he uses the name 'Feynman' – he is merely in a muddle. But if Jones does know that there is just one such person, he can simply identify Feynman by the description 'the person such that (a) he is named "Feynman", and (b) my familiarity with the name "Feynman", as the name of a physicist, derives from having encountered references to him under that name'. (Note that this description may denote even if the description 'the famous physicist called "Feynman"' does not; for example, if there are two famous physicists called 'Feynman', but by chance Jones has only ever encountered references to one of them. But if Jones is not a physicist (or a science writer, or a member of a related profession) this situation is an unlikely one; most probably, if the description 'the famous physicist called "Feynman"' does not denote, nor will the longer description as used by Jones. This explains why Jones would be embarrassed by the information that there were two physicists called 'Feynman', both famous. If there were two physicists called 'Feynman', only one of whom was famous, however, then more than likely Jones, as a non-scientist, would only have encountered references to the famous one, so the longer description, as used by him, would still denote. This explains why this piece of information would not put Jones out of countenance.)

Again, while, as Kripke says, one does not use the name 'Gödel' to refer to the unknown Schmidt just because Schmidt proved the incompleteness of arithmetic and the only biographical detail one associates with the name 'Gödel' is 'prover of the incompleteness of arithmetic', this proves nothing as strong as Kripke claims. For to use 'Gödel' to refer to Gödel in this circumstance, one must know that there is just one person such that (a) he is named 'Gödel', and (b) one's familiarity with the name, as the name of a logician, derives from having encountered references to him under that name. But if one knows this, one can identify Gödel by the description 'the person called "Gödel" such that my familiarity with the name "Gödel", as the name of a logician, derives from having encountered references to him under that name'.

In general, some such egocentric, metalinguistic, causal description is bound to be available, if nothing else is (no description in terms of famous deeds or other distinctive peculiarities and no identifying knowledge in the form of a combination of non-individuating descriptive knowledge with a reference-narrowing recognitional ability), whenever one is capable of referring to an object by a proper name, and, of course, such descriptions are not circular in the manner of 'the person I (here and now) mean by "Jones"' – they are genuinely reference determining. Thus, contrary to the suggestion of Kripke's discussion, the requirement that a description theory of reference not involve the notion of reference in an ineliminable way does not entail that no description theory can be true.

Moreover, there is a difficulty in principle with Kripke's contention that the reference of a proper name might be determined independently of the speaker's knowledge and intentions in a way that is inconsistent with the epistemic constraint on reference embodied in the description theory or the more general Fregean sense theory. For, if a person *intends* the reference of a name he uses to be so-and-so, it must *be* the so-and-so, or nothing. (Of course, he can *believe* the reference of the name to be the so-and-so when it is not). If a person really intends the reference of 'Gödel', when he utters it, to be the person who proved the incompleteness of arithmetic, that is who it will be – even if that is Schmidt. Kripke would not deny this, for he allows the possibility of reference being determined in some cases by description and such cases must be ones where the speaker's intentions are allowed to be dominant in determining, his reference. Thus, when a speaker has intentions capable of determining a specific object as the reference of a name utterance, his reference will be determined by the identifying knowledge in his possession. To find counter-examples to the thesis that the reference of a proper name is determined by the speaker's identifying knowledge one must, therefore, apparently consider cases where no such unambiguous reference-determining intentions exist – where the speaker has *no* intentions capable of determining his reference, or has several intentions which do not determine the same reference. But, however the reference is determined in such a case, it must be in a manner which, if it were described to them, the speaker and the other members of his linguistic community could be brought to acknowledge as correct, i.e. as bound to determine the correct reference on any relevant occasion of utterance. Thus it must be a mode of reference determination implicitly known to the speaker and *intended* by him to determine his reference – for he knows that it will determine his reference in the absence of any specific reference-determining intention on his part, and so, lacking such an intention, he must intend to let it do so. And so once more, the speaker's intentions will be determinative of his reference (Kripke grudgingly acknowledges this point in footnote 38 of 'Naming and Necessity' (1972: 349), where he allows that if any 'causal' theory of reference is correct a 'causal' version of the description theory must be 'trivially true'). The most that could possibly be the case is that sometimes the identifying knowledge of his reference a speaker possesses is inexpressible except by way of a reference to the very name token uttered on the occasion: for example, as 'the causal source of this token: Gödel'. But even if this were so it would not be a counter-example to the thesis that name reference is determined by the speaker's identifying knowledge, or even, in fact, to the description theory as Kripke himself formulates it in 'Naming and Necessity'.

Thus we have not found, in Kripke's argument from ignorance and error, any good reason to reject Frege's contention that proper names have sense as well as reference, and that their reference is epistemically constrained as required by Russell's Principle. Moreover, we are now in a position to cash an earlier promissory note. For the picture of our naming practices now developed is one according to which some of the users of a proper name are deferential in their use of it to others and need have no identifying knowledge of the name's bearer which can be expressed without reference to those others and to their uses of the name. But placed within a Fregean framework of thought, this is a version of the view that the sense of a proper name varies from speaker to speaker, and the correctness of that view, as we saw, would provide a rationale for the convention proposed earlier as an explanation of the fact that proper names function as rigid designators – namely, that speakers must not use proper names with their indirect references, i.e. to speak about the *senses* they associate with them.

That the thesis that names are used deferentially entails variation in sense from speaker to speaker might seem hardly a recommendation of it in view of the apparent challenge such variation poses for the idea of a common understanding of proper names (which led Frege to speak in 'Thoughts' of different users of the same name as not speaking a common language). But actually variation of sense, understood in this way, seems apt to meet the challenge. The idea is that in a typical community of name users, X_1 to X_n, some of X_1 to X_n will attach to a name 'N' such senses as 'what X_3 calls "N"', 'what most of X_1 to X_{23} call "N" ', 'what the people from whom I got the name call "N" ', and so on. Of course, not everyone in a community can refer deferentially if the name in fact has a reference; there must be, or have been, users of the name who are able to identify the object of their reference non-deferentially (something like this distinction is made in Evans 1982, ch.11: Evans calls his non-deferential users 'producers' and his deferential users 'consumers'). But it can be true of some that they can refer only deferentially, and known implicitly by all to be true of some. And so the name will be, and will be known to be, in a sense ambiguous. However, the ambiguity will not be of a straightforward kind; for the users of 'N' will not be referring *merely* coincidentally to the same objects (as two speakers of distinct languages in which fortuitously the same word happens to have the same reference). Rather, in associating such a sense as 'what X_3 calls "N"' with 'N' one guarantees that whatever X_3 refers to by the name one will also refer to oneself. Thus, in a community of name users, some of whom are deferential towards others, it will not be coincidental, given the various senses they associate with the name, that they are all using it with the same reference. If it is coincidental for two name users then this will be traceable back to two non-deferential name users who are coincidentally referring to the same object despite associating different non-deferential senses with the name. And then we can divide our community into two, grouping people according to which of these two non-deferential name users they are (directly or indirectly) deferential to (of course, the answer may be both – and then it *will* be luck that reference is achieved). This suggests a criterion for joint membership in a community all of whom belong to a common name-using practice with respect to a particular name. Two people are members of such a community with respect to their use of a name 'N', if and only if: *either* they attach the same sense to the name, *or* one of them is deferential to the other in his use of the name, *or* one of them is deferential to a third person who is deferential to a fourth . . . who is deferential to the other, *or* both are deferential to a third person, either directly or in the indirect way just indicated.

This is sketchy, but the picture, I hope, is an intelligible one. At any rate, I think it suffices for the point I wish to make, namely that, contrary to Frege's own view, we do not have to think of variation in sense from speaker to speaker as a *defect*, endangering the unity of the linguistic community, as long as such variation in sense is accompanied by an acknowledgement by the individual members of the community (via their linguistic deference if they are 'consumers', or, if they are 'producers', via their acceptance of the linguistic deference of others) of their responsibility to achieving a common reference. Thus to think of sense as varying mode of presentation of reference, rather than as unvarying conventional significance, is consistent with holding that sense is not *merely* subjective.

I conclude that Kripke's attack on the 'Frege–Russell' view fails to refute it. But what it teaches us is the importance of the social dimension of language and the crucial role of deferential intentions in determining reference. This, however, can be accommodated within a Fregean framework, and indeed must be added to it if we are to go beyond Frege's dismissal of ordinary language as a defective instrument and achieve a correct description of it.

Appendix

Frege's two-dimensional conceptual notation, which probably had a negative effect on the first readers of his work, is difficult to print and hard to read. It is now never used. In the text of this book I have used an equivalent modern symbolism to expound Frege's ideas. I set out below the basic elements of Frege's own notation.

The judgement stroke This is a vertical line used to precede an expression for a content which is judged, or asserted. It is used by Frege to distinguish propositions occurring e.g. as suppositions, or as the antecedents or consequents of conditional statements, from asserted propositions, put forward as fact. It is always attached to:

The horizontal This is a horizontal line which in *Conceptual Notation* is called the content stroke and is used to indicate that what follows is an assertable content (whether or not it is actually asserted, in which case the horizontal will have a prefixed vertical line). Later Frege interpreted the horizontal as a function name, in fact, as a name of the concept *is identical with the True*.

In modern logical symbolism there is nothing corresponding to the judgement stroke or the horizontal.

Negation Frege's symbol for negation is a short vertical stroke attached to the underside of the horizontal. Thus, whereas in modern logical notation the negation of A would be written, for example, ¬A, in Frege's notation it is written ⊤ A

The conditional   Frege's symbol for the truth-functional conditional is what gives his script its two-dimensional character. What is written in modern notation as A → B, for example he writes as:

⌐ B
L A

The conditional and negation are Frege's only symbols for truth-functional connectives.

Universal quantification   Frege's notation for this is an old German letter over a concavity in the horizontal line. Thus what is written as '(∀x)' in a modern notation would be written by Frege as:

Frege has no primitive symbol for existential quantification.

Frege uses old German letters as bound variables and italic letters as free variables.

Bibliography

Anscombe, G. E. M. and Geach, P. T. (1961) *Three Philosophers*, Oxford: Blackwell.

Bell, D. (1980) 'On the Translation of Frege's *Bedeutung*', *Analysis* 40: 191–5.

Bell, D. (1990) 'How "Russellian" was Frege?' *Mind* 99: 267–77.

Bennett, J. (1966) *Kant's Analytic*, Cambridge: Cambridge University Press.

Boole, G. (1973) *The Mathematical Analysis of Logic* (1847), repr. in Boole, *An Investigation of the Laws of Thought*, New York: Dover.

Boolos, G. (1993) 'Basic Law (V)', *Proceedings of the Aristotelian Society*, supp. vol., 67: 213–33.

Boolos, G. (1998) *Logic, Logic and Logic*, ed. Richard Jeffrey, with introd. and afterword by John P. Burgess, Cambridge: Harvard University Press.

Burge, T. (1979) 'Sinning against Frege', *Philosophical Review* 88: 398–432.

Carnap, R. (1963) 'Intellectual Autobiography', in Schilpp 1963, 1–84.

Currie, G. (1982) *Frege: An Introduction to his Philosophy*, Brighton: Harvester.

Dedekind, R. (1909a) 'Continuity and Irrational Numbers', tr. of 'Stetigkeit und irrationale Zahlen' (1872), in Dedekind, *Essays on the Theory of Numbers*, La Salle, Ill.: Open Court.

Dedekind, R. (1909b) 'The Nature and Meaning of Number', tr. of 'Was sind und was sollen die Zahlen?' (1888), in Dedekind, *Essays on the Theory of Numbers*, La Salle, Ill.: Open Court.

Demopoulos, W. (1994) 'Frege and the Rigorization of Analysis', *Journal of Philosophical Logic* 23: 225–46.

Demopoulos, W. (ed.) (1995) *Frege's Philosophy of Mathematics*, Cambridge: Harvard University Press.

234   Bibliography

Detlefsen, M. (1995) 'Philosophy of Mathematics in the Twentieth Century', in S. G. Shanker (ed.), *The Routledge History of Philosophy*, vol. 9: *Philosophy of Science, Logic and Mathematics in the Twentieth Century*, London: Routledge.

Donnellan, K. S. (1972) 'Proper Names and Identifying Descriptions', in G. Harman and D. Davidson (eds), *The Semantics of Natural Language*, Dordrecht: D. Reidel.

Dudman, V. (1976) 'From Boole to Frege', in M. Schirn (ed.), *Studies on Frege*, vol. 1: *Logic and Philosophy of Mathematics*, Stuttgart-Bad Canstatt: Friedrich Frommann Verlag.

Dummett, M. (1955) 'Frege on Functions: A Reply', *Philosophical Review* 64: 96–107.

Dummett, M. (1973) *Frege: Philosophy of Language*, London: Duckworth; 2nd edn 1981.

Dummett, M. (1978) *Truth and Other Enigmas*, London: Duckworth.

Dummett, M. (1981) *The Interpretation of Frege's Philosophy*, London: Duckworth.

Dummett, M. (1991a) *Frege: Philosophy of Mathematics*, London: Duckworth.

Dummett, M. (1991b) *Frege and Other Philosophers*, Oxford: Oxford University Press.

Dummett, M. (1993) *The Seas of Language*, Oxford: Clarendon Press.

Dummett, M. (1994) 'Chairman's Address: Basic Law V', *Proceedings of the Aristotelian Society* 94: 243–51.

Dummett, M. (1998) 'Neo-Fregeans: In Bad Company?' in M. Schirn (ed.), *Philosophy of Mathematics Today*, Oxford: Oxford University Press.

Evans, G. (1982) *The Varieties of Reference*, ed. J. McDowell, Oxford: Oxford University Press.

Frege, G. (1879) *Begriffsschrift, eine der arithmetischen nachgebildete Formelsprache des reinen Denkens*, Halle: I. Nebert; tr. in Frege 1972, 101–203.

Frege, G. (1884) *Die Grundlagen der Arithmetik, eine logisch mathematische Untersuchung über den Begriff der Zahl*, Breslau: W. Koebner; tr. as Frege 1968.

Frege, G. (1962) *Grundgesetze der Arithmetik* (vol. 1 of 1893 and vol. 2 of 1903, combined in one vol.), Hildesheim: Olms; preface, introd. and sections 1–52 of vol. 1 and appendix to vol. 2 tr. in Frege 1964; parts of vol. 2 tr. in Frege 1997.

Frege, G. (1964) *The Basic Laws of Arithmetic: Exposition of the System*, ed. M. Furth, Berkeley: University of California Press; tr. of preface, introd. and sections 1–52 of vol. 1 of Frege 1962, and the appendix to vol. 2.

Frege, G. (1968) *The Foundations of Arithmetic*, tr. of Frege 1884 by J. L. Austin, with German text, Oxford: Blackwell.

Frege, G. (1969) *Translations from the Philosophical Writings of Gottlob Frege*, ed. P. Geach and M. Black, Oxford: Blackwell; includes 'Function and

Concept (1891), 'On Sense and Reference' (1892), 'On Concept and Object' (1892), 'What is a Function?' (1904).

Frege, G. (1972) *Conceptual Notation and Related Articles*, tr. and ed. with a biog. and introd. by T. Bynum, Oxford: Oxford University Press.

Frege, G. (1979) *Posthumous Writings*, tr. P. Long and R. White, Oxford: Blackwell; includes 'Numbers and Arithmetic' (1925).

Frege, G. (1980) *Philosophical-Mathematical Correspondence*, tr. H. Kaal, Oxford: Blackwell.

Frege, G. (1984) *Collected Papers on Mathematics, Logic and Philosophy*, ed. B. McGuinness, tr. M. Black et al., Oxford: Blackwell; includes 'Thoughts' (1918).

Frege, G. (1997) *The Frege Reader*, ed. M. Beaney, Oxford: Blackwell; includes tr. of parts of vol. 2 of *Grundgesetze der Arithmetik*, see Frege 1962.

Gauss K. (1863–1903) *Werke*, Leipzig: Teubner.

Geach, P. T. (1956) 'On Frege's Way Out', *Mind* 65: 408–9.

Geach, P. T. (1962) *Reference and Generality: An Examination of Some Mediaeval and Modern Theories*, Ithaca, N.Y.: Cornell University Press.

Geach, P. T. (1972) *Logic Matters*, Oxford: Blackwell.

Geach (1976a) 'Saying and Showing in Frege and Wittgenstein', in K. J. J. Hintikka (ed.), *Essays on Wittgenstein in Honour of G. H. von Wright*, Acta Philosophica Fennica 28, Amsterdam: North-Holland, 54–70.

Geach, P. T. (1976b) 'Two Kinds of Intentionality?' *Monist* 59: 306–20.

Geach, P. T. (1976c) 'Critical Notice of M. Dummett, *Frege: Philosophy of Language*', *Mind* 85: 346–449.

George, A. (1997) 'Has Dummett oversalted his Frege? Remarks on the Conveyability of Thought', in R. Heck (ed.), *Language, Thought and Logic*, Oxford: Oxford University Press, 35–70.

Hale, Bob (1979) 'Strawson, Geach and Dummett on Singular Terms and Predicates', *Synthèse* 42.

Hale, Bob (1984) 'Frege's Platonism', in Wright 1984, 40–56.

Hale, Bob (1994) 'Dummett's Critique of Wright's Attempt to Resuscitate Frege', *Philosophia Mathematica* (Series III) 2: 122–47.

Hale, Bob (1996) 'Singular Terms (I)', in M. Schirn (ed.), *Frege: Importance and Legacy*, Berlin: Walter de Gruyter, 438–58.

Hale, Bob (1999) 'Intuition and Reflection in Arithmetic', *Aristotelian Society*, supp. vol. 73: 75–98.

Heck, R. (1993) 'The Development of Arithmetic in Frege's *Grundgesetze der Arithmetik*', *Journal of Symbolic Logic* 58: 579–601; repr. with postscript in Demopoulos 1995, 257–94.

Heck, R. (1997) 'The Julius Caesar Objection', in R. Heck (ed.), *Language, Thought and Logic*, Oxford: Oxford University Press.

Kant, I. (1929) *The Critique of Pure Reason* (1781), tr. Norman Kemp Smith, London: Macmillan.

Kant, I. (1959) 'Prolegomena to any Future Metaphysic that will be able to present itself as a Science' (1783), tr. Peter G. Lucas, Manchester: Manchester University Press.

Kaplan, D. (1969) 'Quantifying In', in D. Davidson and J. Hintikka (eds), *Words and Objections*, Dordrecht: D. Reidel, 206–42.

Kenny, A. (1995) *Frege*, London: Penguin.

Kneale, W. and Kneale, M. (1962) *The Development of Logic*, Oxford: Oxford University Press.

Kripke, S. (1972) 'Naming and Necessity', in G. Harman and D. Davidson (eds), *The Semantics of Natural Language*, Dordrecht: D. Reidel, 253–355.

Kripke, S. (1980) *Naming and Necessity*, repr. of Kripke 1972 with Introduction, Oxford: Blackwell.

McCulloch, G. (1989) *The Game of the Name*, Oxford: Clarendon Press.

Mill, J. S. (1936) *A System of Logic Ratiocinative and Inductive being a connected view of evidence and the methods of scientific investigation* (1843), 8th edn, London: Longman.

Noonan, H. (1979) 'Rigid Designation', *Analysis* 39: 174–82.

Noonan, H. (1984) 'Fregean Thoughts', in Wright (1984), 20–39.

Parsons, C. (1965) 'Frege's Theory of Number', in M. Black (ed.), *Philosophy in America*, New York: Cornell University Press.

Perry, J. (1977) 'Frege on Demonstratives', *Philosophical Review* 86: 474–97.

Perry, J. (1979) 'The Problem of the Essential Indexical', *Nous* 13: 3–21.

Potter, M. (1999) 'Intuition and Reflection in Arithmetic', *Aristotelian Society*, supp. vol. 73: 63–72.

Putnam, H. (1975) *Mind Language and Reality*, Cambridge: Cambridge University Press.

Quine, W. V. O. (1955) 'On Frege's Way Out', *Mind* 64: 149–55.

Quine, W. V. O. (1960) *Word and Object*, Cambridge, Mass.: MIT Press.

Resnik, M. (1980) *Frege and the Philosophy of Mathematics*, Ithaca, N.Y.: Cornell University Press.

Rosen, Gideon (1993) 'The Refutation of Nominalism', *Philosophical Topics* 21: 149–86.

Rumfitt, I. (1994) 'Frege's Theory of Predication: An Elaboration and Defense, with Some New Applications', *Philosophical Review* 103: 599–637.

Rumfitt, I. (1999) 'Logic and Existence', *Aristotelian Society*, supp. vol. 73: 151–80.

Russell, B. (1903) *The Principles of Mathematics*, London: George Allen and Unwin.

Russell, B. (1946) *A History of Western Philosophy*, London: George Allen and Unwin.

Russell, B. (1956) *Logic and Knowledge: Essays 1901–1950*, ed. R. C. Marsh, London: George Allen and Unwin; includes 'On Denoting' (1905).

Russell, B. (1959) *My Philosophical Development*, London: George Allen and Unwin.

Schilp, P. A. (ed.) (1963) *The Philosophy of Rudolf Carnap*, LaSalle, Ill.: Open Court.

Sluga, Hans (1980) *Gottlob Frege*, London: Routledge.

Strawson, P. F. (1959) *Individuals*, London: Methuen.

Strawson, P. F. (1950) 'On Referring', *Mind* 59: 320–44.

Sullivan, P. and Potter, M. (1997) 'Hale on Caesar', *Philosophia Mathematica* (Series 111) 5: 135–52.

Wittgenstein, L. (1961) *Tractatus Logico-Philosophicus*, tr. D. F. Pears and B. McGuinness, London: Routledge and Kegan Paul.

Wittgenstein, L. (1968) *Philosophical Investigations*, tr. G. E. M. Anscombe, Oxford: Blackwell.

Wright, C. (1983) *Frege's Conception of Numbers as Objects*, Aberdeen: Aberdeen University Press.

Wright, C. (ed.) (1984) *Frege: Tradition and Influence*, Oxford: Blackwell.

Wright, C. (1998) 'On the Harmless Impredicativity of N ("Hume's Principle")', in M. Schirn (ed.), *Philosophy of Mathematics Today*, Oxford: Oxford University Press.

Index

Undergraduate Lending Library